# Elizabeth Woodville

*To my wife*

# Elizabeth Woodville

## A Life

DAVID MACGIBBON

AMBERLEY

This edition first published in 2013
First Published 1938

Amberley Publishing
The Hill, Stroud
Gloucestershire, GL5 4EP

www.amberley-books.com

Copyright © David MacGibbon, 1938, 2013

The right of David MacGibbon to be identified
as the Author of this work has been asserted in
accordance with the Copyrights, Designs and
Patents Act 1988.

ISBN 978 1 4456 1275 1 hardback
ISBN 978 1 4456 1298 0 ebook

British Library Cataloguing in Publication Data.
A catalogue record for this book is available
from the British Library.

Typesetting and Origination by Amberley Publishing
Printed in the UK.

# CONTENTS

# PREFACE

Now that we are fortunate enough to have another Queen Elizabeth on the throne, a biography of our first Queen Elizabeth, the quincentenary of whose birth coincided most happily with the coronation of our present queen, will not, perhaps, be considered as altogether out of place.

Considering the extraordinary changes of fortune experienced by Elizabeth Woodville in the course of her short life, it seems a most remarkable fact that she has not, for a great many years, been made the subject of a biography. However, the times in which she lived are so full of incidents connected with the state of the country as a whole, that the life of an individual, however illustrious he or she may be, can occupy but a quite insignificant place among the many important events with which that period of history is filled. Thus in selecting Elizabeth Woodville as the central figure of this work, I have made it my aim not only to give as complete an account as possible of a person whom most historians have hitherto looked on rather as the graceful ornament of a throne than as ruling the destiny of the nation, but at the same time to attempt a satisfactory solution of the many obscure events, such as the murder of the Princes in the Tower, with which her life was so largely connected.

Elizabeth was barely eighteen years old at the time of the First Battle of St Albans (22 May 1455), and the disastrous Wars of the Roses ended a few years before her death. It is with that period – one of the most eventful, and at the same time the most obscure, in the whole of our national history – that this work is concerned.

For help received in the consultation of manuscripts and books my thanks are specially due to Mr Arthur Ellis, Superintendent, to Mr F. G. Rendall, and the whole staff of the Reading Room at the British Museum, whose ever-willing helpfulness and unfailing courtesy cannot be too highly praised; to Dr Eric Miller of the Department of Manuscripts and to Mr A. M. Hind, Keeper of the Department of Prints and Drawings at the British Museum.

My thanks are also due to Sir Eric Maclagan, Director of the Victoria and Albert Museum, for permission to photograph and reproduce the portrait of Elizabeth Woodville in the window of the Martyrdom Chapel at Canterbury Cathedral; to Mr Lawrence E. Tanner, Keeper of Muniments at Westminster, who, besides showing me Elizabeth's lease of the Abbots' House, was good enough to write to me at considerable length on more than one occasion, and whose expert knowledge on the period, especially the episode of the Princes in the Tower, was of the greatest value; to Mr George Smith, who showed me the original manuscripts containing the details of Elizabeth Woodville's coronation, besides giving me some important clues for my research work; to Mr A. E. Stamp of the Public Record Office, who not only drew my attention to many important documents, but wrote to me on several occasions; to Dr W. A. Shaw of the Public Record Office, who went to the trouble of bringing his panel portrait of Elizabeth Woodville to London for my edification; to Mr Eric Partridge for many useful suggestions, together with some much-needed encouragement and advice; to the Worshipful Company of Skinners for permission to reproduce the portrait of Elizabeth from the Illuminated Book of the Fraternity of Our Lady's Assumption; to the Society of Antiquaries for permission to reproduce Elizabeth Woodville's seal; to the Committee of the Guildhall Library for permission to examine and quote extracts from the *Great Chronicle*; to Mr Herbert Norris, Miss Margaret Babington of the Friends of Canterbury, and Miss Mary A. S. Hickmore, who all wrote to me in answer to various important questions; to Mr William C. Wells, whose knowledge of Northamptonshire was of the greatest assistance; finally to Miss Cora L. Scofield, whose *Edward IV*, a work of monumental greatness, has proved quite invaluable for many points concerning the reign of Edward IV.

# HISTORICAL INTRODUCTION

From the point of view of the student of history one of the most interesting periods in the annals of our country was that immediately following the deposition, captivity and subsequent murder of Richard II in 1399. With the usurpation of the throne by Henry IV began that long period of unrest and misery which was destined to last throughout six reigns, and which was only terminated by the accession to the throne of Henry VII and Elizabeth of York.

Those who are interested in English history will know that Henry VI, the only son of Henry V, ascended the throne in 1422, when only nine months old, Henry V leaving him in possession of a large part of France, which was his by right of conquest.

Prior to his death Henry V had appointed his two brothers, the dukes of Bedford and Gloucester, to the regencies of France and England during his son's minority; since, however, this arrangement did not meet with Parliament's approval, they named Bedford Protector of England so long as he remained in the country; and Gloucester was commissioned to act in his absence. The person and the education of the infant king were committed to the care of the late king's uncles, Henry Beaufort, Bishop of Winchester (later Cardinal Beaufort), and Thomas, Duke of Exeter, his brother.

Charles VI of France died within two months of Henry V, with the result that his grandson, Henry VI, was duly proclaimed King of France. The Dauphin, the youngest and only surviving son of Charles VI, was also proclaimed, and crowned at Poitiers as Charles VII; the Duke of Bedford, however, took possession of the kingdom in the name of his nephew, and the war between the two countries continued with unremitting fury.

The Dauphin (Charles VII), who hoped to rally his party now that his greatest rival was dead, led his army into Burgundy. He was defeated at Crevant (1423), and the next year still more decisively at Verneuil (16 August 1424). Meanwhile, however, the Duke of Gloucester had contrived, by marrying Jacqueline of Hainault, to alienate Burgundy from the English interests, and though Bedford did his best, by enormous concessions, to retain his friendship, the breach between them gradually widened. Pope Martin V, too, at this time wrote an appeal to Bedford to desist from his attempts to force upon the French people a sovereign in defiance of the rights of succession, and the public opinion of Europe was steadily turning against England.

It was at this time that Joan of Arc came forward, alleging her divine commission to rescue her country from the invader. At the moment when Joan obtained her first audience with Charles VII the English were in the midst of the protracted Siege of Orleans. Bedford had been induced, contrary to his own judgement, to undertake this siege with a view to carrying the war into the country beyond the Loire, which adhered to the party of Charles. All France had begun to look upon the Siege of Orleans as the decisive issue of the whole war. Joan of Arc made her way into the city on 29 April 1429, and nine days later compelled the English to raise the siege. Joan of Arc's next act was to conduct the king to be crowned at Rheims, which she duly did on 17 July, after having defeated the English at Patay in the preceding month. These events ended the achievements which Joan had proclaimed it her mission to perform. However, she accomplished still more for the cause of France's deliverance by her death. Captured by the English at Compiègne on 23 May 1430, she was taken to Rouen, unjustly condemned for sorcery, and burnt in May of the following year. But her death served only to encourage the national spirit of France, which she had succeeding in rousing, the result being that the struggle now became a national effort to expel the alien invaders. From that moment onward the cause of England was virtually lost. It is not necessary here to follow in detail the varying stages of its decline. By the Treaty of Arras (21 September 1435), Burgundy, still further alienated from Bedford by the latter's marriage without his consent to Jacquetta of Luxembourg, finally threw in his lot with Charles VII, and the event is said to have caused the death of Bedford, which followed soon after. The war dragged on with diminishing hopes on the English side, and increasing discontent at home, for ten years more. In 1444 a truce was made between the two countries; and in the following year a marriage was arranged between Henry VI and Princess Margaret, daughter of René of Anjou and the niece of the King of France. The marriage, which took place on 22 April 1445, was to be accompanied by the cession of Anjou and Maine to King René, and it was hoped to found on it a permanent peace.

Henceforward, the interest of events abroad depends mainly upon the effect which they had upon public feeling at home – the degree in which they embittered the different parties of English statesmen and tended to bring about the War of the Roses, which shortly ensued. Two years after the king's marriage (1447), the two rival statesmen, the Duke of Gloucester and Cardinal Beaufort, died. The Duke of Suffolk[1] now became the most trusted Minister of the Crown. He had been chiefly instrumental in bringing about the king's marriage, and he was on that account the favourite of Queen Margaret, by whom the king was entirely governed. But as the royal marriage and the queen herself became every day more unpopular in the country, the general distrust of the duke kept pace with his favour at Court Richard Duke of York,[2] now occupied, and that deservedly, the place in popular estimation that Gloucester had held a few years before his death, while the continued losses of the English were attributed to the treachery of Suffolk and the queen. At length Suffolk was, at the instance of York and his party, impeached of high treason, banished by the king, and seized and beheaded in the course of his passage to the coast of France (1450). He was succeeded in the queen's favour by the Duke of Somerset,[3] to whom the defence of the possessions in France was entrusted. York had in the meantime been removed from the country by appointment as Lord-Lieutenant of Ireland (1447). In 1450 a foretaste of the civil war was experienced in the rebellion of the men of Kent, under Jack Cade, who professed to be John Mortimer, a cousin of the Duke of York. Soon after this rebellion had been suppressed, York returned to England, with a following of several thousand men, and insisted on his admission to the council. This was granted, and the appeal to arms was, for a while, deferred.

Meanwhile, the affairs of the country across the Channel had gone from bad to worse. There was no longer any question of retaining the more recent acquisitions. Indeed, the most ancient possessions were about to be lost – Normandy in 1450, and Guienne in 1453. During the defence of the latter place, the Earl of Shrewsbury[4] and about thirty knights fell in one battle at Castillon.

In August 1453 Henry VI began to show signs of that mental disorder which he had inherited from his grandfather, Charles VI of France. It had now become clear to all that, sooner or later, the queen and Somerset on the one hand, and the Duke of York and his partisans, among whom was the powerful Earl of Warwick, better known as the Kingmaker, on the other, would have recourse to the sword to settle their disputes, with the result that the noblemen throughout the country began to arm their retainers. The prospect of war was increased by the birth of a son to Henry VI and Margaret in October 1453. This event destroyed York's prospects of succeeding peacefully to the English throne, and increased the suspicion with which Queen Margaret regarded him. York was appointed protector in April 1454; but in January 1455 the king recovered his faculties and the appointment was automatically annulled. The queen and Somerset now began to think of taking vengeance on York, who was obliged to retire to the North. There he was joined by the most powerful of his adherents, and taking up arms, marched upon London. On 22 May 1455, York's army encountered the king's forces at St Albans, and there was fought the first battle of the Wars of the Roses. Somerset was slain, the Yorkists being everywhere victorious; with the result that, on the king's again becoming deranged, York was once more appointed Lord Protector (1455–56). Hostilities were not renewed till the autumn of 1459, when Queen Margaret felt herself strong enough to renew the struggle. By this date Elizabeth Woodville had already begun to take her place in the history of the nation.

# I

# BIRTH & EARLY LIFE

Elizabeth Woodville or Wydeville, first child and eldest daughter of Sir Richard Woodville, later first Earl Rivers, and his wife Jacquetta,[1] daughter of Peter, Duke of Luxembourg and Count of St Pol, and window of John, Duke of Bedford, was born, in all probability, at Grafton,[2] sometime in 1437.[3]

Her father, Sir Richard Woodville, was the son of Richard Woodville of the Mote, near Maidstone, and (after the death of his elder brother Thomas) of Grafton, Northamptonshire.[4]

The Woodvilles had been settled at Grafton as early as the reign of Henry II.[5] A Willelmus de Widuill of Northamptonshire is mentioned in the *Liber Niger Scaccarii*,[6] the earliest extant register of English tenants-in-chivalry and their holdings, which was probably compiled with a view to the assessment of the aid levied by King Henry II for the marriage, in 1168, of his eldest daughter, Matilda, to Henry the Lion, Duke of Saxony.[7] By a subinfeudation which could not have been later than this reign, a William de Wivill had lands in Grafton, for which he rendered 25s yearly to the Abbot of Grestein;[8] and in 1205 a jury was was summoned to inquire whether Hugh, father of Robert De Wivill, was seised in demesne of three virgates there which Robert claimed against Richard de Wivill, and whether Hugh did homage to the Abbot of Grestein who granted to him 5s out of the 25s which William de

Wivill was accustomed to render; when they presented that William de Wivill father of Hugh rendered 24s yearly, and after process of time William permitted his son Hugh on his marriage to build a house in his chief court; and he died in that house, and his father afterwards held all the land for his life and his wife also.[9]

The same year Robert de Wivill levied a fine of three virgates of land to Richard de Wivill at a reserved rent of 7s yearly, and held besides in birthright a virgate of land, a capital messuage, and 4 acres asart, which Hugh his father held in Grafton.

By another plea in the same reign, this Robert de Wivill claimed against another Robert de Wivill, brother of Richard de Wivill, two virgates and a half of land in Grafton, as his right; land of which Hugh his father, by command of William his (Hugh's) father and Emma, his mother, of whose marriage the land was, received homage of the said Robert for one virgate, and died seised of the service, and the residue of the land he claimed to hold in demesne.[10]

In 1234 the Abbot of Grestein resisted the claim of Walter de Wyvill to suit at the hundred court at Cleley;[11] and the confirmation charter from Edward II to the abbey states that John, son of Walter de Widevil of Grafton, had released and quitclaimed the abbot and convent and their tenants at Grafton from suit at the said hundred court.[12]

The family of Woodville gradually came to hold a more important position in the locality. In 1297 John de Wyvill, Esquire, was returned from the county of Northampton as holding lands to the amount of £20 yearly and upwards, either *in capite* or otherwise, and as such summoned under the general writ to perform military service in person with horse and arms in parts beyond the seas.[13] His grandson Richard de Widevill was one of the most influential men in the county. He executed the office of High Sheriff no less than eight times in the reign of Edward III, and was one of its representatives in seven parliaments.[14] The same county honours were almost as frequently conferred on his son John Widevill,[15] and grandson Thomas Widevill, who in 1435 first acquired the manorial rights from William de la Pole, Earl of Suffolk, thus becoming Lord of Grafton, where his ancestors had been settled as tenants for close on three centuries.[16] This Thomas, to whom we have already referred, was the uncle of Sir Richard Woodville, the father of Elizabeth.

Sir Richard's mother was Mary, daughter and heiress of John Bedleygate by Mary, daughter and co-heir of William Beauchamp of Wellington, Somerset.[17]

Sir Richard's father, Richard Woodville, Esquire, the elder,[18] was a trusted servant of Henry V and the regent Bedford in the French wars. He held a command in the expeditions of 1415 and 1417, and in 1420 became esquire of the body to Henry V and seneschal of Normandy.[19] In 1418 the king granted him the Norman seigniories of Préaux and Dangu.[20]

Bedford, on becoming regent for Henry VI in France, made Woodville his chamberlain, and rewarded his 'grans notables et aggreables services' with yet further grants.[21] His connection with Bedford probably induced Cardinal Beaufort and the council to entrust the Tower to his keeping when Humphrey, Duke of Gloucester, attempted a *coup d'etat* with the aid of the citizens of London in 1425.[22]

In the spring of 1427, Woodville returned with the regent to France to take up the post of Lieutenant of Calais,[23] where the marriage between his daughter Joan and William Haute, an Esquire of Kent, was apparently solemnised.[24] He still held this position in October 1435,[25] although he seems, in 1431, to have been detached for a time to serve on the council of Henry VI, during the latter's stay in France.[26]

During the next few years there is the greatest difficulty in distinguishing him from his son. He seems, however, to have settled down at Grafton after the death of his elder brother Thomas,[27] and died sometime about 1441–42.[28]

Richard Woodville the Younger was knighted by Henry VI at Leicester on 19 May 1426.[29] It was probably he who commanded a troop in France in 1429 and conveyed the wages of the Duke of Burgundy's forces to Lille in the following year.[30] He seems also to have been in the household of the Duke of Bedford,[31] where he probably met for the first time the Duchess of Bedford, who was destined to become his wife.

He is said to have been captured in the attack on Gerberoi in May 1435,[32] but must have been released soon afterwards, as he is reported to have served under Suffolk in 1436.[33]

On the death of Bedford (15 September 1435) his widow had been granted her dower by a patent of 6 February 1436, her uncle, the Bishop of Thérouanne, 'King's Chancellor in France', being 'empowered to receive her fealty, and that she do not marry without the king's consent under the Great Seal of England'.[34] However, less than a year later she was pleading to King Henry VI that 'for causes as she trusteth to God agreeable to him' she 'toke but late ago to Husband youre trew liegeman of youre Roialme of England, Richard Wydeville knight not having thereto youre Roiall licencse and assent ... for which the offense, they have suffred right grate stretness, as well in their persones as in their goddes', for which cause she begged the king 'to assesse ... a reasonable fine, and thereupon to grant your gracious letters of pardon'.[35]

The bride's brother Louis, Count of St Pol, and her uncle Louis, Bishop of Thérouanne, were also greatly disgusted at this marriage.[36]

The consequence of the appeal to the king was that on 23 March 1437, Jacquetta had to pay the king a fine of 1,000 pounds for marrying without the royal licence.[37]

For his father's sake,[38] the king's advisers were inclined to take a lenient view of Sir Richard Woodville's daring love-match, with the result that the young couple were pardoned on 24 October 1437.[39] Their fine would seem to have been found by Cardinal Beaufort, who ever since 1425 had been a great friend of the Woodvilles, in exchange for the Duchess of Bedford's life-interest in the manor of Charleton Canville in Somerset, besides other manors in Dorset and Wiltshire.[40]

Once Sir Richard Woodville had been granted his pardon, he received evidence of return to royal favour by the grant, in July, of the office of Chief Rider of the Forest of Saucy.[41] This forest was not far from the ancestral home of the Woodvilles at Grafton, where Sir Richard and his bride probably went to live.

Sir Richard was among those who escorted Margaret of Anjou when she came to England, as the bride of Henry VI.[42]

It was only natural that the Duchess of Bedford should become a great favourite of Margaret of Anjou; not only was she a fellow-countrywoman, but inasmuch as her sister Isabel was married to Margaret's uncle, Charles d'Anjou, their families were closely allied, and her own status as widow of the king's uncle enabled her to take precedence of all the other ladies at the queen's Court.

Queen Margaret gave her some personal gifts, noted by the Keeper of the Queen's Jewels as having been for her, which were worth as much as those given to the king's nearest relatives.[43]

It seems probable, however, that the duchess found her chief reward in the appreciation of her husband's services. Sir Richard served under Somerset and Talbot in the attempt to relieve Meaux in September 1439.[44] His reputation as an accomplished knight caused him to be selected to perform a 'feet of armes' with the famous Pedro Vasque de Saavedra, chamberlain of the Duke of Burgundy, who came to London in 1440 to 'run a course with a sharp spear for his sovereign lady's sake'.[45] They duly met 'within lists' at Smithfield on 26 November, but the king 'took up the matter into his hands', after the third stroke.[46] In June 1441 he once more went to France with the Duke of York, being present at the siege and capture of Pontoise.[47] Substantial estates were made to him in recognition of his good services in the French wars.[48] On 25 September 1442, he was made a Knight Banneret and Captain of Alencon,[49] while on 8 May 1448, he was created Baron Rivers.[50]

Rivers took part in the suppression of Jack Cade's rebellion in 1450,[51] riding into the city, on 12 June, accompanied by the Duke of Buckingham with 'greet power of people in lyveries with veensd and arraid for werr'.[52] He fought in the battle near Sevenoaks on 18 June, in which the Royalists were routed, their leaders, Sir Humphrey and William Stafford, being slain.[53]

Although the rumour that Rivers was to succeed the murdered Suffolk as Constable of England[54] was proved to be baseless, he was soon afterwards admitted to the Order of the Garter (4 August) and the Privy Council.[55]

The French having begun the conquest of Aquitaine, Rivers was, on 18 October 1450, named seneschal of that province,[56] being placed at the head of a force of 300 spears and 2,700 bows. A fleet for his transport was collected at Plymouth in October and November 1450, and kept waiting till July or August 1451,[57] when, news having been received of the fall of Bordeaux, the expedition was finally abandoned.[58]

Rivers appears to have spent the next few years at Calais as one of the lieutenants of the Duke of Somerset, who had been appointed its captain in September 1451, with the result that he was unable to fight for Henry VI at the First Battle of St Albans.[59] After the victory of the Yorkists in this battle, the Earl of Warwick superseded Somerset, who had fallen in the battle, as Captain of Calais,[60] Rivers being recalled to England. He refused, however, to hand over his charge to Warwick, and it was not until the garrison had been propitiated by a Parliamentary arrangement for the payment of their arrears that Warwick was permitted, on 20 April 1456, to take over the command.[61]

In January 1458 Rivers was summoned to the Great Council at Westminster, which arranged a temporary reconciliation between the two parties, the unreality of which was illustrated in the following July by his appointment to inquire into Warwick's piratical attack upon the Lübeck salt fleet.[62] It is highly probable that Warwick's hatred of the Woodvilles was first caused by this inquiry, which must have sorely wounded his pride.

Sir Richard was regarded as the handsomest man in England, his bride, too, being remarkable for her beauty. They had a family of five sons and seven daughters, of whom the eldest, Elizabeth, was, as we have already stated, born, probably at Grafton, in 1437, within a year of her parents' marriage.[63]

Meanwhile the Duchess of Bedford was still the second lady of the land and continued, with her husband, high in Queen Margaret's favour.[64]

Therefore as her children grew up, she was able to provide for them at Queen Margaret's Court. Thus it was that Elizabeth was appointed maid of honour to the queen:[65] little dreaming that she was destined to fill her place on the throne.

Little more is known of her early life except that there exist two letters addressed to her before her first marriage, one by Richard, Duke of York, and the other by Richard Neville, Earl of Warwick, both in favour of a certain Sir Hugh Johns, who sought her hand in marriage.[66]

In the first of these letters[67] the Duke of York recommended Sir Hugh to Elizabeth in the following terms:

To Dame Elizabeth Wodehille.[68]

Right trusty and welbeloved, we grete you wel; and forsomoche as we are credibly enformed that our right herty and welebilovede knyght, Sir Hugh John, for the grete wommanhode and gentillesse approved and knowen in your persone, ye beyng sooule and to be maried, his hert holy have, wherof we are rigth wel pleased. How it be of your disposicioun towardes him in that hihalve as yet to us is unknowen, We, therefore, as for the feith, true and good lorsdhip we owe unto him at this tyme, and so wel continue, desire and hertly praie you ye wol on your partie be to him wel willed to the perfourmyng of this por writyng and his desire. Wherein ye shal do not onely to our pleasire, but we doubte not to you grete wele to worshipe in tyme comyng. Certefying you, if ye fulfille our entent in this matier, we wol and shul be to him and you suche lord as shal be to your brother grete wele and worship by the grace of God, who precede and guyde you in all hevenly felicitee and welfare.

Writen etc. by Richard Duk of York.

In the second of these two letters[69] Richard Neville, Earl of Warwick, the Kingmaker, wrote to her,

To Dame Elizabeth Wodehill.[70]

Worshipful and welebiloved, I grete you wele, and forasmoche as my right welebiloved, Sir Hugh John, knyght, which now late was with you unto his ful grete joie and had grete chere as he seith, whereof I thanke you, hath enfourmed me how that he for the greet love and affectioun that he hath unto your persone, as wele for the grete sadness and wisome that he founde and proved in you at that yme, as for your grete and presied vertues and wommanly demeanyng, desireth with al his hert to do you worship by wey of mariage, bifore ony other creature lyvynge as he seith. I, consideryng his seid desire, and the greet worshipe that he had, which was made knyght at Jerusalem; and after his comyng home, for the grete wisdome and manhode that he was renoumed of, was made knight Marcha of Fraunce, and after that knyght Marshal of England,[71] unto his grete worshipe, with other his grete and many vertues and desertes: and also the gode and notable service that hath done and daily doth to me, write unto you at this tyme, and pray you affectonsly that ye wil the rathere, at this my request and praiere, to condescende and applie you unto his seid lawful and honest desire, wherein ye shal not onely purvey right notably for yourself unto your wele and grete worshipe in tyme to come, as I verely trust, but also cause me to shewe unto you such gode lorship, as ye by reasoun shal holde you contene and pleased, with the grace of God, which everlastyngly have you in his blissed proteccioun and governaunce.

Written by Richard Erle of Warr.

These letters appear to have been written sometime after 1451, when Elizabeth was about fifteen years old.

However, some worldly considerations, besides her duty to her royal mistress, Queen Margaret, seem to have led Elizabeth to reject the Yorkist partisan, Sir Hugh Johns, and to accept the hand of Sir John Grey, son and heir of Edward Grey, Lord Ferrers of Groby. Sir John was a strong supporter of the House of Lancaster, and should have succeeded to his father's title in 1457,[72] but is referred to by all historians as Sir John Grey.[73] So unsettled was the state of the kingdom that Elizabeth's husband was never summoned to parliament.[74] The actual date of Elizabeth's marriage with Sir John Grey is not known, but it probably took place soon after her rejection of Sir Hugh John about 1452.[75]

Little is known of Elizabeth during the few years which followed her marriage to Sir John Grey, save that she was appointed one of the four ladies of the bedchamber of Queen Margaret, in whose wardrobe-book she is mentioned as 'Domina Isabella Grey in attendance on the queen's person'.[76]

Tradition declares her marriage with Sir John Grey to have been a happy one.[77] Despite the fact that Elizabeth was frequently separated from her husband by the stubborn struggle between the rival houses of York and Lancaster, which began almost directly after their marriage, no period of Elizabeth's life was perhaps so free from care as the few years she passed sometimes in attendance on Queen Margaret at her favourite palace of Greenwich, but more often at the stately manor of Bradgate with the husband of her choice. Two sons were born of this marriage, the elder, Thomas, about 1456,[78] and the younger, Richard, a few years later.[79]

It so happened that the Duke of York's son, young Edward Plantagenet, then Earl of March, and Earl Rivers, Elizabeth's father, were destined to meet for the first time in the most extraordinary circumstances.

For eighteen months following the great reconciliation at St Paul's (25 March 1458), England enjoyed at least the outward signs of peace. When, however, hostilities were resumed in 1459,[80] the Yorkist leaders, Warwick, and Edward, Earl of March, had, after the Battle of Bloreheath (23 September 1459), been forced to seek safety in flight from Ludford (12 October). After many adventures they succeeded, on 2 November, in reaching Calais,[81] and immediately began to prepare for a descent on the Kentish coast, where the population regarded them with a favourable eye.

To Rivers was entrusted the task of raising the force necessary to oppose this threatened invasion.

On 15 January 1460,[82] Rivers and his son Anthony, both ardent partisans of the Lancastrian cause, were fitting out ships at Sandwich in obedience to the order which they had received. Sir John Dynham, a naval captain in the service of Warwick, made a brilliantly successful raid on Sandwich, and surprising Rivers in his bed, conducted him, and Sir Anthony, who had the misfortune to arrive in London a little later, as prisoners to Calais.[83]

'As for tidings,' wrote William Paston,[84]

my lord Rivers was brought to Calais and before the lords with eight score torches, and there my Lord of Salsbury rated him, calling him knave's son, that he should be so rude to call him and these other lords traitors, for they shall be found the king's true liegemen when he should be found a traitor. And my Lord of Warwick rated him and said that his father was but a squire and brought up with King Henry the Fifth, and sithen himself made by marriage, and also made lord, and that it was not has part to have such language of lords, being of the king's blood.

And my Lord of March rated him in like wise. And Sir Anthony was rated for his language of all three lords in like wise.

As the Duke of York had at this time not yet claimed the crown, but only the right of succession, neither his son nor Warwick dared to take the lives of Henry VI's subjects in cold blood, with the result that they were permitted to return to England in time to fight for King Henry at the Second Battle of St Albans and at Towton.[85]

Meanwhile the struggle between the houses of York and Lancaster continued with unremitting fury. On 26 June[86] Warwick and Edward left Calais, and on 2 July 1460 entered London in triumph.[87] On 10 July was fought the Battle of Northampton,[88] which resulted in an overwhelming victory for the Yorkists, Henry VI himself being taken prisoner. On 16 October[89] Richard, Duke of York, for the first time, laid claim to the crown. Finally on 31 October an agreement was concluded whereby Henry was to continue to wear the crown during his lifetime, but was to be succeeded by the Duke of York to the exclusion of Henry VI's son, the young Prince Edward.[90]

Queen Margaret, roused to action by this attack on the rights of her son, had fled to the North, where she succeeded in raising an army. On 30 December took place the Battle of Wakefield, in which the Yorkists were completely defeated, the duke himself being slain.[91] Edward, Earl of March, now succeeded to his father's claims. Margaret, however, defeated his chief supporter, the Earl of Warwick, at the Second Battle of St Albans on 17 February 1461. In this battle fell Elizabeth's first husband, Sir John Grey, the commander of the Lancastrian cavalry, while leading the last furious assault on the enemy's line.[92]

Her late husband's lands having been declared by the Yorkists forfeit to the Crown, Elizabeth sadly retired with her children to her old home at Grafton, an outcast and unhappy widow. Little did the sorrowing woman dream that she was to leave that home a queen.

# 2

# THE ACCESSION OF EDWARD IV & HIS MARRIAGE WITH ELIZABETH

Although defeated by the Lancastrians at the Second Battle of St Albans, Warwick had lost no time in collecting the remains of his army. He hastened westwards to meet Edward, now Duke of York, who was advancing from Gloucester. On 2 February Edward had completely defeated the Earls of Pembroke and Wiltshire at Mortimer's Cross, between Wigmore and Leominster. On 22 February, five days after the Battle of St Albans, a junction was effected at Chipping Norton in Oxfordshire, or at Burford-on-the-Wold nearby.[1] On 27 February, ten days after Warwick's defeat, the two Yorkist leaders reached London,[2] and the gates which had been locked against Queen Margaret, causing her to retire to the North, were opened wide to receive them. All the city was glad and said, 'Let us walk in a new wine-yard, and let us make us a gay garden in the month of March with this fair white rose and herb, the Earl of March'.[3]

> The Rose came to London, full royally riding,
> Two archbishops of England they crowned the Rose King
> Almighty Lord! Save the Rose, and give him his blessing,
> And all the realm of England joy of his corowning,
> That we may bless the time that ever God spread that flower.

For a few days Edward took up his abode in the Bishop of London's Palace, numbers of the gentry of the South and East of England coming up to show their devotion to him. On Sunday 1 March, George Neville, Bishop of Exeter, who had been appointed Chancellor by the Yorkists shortly after the Battle of Northampton,[4] addressed a large gathering at Clerkenwell, composed partly of the citizens and partly of Edward's soldiers,[5] declaring how Edward might rightly claim the Crown. On 3 March a great council was called at Baynard's Castle, a mansion which had belonged to the Duke of York, Edward's father, and it was agreed that Edward was now the rightful king, Henry VI having forfeited his crown by breach of the late Parliamentary settlement.[6] On the next day, 3 March, Edward entered Westminster Hall, seated himself on the royal throne, and declared his title to the people with his own mouth. The people were then asked if they would accept him, and there was a general cry of 'Yea! Yea!', after which he entered the abbey and offered at St Edward's Shrine.[7] Next day proclamations were issued in his name as Edward IV 'King of England and France and Lord of Ireland'.[8]

A few weeks later, at Towton, on Palm Sunday – 29 March – Edward met the Lancastrian army and utterly defeated it, no less than 22,000 Lancastrians being slain.[9] By this overwhelming victory Edward secured for himself the possession of the throne. He was duly crowned at Westminster Abbey on Sunday 28 June 1461.[10]

All his contemporaries speak of Edward IV as being tall, fair-headed and remarkably good-looking.[11] All foreigners who saw him appear to have been struck by his masculine beauty and kingly air, while his ingratiating manners contributed to render him exceedingly popular.[12] The good fortune which attended him throughout his life may have been partly due to this cause, as well as to his undoubted valour and skill as a general and a leader of men. Although he never lost a battle, nothing is more astonishing than his imprudence and the easy conscience with which he trusted such traitors as Warwick, Somerset and Montagu. Careless and self-indulgent, he allowed dangers to accumulate, but whenever it came to action, he was firm and decisive. His familiarity with the wives of London citizens was the subject of much comment, as were his exactions, whether in the form of Parliamentary taxations, benevolences, or debasement of the currency, to which last device he had recourse in 1464.

Edward may rightly be considered as the first of our modern kings and the last of our medieval ones. He had many faults: he was ungrateful to his friends; he was easy prey to flatterers, and a bad judge of men – and women; he was fond of rich foods and comfort; he liked wine and beautiful women. But against these venial sins must be put his good points: he was a lover of books, the patron of Caxton, a brilliant general,[13] and a good Catholic. He also manifested in many instances an ardent attachment to his many brothers and sisters, actually finding time after the Battle of Northampton to visit them every day.

> Decently educated, with a taste for the refinements of life as well as its grosser pleasures, he introduced into the English Courtan order combined with splendour which made it an asset of real value in the intellectual and social life of the nation, reflecting onto it the rays of the sunrise of the Renaissance. There is a largeness and open-handedness about him that is surprising to find in combination with financial strictness and methods of extortion generally suited with miserliness.[14]

It may be an extreme ting to say that Edward's greatest gift to his country was his own personality. One thing, however, is certain – namely, that the new blood and new life which he brought to the monarchy have been of lasting benefit to England. Edward introduced a new element into the loyalty of subjects to the Crown. Other kings had been popular – such great warriors as Richard *Coeur de Lion*, Edward III and Henry V – while his immediate predecessor's piety and helplessness had won him a lasting affection in the hearts of his subjects. Edward IV came out from the barriers which kept the kingship to the council chamber and the field of battle, and established it firmly in the everyday affections of the people.[15]

Following Towton a short but welcome peace had settled on the country, and the people began once again to go about their business and pleasures without fear. In the autumn following Edward's accession, Hardywcke Hall was filled with guests of the owner, Roger de Hardwycke. This gathering had been brought together ostensibly for the purpose of hunting, though it was intended also by the host and his near relatives to utilise the occasion for the consideration of the cruel confiscation by the new king of the Bradgate estates belonging to Elizabeth (Woodville), Baroness of Groby, whose husband, Sir John Grey, had, as we have already stated, fallen at St Albans.[16]

It is not improbable that the real instigator of the Bradgate confiscation was the Earl of Warwick, the Kingmaker, who bore Elizabeth Woodville a grudge for having married the Lancastrian Sir John Grey instead of Sir Hugh Johns, through whom he and his uncle Richard, Duke of York, may have hoped to win over to their side Elizabeth's mother, the then-powerful Duchess of Bedford. As Thomas, Baron Stanley, had married Warwick's sister Eleanor, cousin-german to the king,[17] and as the Dowager Duchess Catherine of Norfolk was their aunt,[18] as was also the king's mother, Cecily, Duchess of York, it was thought that some plan might be devised by which the influence of these ladies could be brought to bear upon Warwick, who, it was hoped, might be persuaded to abandon his abandon his animosity towards the Woodvilles and advise the king to restore Bradgate to its rightful owner. The efforts of these worthy relatives were destined to be of no use whatsoever, the restoration being finally accomplished by a process far different from the one expected.

In those days it was customary for widows to marry again almost immediately, and during the half-year that had elapsed since her husband's death at St Albans, the widowed Baroness Ferrers, had doubtless received offers of marriage from not a few Court gallants and county nobles and gentlemen, among whom was young Jocelyn, nephew of the 'Stag of Hardwicke' and son of Sir John de Hardwycke of Bolsover. During her visit to Hardwycke she made her choice and gave her heart to Jocyelyn[19] in secret, but it was deemed prudent to withhold the public gift of her hand owing to Warwick's enmity and the forthcoming negotiations concerning Bradgate.

There is a tradition that after the last meet of the hunting party a large cavalcade was returning from Haddon Hall to Hardwycke, when on Astwith Gorse the riders encountered a gipsy encampment. The younger ones of the party seized the opportunity of having their fortunes told, and immediately asked an old gipsy woman to do this. The woman is said to have singled out Elizabeth from the others, and after requesting her to place her hands upon those of Ralph Vernon, Jocelyn de Hardwycke and Roger de Hardwycke of Pattingham, she solemnly repeated the following words:

> A royal prince fair lady shalt thou wed,
> But troubles dire shall fall upon thine head;
> Bone of thy bone shall by a future fate
> With blend of these three houses surely mate.

Elizabeth returned to Grafton at the close of these festivities; and having noticed, during long months of weary waiting, that the family negotiations appeared to be making little or no progress, she determined to seek the king and plead her cause in person.

Nothing, however, can be more evident than that all the connections of Elizabeth, both parental and matrimonial, were viewed with considerable hostility by the newly crowned king. However, her mother, Jacquetta, was a diplomat of the most consummate ability, so much so that the populace attributed her influence over the minds of men to sorcery. The manner in which she reconciled herself to Edward, when she had so recently been aiding Queen Margaret, quite apart from the stormy scene which had occurred between that prince and her husband and son at Calais, is almost inexplicable. Be that as it may, the effect of her influence is to be found, in no uncertain terms, on the Issue rolls of Edward's exchequer. In the first year of his reign there is an entry declaring that 'the king, affectionately considering the state and benefit of Jacquetta Duchess of Bedford and Lord Rivers, of his especial grace', not only pays her the annual stipend of the dower she held of the Crown, 'three hundred and thirty-three marks, four shillings, and a third of a farthing', but actually pays £100 in advance.[20]

It is highly probable, as Miss Scofield suggests,[21] that Sir John Grey's fair widow first became acquainted with Edward in the depths of her distress for the loss of her husband, and that Edward's sudden passion for her was the cause of his extraordinary profession of affection for her mother and father, who were, even after the death of Sir John Grey, such staunch supporters of the House of Lancaster.

It is well known that after the Battle of Mortimer's Cross, Edward turned westwards and spent two days at Stony Stratford.[22] During those two days he probably rode over to Grafton Regis, the home of Lord Rivers, as he did on a famous occasion three years later; for just before he started on his way again he sent word to the Chancellor that 'of our grace especial', he had pardoned 'Richard Woodville, knight, Lord Rivers, all manner offences and trespasses of him done against us'.[23]

Who, then, can doubt but that a pair of bright eyes which Edward had just seen very probably for the first time[24] – the eyes of Elizabeth Woodville – had pleaded for her father's and her brother's pardon? If this singular entry in the Issue rolls may be permitted to support this surmise, then Elizabeth and Edward met two or three years earlier than most historians generally lead us to believe.

Recent discoveries, while proving this to be almost certain, have, at the same time, thrown considerable light on Elizabeth's first marriage and her difficulties following her first husband's death.[25]

In the year 1456, in the Court of Common Pleas, the manors of Newbottle and Brington in Northamptonshire and Woodham Ferrers in Essex were enfeoffed by Edward Grey and his wife Elizabeth to certain persons, among whom were Robert Isham, William Boldon and William Fielding.[26] This act appears to have been connected with the marriage of their son John Grey to Elizabeth Woodville.

There are among the early proceedings in Chancery some pleas which may well have been the actual cause of Elizabeth's petition to the king, and their resultant love-story and marriage.

Sir John Grey's father died in 1457, and by May 1462 his mother Elizabeth, Lady Ferrers, had married again,[27] her second husband being Sir John Bourchier, one of the sons of Henry, Earl of Essex, and his wife Isabella Plantagenet, aunt to Edward IV.

There is a petition to the Lord Chancellor from Sir John Bourchier and his wife asking that the Lord Chancellor would require Robert Isham, William Boldon and William Fielding, the surviving feoffes of the manors of Newbotell, Brington and Woodham Ferrers to 'make astate' to her.

There are also two petitions from Dame Elizabeth Grey to the Lord Chancellor, stating that by the agreement for her marriage to John Grey made by her father Richard Woodville, Lord Rivers, with Sir Edward Grey, the former on his part undertook to pay a sum of CC marks, while the latter and his wife enfeoffed these three manors to provide an income for John Grey and his wife and heirs. Though Robert Isham and William Boldon had taken the necessary steps to 'make astate' to Sir John Grey's widow, William Fielding hesitated to do so. A further petition from Lord Rivers states that he had paid his daughter's marriage portion to Sir Edward Grey, but for the trust he had in him took no receipt nor discharge, and now Sir Edward's widow was dunning him for CXXV marks of the marriage portion.

In their answers Robert Isham and William Boldon set out that the intent of the assignment was to provide an income of 100 marks yearly 'for the saide John Grey and Elizabeth his wife, and to the heires of the saide John's bodie'. William Fielding was non-committal, saying 'that he was uncertain as to the intent of the assignment'.[28]

It is evident that the claims of Elizabeth and her sons to these manors were preferred to those of her mother-in-law, Lady Ferrers. In any case, the matter would seem to have been settled in her favour before she entered into negotiations with William, Lord Hastings, Edward IV's chamberlain, for the marriage of one of her sons to his unborn daughter. The matter may have been in course of arrangement for some time, but the agreement[29] was signed by her under the date of 13 April 1464, just over a fortnight before her marriage to the king. It is an indenture

> made between Elizabeth Grey, widow of Sir John Grey, knight, son and heir of Edward Grey, late Lord Ferrers, and William, Lord Hastings for the marriage of Thomas Grey, her son or in case of his death of Richard his brother, with the eldest daughter to be born within the next five or six years to Lord Hastings;[30] or, failing such a daughter, with one of the daughters to be born within the same period to Ralph Hastings, his brother, or failing such a daughter, with one of

the daughters of Dame Anne Ferers his sister. If any manors or possessions once belonging to Sir William Asteley, knight, called 'Asteley land',[31] or any of the inheritance of Dame Elizabeth 'called Lady Ferrers of Groby' (save all manors, lands and tenements in Nobottle (Newbotell) and Brighton Co. North Hants and Woodham Ferrers Co. Essex) were at any time recovered in the title and right of Thomas or Richard from the possession of any other person having an interest in them, half of the rent and profits thereof while Thomas, or, if he died, Richard, was under the age of twelve years was to belong to Lord Hastings and half to Dame Elizabeth. Lord Hastings to pay her the sum of 500 marks before such marriage, or if there was no female issue as above she to pay him the sum of 250 marks.[32]

It was quite clear to Elizabeth that, in the circumstances of her mother-in-law's marriage, all her lands as well as the property which Lady Ferrers herself had inherited might pass away to the Bourchiers, unless someone sufficiently strong was able to uphold her children's claims. Thus it would seem that in the interests of her children she had entered into this agreement with Hastings, who was on terms of intimate friendship with the king, and able to wield an influence which even the Bourchier family was forced to respect.

In the same month a belated inquiry was made into the affairs of her late husband, Sir John Grey, establishing that their son Thomas was heir.[33] Thus by the agreement with Lord Hastings and the official recognition of her eldest son as heir to his father, Sir John Grey, Elizabeth probably felt that her children's interests were safeguarded as far as possible.

In view of the fact that Elizabeth became his wife less than three weeks after the agreement was signed, it appears highly probable that the king was to a large extent responsible for the agreement made with Hastings, and that this and the above-mentioned inquiry were made at his command in order not only to set Elizabeth's anxiety for her children's welfare at rest, but to prove to her how very deeply he was in love with her.

Whatever the actual date of this celebrated triumph of love over sovereignty may be, tradition points out the exact spot of the first interview between Elizabeth and the king. She is said to have waylaid him in the forest of Whittlebury, when he was hunting in the neighbourhood of Grafton. There she waited for him, under a tree still known in Northamptonshire as 'the Queen's Oak'.[34] Beneath the shade of its branches the fair widow is said to have accosted Edward, holding her fatherless boys by the hands; and, on Edward stopping to listen to her, she threw herself at his feet, and pleaded for the restoration of Bradgate,[35] the inheritance of her children, which was destined in later years to derive such lustre from being the home of Elizabeth's equally unhappy descendant, Lady Jane Grey.[36] Her downcast looks and mournful beauty gained not only her suit, but the heart of the young king.[37]

Hall[38] gives the following attractive description of Elizabeth.

> She was a woman more of formal countenance than of excellent beauty, but yet of such beauty and favour with her sober demeanour, lovely looking and feminine smiling (neither too wanton nor too humble), beside her tongue so eloquent and her wit so pregnant.

Whether or not the two lovers actually met for the first time beneath its branches, 'the Queen's Oak' still stands in the direct track of communication between Grafton and Whittlebury Forest, its hollow trunk a venerable witness of one of the most romantic love-matches in history.

Edward's first thoughts appear to have been to take dishonourable advantage of Elizabeth, and he seems to have tried every art to induce her to become his on other terms than as sharer of his regal dignity.[39] However, she withstood all his advances,[40] and so increased his passion by her constant refusals that he came to realise that he could not live without her. Thus, without asking the advice of his councillors, who, he knew, would strenuously oppose his wishes, he made up his mind to marry her as soon as possible.

He is said to have communicated his intentions to his mother, Cecily, Duchess of York, who, not unnaturally, was infuriated at the thought of having to give place to the daughter of a man whom she despised as being far beneath her in blood.

The duchess is said to have pointed out the consequences of the proposed step, dwelling with much emphasis on the dishonour to his throne in marrying a subject, and setting before her son the certain anger of his people and friends, more especially the Earl of Warwick. She objected to Elizabeth as a widow with children, to which Edward replied, 'She is indeed a widow, and hath children; and by God's blessed Lady! I, who am but a bachelor, have some too. Madame, my mother, I pray you to be content.'[41] The duchess also appears to have reproached her son with the breach of his marriage contract with Elizabeth Lucy, the predecessor of Elizabeth Woodville in Edward's affections.[42] Elizabeth Lucy, having been sent for and questioned, declared that no pre-contract had ever existed between them, 'although his Grace spake such loving words to her, that she verily hoped that he would have married her, and that if such kind words had not been, she would never have showed such kindness to him, to let him so kindly get her with child'.[43]

Since by this examination 'it was clearly proved that there was no impediment to let the king marry',[44] the duchess was soon to learn that all her protests had been made in vain.

At a Chapter of the Order of the Garter held at Windsor on 29 April 1464,[45] it was recorded, 'The sovereign was absent elsewhere, being involved in the great and weighty matters of the kingdom, and continually taken up with them. The Earl of Warwick, Lord Montagu and Lord Scripp were guarding the Northern border,' while several other knights, including Lord Hastings and Lord Rivers, were, by the king's orders, 'attending on those nobles who were assigned for the defence of the Northern borders or engaged in some other necessary employments elsewhere'.[46] The king's presence was most certainly needed in the North, for a Lancastrian rising under Somerset and Percy had just occurred there. Edward, however, was concerned with other matters besides his Lancastrian foes.

Leaving London on 28 April,[47] Edward spent that and the following night under Abbot Whethamstede's roof at St Albans,[48] reaching Stony Stratford on 30 April. Early the next morning, without confiding his intentions to anyone, he rode over to Grafton, where he was secretly married to Elizabeth. Fabyan[49] thus describes this marriage, destined to have such far-reaching effects not only on the bride and bridegroom, but on the whole future of England as well.

> In most secret manner, upon the first day of May, King Edward spoused Elizabeth, late the wife of Sir John Grey … Which spousailles were solemised early in the morning at the town named Grafton, near unto Stoney Stratford. At which marriage was no person present but the spouse, the spousesse, the Duchess of Bedford her mother, the priest,[50] and two gentlemen and a young man who helped the priest sing.

A few hours later the king rode back to Stony Stratford, explained to his attendants that he had been hunting, and went to bed again as if to sleep off fatigue.[51] Later in the same day he went to Northampton, where the Court remained for the next five days.[52] Two days later (3 May) Edward 'sent to Grafton, to the Lord

Rivers, fader unto his wyfe, shewynge to hym that he wolde come and lodge with hym a certeyne season, where he was receyved with all honoure, and so taryed there by the space of iiii days'.[53] To divert the attention of the courtiers their time was wholly occupied with hunting parties – nor did the king and his bride ever meet in private till her mother had made certain that the whole household had retired to rest, when she was brought to him so secretly that 'almoste none but her mother was of counsayll'.[54]

Thus, after spending four days with his bride, the king moved on to Leicester, where he stayed from 8 to 13 May, waiting for troops to join him.[55]

Prior to the king's arrival in the North, the Lancastrian rebels had already been defeated by Montagu at Hedgeley Moor[56] (25 April), and three weeks later (15 May) they were again defeated at Hexham. In this latter engagement the Lancastrian army was almost annihilated; thus was Edward yet more securely established on the throne.

When the king next saw his bride is somewhat uncertain. He was not in that immediate neighbourhood again until July. Following a visit to York, where he remained about two months, he returned to London in July. On his journey to London he stopped, on 15 July, at Stony Stratford, 5 miles from Grafton, and it seems probable that he found time to ride over there and spend a few hours with his bride. On 28 July he was at his manor of Penley, halfway between London and Grafton, whence he went to Stamford via Leicester; he remained at Stamford four days (7–11 August), whence he went to Ludlow and then returned to Penley on 15 August. For the next month Edward passed his time at Penley and Woodstock, whence he almost certainly visited his lovely young queen.[57]

The marriage was carefully kept secret for some time, since matches had already been suggested for Edward in various quarters. Isabella, Princess of Castile, might have been his bride.[58] At the time of his marriage the council were inclined to favour a match with Bona of Savoy, sister-in-law of Louis XI of France. The chief promoter of this match was his powerful supporter, the Earl of Warwick, who was expected to go to France in the course of the year to arrange it.[59] Not only would Warwick be disgusted by the failure of his plans, but the earl's policy, which was to establish a lasting peace with France, would probably be disconcerted. A truce with France had already been arranged in April to last till October, and a diet was meanwhile to take place at St Omer with a view to a more lasting peace.[60]

Edward made no open opposition to Warwick's plans. The project was mooted to Louis XI, safe conducts for the English Embassy were obtained, and Warwick and Wenlock were expected at St Omer about 4 October.[61] At the very last moment, when Warwick attended the council at Reading on 4 September to receive his master's final instructions, Edward, finding himself driven into a corner, was forced to confess to him that he was already married to Elizabeth Woodville.[62] The council had met for the formal purpose of approving Warwick's negotiations for Edward's marriage with Bona of Savoy. A speaker, probably the earl himself, had 'moved him, and exhorted him in God's name to be wedded and to live under the law of God and the church'.[63]

Then the king answered that of a truth he wished to marry, but that perchance his choice might not be to the liking of all present. Then those of his council asked to know of his intent, and would be told to what house he would go. To which the king replied in right merry guise that he would take to wife Dame Elizabeth Grey, the daughter of Lord Rivers. But they answered him that she was not his match, however good and however fair she might be, and that he must know well that she was no wife for such a high prince as himself; for she was not the daughter of a duke or earl, but her mother the Duchess of Bedford had married a simple knight, so that though she was the child of a duchess and the niece of the Count of St Pol,[64] still she was no wife for him. When King Edward heard these sayings of the lords of his blood and his council, which it seemed good to them to lay before him, he answered that he should have no other wife and that such was his good pleasure.[65]

This announcement was greeted almost with incredulity – indeed, when the news became known over the country, so extraordinary was it considered that people could only suppose that Elizabeth's mother had used either witchcraft or love philtres to ensnare the young king.[66] However, Edward gave no encouragement to any such fancies, and still less indication of any desire to reverse what he had done, nor indeed any appearance of regretting it.[67]

Warwick and the council were as angry as they were astonished;[68] nevertheless there was nothing to be done at the moment but to accept the *fait accompli* and dissemble their anger at never having been consulted. For Warwick this revelation must indeed have been a bitter blow. He saw that he had been wilfully deceived in everything that he had undertaken since the previous May. It was a mortifying situation. Nevertheless, vexed as he might be at Edward's marriage, it did not necessarily threaten the great position he held in the country, or that of the Neville family, although his pride was hurt, and his prestige was, for the time at least, badly shaken. Edward actually sought to calm his rage by translating his brother, George Neville, from the bishopric of Exeter to the archbishopric of York,[69] vacant by the death of William Booth. Even if this attempt at a peace-offering proved to be quite insufficient, Warwick, for the time at least, accepted the awkward situation with good grace.

# 3

# THE CORONATION OF ELIZABETH

Once Edward had confessed himself to be a married man, he lost no time in giving the lady of his choice the position to which she was entitled.

On St Michael's Day, three weeks after the momentous council meeting at the ancient palace of Reading, Edward introduced his wife publicly to Court.[1] She was led, in solemn pomp, by the Duke of Clarence, King Edward's brother, and the Earl of Warwick,[2] into the chapel of the abbey, where she was acknowledged as queen by all present.

Warwick, however, was not the only person to be vexed at the king's choice of queen. Elizabeth's marriage with Edward IV drew upon him the enmity of the celebrated Isabella of Castile, sister of Henry IV, the Impotent, and afterwards queen and joint ruler with Ferdinand of Aragon. At the end of February 1464, the ambassadors from the King of Castile came to England to offer Edward the hand of his sister Isabella.[3] This offer was, however, declined, and though she knew little or nothing about the husband proposed for her, Isabella never forgave the slight she felt she had suffered. Years later, when Edward was in his grave, and Isabella herself was Queen of Castile, her ambassador, Graufidius de Sasiola, in a letter dated 8 August 1483, informed Richard that she had been 'turned in her hart from England in time past, for the unkindness the which she took against the king last deceased, for his refusing of her and taking to his wife a widow of England; for the which cause also was a mortal war betwixt him and the Earl of Warwick, the which took ever her part to the time of his death'.[4]

Isabella's remarks were indeed not far from the truth. The marriage of Edward to Elizabeth may be considered as a turning-point in the story of his character and the history of his reign.[5] From that time onwards began the rivalry between the houses of Woodville and Neville which was to end only with the Kingmaker's death.

Elizabeth seems, from some accounts,[6] to have been a person of a cool, calculating decision of character, without any deep affection, but of steady dislikes and revengeful disposition. She was destined to retain a lasting power over the mind of her husband – a most dangerous weapon in the hands of a woman possessed of great cunning and powers of intrigue – and was able to influence him to her will without publicly appearing in political affairs. She was to bear him a large family:[7] but she soon lost her sole dominion of his fancy, and seems to have resigned herself to this rather disagreeable situation without any outward signs of difficulty. She showed the greatest ability in the way in which she forwarded the interests of her family. Even if, as Stratford asserts,[8] she herself brought nothing of very great value into either public of Court life, the rise of her kindred introduced some far more intellectual, accomplished and literary persons into the Court. It seems almost certain that her brother Anthony, Lord Scales, was chiefly responsible for the interest taken by the king and queen in William Caxton's printing press, for which fact alone the family of Woodville is worthy of a memorable place in history.[9]

The chief characteristic of the new queen was, however, her devotion to her brothers and sisters, and the grasping haste with which she pushed their fortunes. Indeed, the advancement of her own relatives, and the depreciation of her husband's friends and family, were her chief objects.[10] She appears to have gained her own way with her husband by an assumption of the deepest humility; her words were soft and caressing, her glances timid.

Elizabeth's apparent freedom from jealousy, the consequence of cold affection and prudent calculation, was the principal cause of the dominion she held over her husband's powerful but indolent temper. By suiting his humour, by winking at his gallantries, by a submissive sweetness of temper which soothed his own hasty moods and contrasted in the most singular fashion with the rough pride and domineering manner of Warwick, Elizabeth had succeeded in swaying Edward's mind even when she had lost his heart.

A striking example of Elizabeth's influence over Edward is to be found in her treatment of Thomas FitzGerald, 8th Earl of Desmond, who, in 1463, had been appointed Deputy Governor of Ireland. Desmond is said to have told the king that he ought to divorce Elizabeth and marry some foreign princess whose connections would help stabilise his throne.[11] When in May 1467[12] the Earl of Worcester was made Deputy Governor in Desmond's place,[13] it was commonly reported that Worcester's new office had been obtained for him by the queen, who intended through him to avenge herself on Desmond.

On his arrival in Ireland, Worcester summoned a Parliament, and somehow succeeded in excluding Desmond's friends from it, with the result that he further succeeded in having Desmond attainted. On the latter coming to face his enemies, Worcester immediately caused him to be seized and beheaded at Drogheda, on 14 February 1468.[14]

In everything he did in Ireland, Worcester appears to have been acting for Elizabeth, who is said to have secretly procured a privy seal warrant for Desmond's arrest and execution.[15] Although Edward was certainly very angry at Desmond's death,[16] Elizabeth seems to have quickly won him over to her side again, as not only did he refrain from calling Worcester home, but on the birth of a son to Worcester in Ireland,[17] the king saw fit to send him a large cup of silver and gilt as a christening present.[18]

Edward must soon have realised that his position in the country, especially with the powerful group of nobles who had supported him and his father, was seriously weakened by his choice of queen; thus he acceded to her desire for the advancement of her family the more readily in that he saw the dire necessity of creating a body of nobles destitute of territorial and semi-feudal authority, a body of supporters who owed their fortunes to him, and whose unpopularity with the rest of the Peerage would make it necessary for them to stand by him. Now, the House of Rivers was almost as prolific as the House of Neville; the new queen had five brothers, seven sisters,[19] and two sons by her first marriage, and for them the royal influence was utilised in the most extraordinary way during the next two years. Nor was it merely inordinate affection for his wife that led Edward to squander his wealth and misuse his power for the benefit of her relatives. It soon became evident that he had resolved to build up, with the aid of the queen's family, one of those great allied groups of noble houses whose strength the fifteenth century knew so well – a group that would make him independent of the Nevilles.[20] Therefore, almost immediately after the announcement of his own marriage, he consented to the betrothal of the queen's next sister, Margaret, to Thomas, Lord Maltravers, son and heir of the Earl of Arundel.[21] This was destined to be the first of a series of marriages in the Woodville family which was not to end for two years.[22]

Edward and his bride spent several weeks in the monastery at Reading after the council meeting ended.[23] The last day of November found the king and queen at Windsor. On 8 December, however, they went to Eltham, and on that day Edward commanded the treasurer and chamberlains of the Exchequer to pay £466 13s 4d 'to our right entirely well beloved wife, the queen, for the expenses of her chamber, wardrobe, and stable against this feast of Christmas next coming'. Permanent provision was made for the queen about the same time, when the great council was summoned to Westminster and lands worth 4,000 marks a year were given to her. A few months later the king also granted her his 'manor of pleasance in Greenwich', and finally his manor of Shene as well.[24] The honeymoon Christmas was celebrated at Eltham, when Edward distributed £207 worth of gift-rings. Early in January, however, he returned to Westminster Palace to prepare for the opening of Parliament.[25]

Preparations for the queen's coronation had been going on for some time past. As early as January 1465, Edward had sent his envoys to Philip of Burgundy to inform him that his queen was to be crowned on the Sunday before Pentecost, and to invite him to send a fitting delegation to represent the Burgundian Court on that auspicious occasion.[26] Since Elizabeth Woodville, on her father's side, was of '*assez petite* extraction', Edward was especially anxious that his subjects should be reminded that her mother, Jacequetta of Luxembourg, was descended from a family quite as noble as his own,[27] and with this end in view he requested Philip to send to his wife's coronation her uncle Jacques de Luxembourg, Seigneur de Richebourg, to whom he had already granted a safe conduct in October 1464.[28]

It is evident that expense was not spared, as the Treasurer of the Household received £400 at the Exchequer to meet the additional outlay on the occasion. 'Against the coronation of our most dear wife, the queen,' the king also caused one Gerard van Rye to import for him 'divers' jewels of hold and precious stones, and he bought 'at our own price', 50 marks, 'two bay coursers and a white courser' for the queen's chairs. Elyn Longwith, a London silkwoman, provided certain stuffs worth £27 10s for the queen's 'chars, saddle and pillion', Matthew Philip supplied a cup and basin of gold costing £108 5s 6d, John de Bardi of Florence two cloths of gold valued at £280, and Sir John Howard, at a cost of £20, 'the plate that the queen was served with the day of her coronation'.[29] The king also ordered 'a robe of crimosin Damaske for Garter and the usual scarlet robes for the many heralds and pursuivants',[30] who were to play a conspicuous part in the coming ceremony, and whose gorgeous apparel was expected to appeal to the Londoners' almost insatiable love of pageantry.

On 14 April Edward sent a letter 'from our manor of Shene to the Maire of oure Citie of London' informing him that 'we have certainly appynted and concluded the Coronacion of our mooste dere and moost entierly beloved wiff the Quene to be at our palois at Westminster upon the Sonday before Witsonday next comyng'.[31]

On 23 May the king rode up to London[32] and, in the queen's honour, created at the Tower nearly fifty Knights of the Bath. This was a good many more knights than he had seen fit to create at the time of his own coronation, and among those whom he thus honoured were not only such young noblemen as the Duke of Buckingham and his brother, Humphrey Stafford, both minors and wards of the king, but also the eldest son of Lord Grey of Ruthyn, a cousin of Elizabeth's first husband, Lord Maltravers, the husband of Elizabeth's sister Margaret, and two of the queen's brothers, Richard and John Woodville. The latter was now the king's uncle by marriage, since he had recently taken to wife Warwick's aunt, Catherine, Dowager Duchess of Norfolk, a woman almost four times his age, and who had been already three times married.[33]

The queen came up to London, whose citizens had spent 200 marks on decorations and prepared a gift of 1,000 marks, on Friday 24 May, when the mayor[34] and aldermen went to meet her on Shooter's Hill and escorted her to the Tower.

State entries into London necessitated royal pageantry. If, as in this case, the sovereign were coming from the south crossing the bridge, then the Bridge Wardens were expected to prepare a welcome befitting the City, as a prelude to the many other entertainments to be seen in the streets.

Great preparations had already been made for the reception of Elizabeth; the bridge had been sprinkled with forty-five loads of sand to make it safe, at a cost of 4*d* a load, and the drawbridge had been fumigated at a charge of 3*s* 4*d*.[35]

The arrangement seems to have been that Elizabeth should be greeted on the south side of the bridge by 'St Paul', impersonated by a clerk of St George's, who received 20*d* for his pains. There also some clerks sang to her from a room hired in one of the houses on the bridge. The main pageant appears, however, to have been in the centre of the bridge, where twenty-six singers awaited to greet Elizabeth. There was also a stage on which eight carpenters had worked for twelve days, assisted by others, some of the time, during which they used 5,000 nails. It took two men fifteen days between them to fit the ninety-six ells of 'Sultwych' (a coarse cloth) which had been procured to cover the platform. The stainers (with the tailors) were the best-paid workers, receiving 12*d* a day for their labour. It was for them that brushes and hogs' bristles were bought, and flour for making paste. Moreover, other workmen used the papers – gold, green and 'cinopre' (red), black and white in colour, as well as red and purple buckram – for the figures that were to be on the staging.

There were eight of these figures, six women and two angels' for their hands, gloves were bought and stuffed with flock; their wigs were made of flax dyed with an ounce of saffron. The women wore fine kerchiefs, and for the angels' wings 900 peacock feathers were purchased. Other property for the angels had to be hired. All these preparations seem to have made the workers very thirsty, since there was a bill at the Crown for 46*s* 10*d*.

The pageant must have been both gay and colourful, with all its figures, its paint, its ballads written on six boards and fixed to the side of the platform, and with the two saints who appeared with it. In compliment to the queen, St Elizabeth – impersonated, as were all women's parts, by a man – greeted her with a speech.

Thus edified, Elizabeth passed on to St Thomas's chapel, before the door of which a cantor and his boys sang, and so over to the London side of the bridge, where the clerk of the church of St Magnus, with his boys, supplied the queen with more music; for them, the warders had paid for laundering of albs and amices.

Through the gaily decorated City streets Elizabeth slowly progressed, past the pageants prepared for her by the mayor and aldermen, to the Tower.[36]

On the next day, seated in her open horse-litter, Elizabeth was conducted to Westminster Palace, accompanied by all the newly created Knights of the Bath, wearing blue gowns with white silk hoods. On the following day, the Sunday before Whit Sunday,[37] she was crowned with great pomp in Westminster Abbey by the Archbishop of Canterbury.[38]

To judge from the account given in a contemporary manuscript,[39] no expense was spared in making the whole ceremony, including the ensuing banquet, as gorgeous as possible, in order to impress on the nation that Elizabeth was in very truth a queen. When Elizabeth, with the Bishop of Durham on her right hand and the Bishop of Salisbury on her left, entered Westminster Hall, where both the Duke of Clarence, the king's brother, and the Duke of Norfolk, Marshal of England, awaited her, 'ryding about the hall on horseback', their chargers 'rychely trapped hede and body to the grounde with Crapsieur[40] rychely embroidered and garnyst with spgnyls of golde, to avoyde the peple agenste the comyng of the queen into the hall', she was 'clothed in a mantyll of purpull and a coronall upon hir hede,[41] under the canapye' which was carried by the Barons of the Cinque Ports, while the Duchess of Buckingham bore her train.

And the queen standing in her place of estate between the said two bishops held in her right hand the sceptre of St Edward and in her left the sceptre of the realm and was so led through the hall to the monastery of Westminster, being followed by the Duchess of Suffolk, the king's sister, her sister Margaret and her mother, the Duchess of Bedford, and thirteen duchesses and countesses wearing surcoats of red velvet and ermine, and fourteen baronesses in scarlet and miniver, and twelve ladies bannerettes in scarlet.

And so with the said solemn procession she was received into the monastery at the North Door and was conveyed through the choir and so proceeded to the High Altar, there kneeling while the 'solempnyte apteyneng' was read over her by the Archbishop of Canterbury. And that done she lay before the altar while certain supplications were said over her by the Archbishop, and that done she was 'reivently thatyre of vrgins taken of hir hede' anointed first the head and so forth as apertained. And then crowned by the archbishop, the Archbishop of York holding the Holy Unction. And all the archbishops and bishops at the solemn coronation conveyed her to the place of state with great reverence and solemnity, the Abbot of Westminster[42] waiting on the 'Sceptres' spiritual and the Earl of Essex on the 'Sceptres' temporal. And at the beginning of the Gospel she sitting in her state the said abbot and Earl delivered unto her the finishing of the Gospel. And they were then received by the said abbot and earl giving attendance as apertained and at thoffering. The said abbot and earl bore the sceptre before her to the altar and so thence to the place of state and also the Duchess of Suffolk the young[er], and the Duchess of Bedford in the mass time attending upon the Crown reverently at certain times of response held the Crown on her head. And also after finishing of mass, all this while barefoot, going to the High Altar again and then Mass, and then was conveyed in the dignity of the chivalry unto the place of state. And that done the choir sang solemnly *Te Deum*. From the monastery she was led crowned between the two bishops under the canopy and the said abbot [of Westminster] with them under the same.

And the Duke of Suffolk being next on her right hand bearing the sceptre of St Edward. And the Earl of Essex on the left hand bearing the sceptre of England. And all the lords and ladies in 'semblabe wise' before and behind at the returning as at the going out. And so [she] was led from the monastery through the Great

Hall unto her chamber and then was 'newe revestyd in a surcote of purpull'. And from the chamber was brought between the said two bishops into the Banquet Hall unto her place of state.

In the same contemporary manuscript, the following description is given of the banquet which followed the coronation.

And when the queen did wash the Duke of Suffolk stood on her right hand and the Earl of Essex on the left hand holding the said sceptres as before. The Earl of Oxford served of water the Duke of Clarence held the basin and gave 'th assay'.

And the queen then was set in her state to meet crowned the said lords kneeling on either side of her at the table holding the said sceptres in their hands. And the Countess of Shrewsbury the younger, the Countess of Kent on the left hand kneeling held the veil before the queen at all times when took any 'repace' and kneeled next unto 'thastate'. And at any time when she so did she herself took off the Crown and when she had done she put it on again.

And on the right hand of the queen sat the Archbishop of Canterbury primate of England and at all times his service covered as the queen's. And on the left hand sat the Duchess of Suffolk and my Lady Margaret her sister. The officers were Sir John Howard, server; Lord Cromwell, carver; Lord Scales and William Allington of Cambridge, cupbearers; the Duke of Clarence Steward of England; the Earl of Arundel as Constable, on his right hand, the Duke of Norfolk as Marshal on the left hand. And these rode before the service on coursers richly trapped to the ground as before, and the Constable and Marshal 'some dele' before my Lord Steward, and before them on foot earls, barons, and other noble knights. And serving the said course of any dish the Knights of the Bath new made, and at that course seventeen dishes.

And at the middle table in the hall on the right hand sat thirteen bishops and abbots … and beneath them at the side table the chief judges of the King's Bench and of the Common pleas, the Chief Baron and their fellow judges and 'Barons Sargeants' and divers others.

At the middle table in the hall on the left hand sat the Duchess of Bedford and queen's mother 'and of countesses and baronesses many others'. And beneath them the Knights of the Bath new made at the same table … And at the table sat next to the wall on the left hand sat the Mayor of London and his brethren aldermen, divers officers and citizens of the same.

And at the 'Second Course' was served … nineteen dishes … and at the third fifteen dishes. And hypocras was served with my Lord Scales cupbearer. And the queen's almoner and a chaplain folded up the tablecloth unto the middle of the table and before her reverently took it up and bore it from the table.

And at washing after dinner Sir John Howard laid the 'Surnape' before the queen. The Duke of Norfolk Marshal of England went before and commanded and Sir Gilbert Debenham 'draweth the Surnape after'.

And at serving of the water the Duke of Clarence Steward of England stood in the middle, and on his right hand the Duke of Norfolk Marshal and on the left hand the Earl of Arundel Constable for the feast. The Earl of Oxford as Chamberlain brought in the basin, and the Duke of Clarence held the basin and gave the assay. And the Knights of the Bath new made brought the spice plates unto the cupbearer. Sir John Say brought the spice plate unto Sir William Bourchier son and heir to the Earl of Essex and he thereof served the queen. The Duke of Clarence delivered the assay (taste) of the spice plate. The Mayor of London bore the cup, with 'wyne of voyde'[43] and the 'Coupe of assay'.

And at the coming in of every course and during the service thereof the trumpets blowing up solemnly. And between certain courses the king's minstrals and the minstrals of other lords playing and piping in their instruments great and small before the queen full melodiously and in the most solemn wise.

And the feast done and the table cleared the queen was brought in to her chamber between the said Bishops of Durham and Salisbury, and the sceptres were borne before her 'with the said astates in semblable wise as they were brought in'.

And at the departing of the queen from the Hall the cup [that] the 'Wyne of Voyde' was served in to the queen was borne through the hall before the Mayor of London.

After the coronation, the queen sat in state at the great banquet in Westminster Hall, to which reference has already been made, where the Archbishop of Canterbury, who sang the Mass at her consecration, took his place at her right hand.[44] Charles the Bold fulfilled his promise of sending to England a sovereign-prince of Elizabeth's kin, to convince the Londoners that Edward 'had taken to himself a helpmate of princely alliances'. Count Jacques du Luxembourg, Elizabeth's uncle, landed at Greenwich some days before the coronation, bringing with him 100 knights.[45]

A largess of £20 for Garter and the other kings and heralds was proclaimed, probably at the coronation banquet, and Walter Halyday, marshal of the king's 'still minstrels', was granted a like sum to distribute among the minstrels, more than 100 in all, who had come up to the City in attendance on certain lords of the realm.[46] The following day, Monday, a grand tournament was held at Westminster, the honours of the day being carried off by Lord Stanley, who received as a prize a ring set with a ruby.[47] The Sacrists' Rolls of Westminster Abbey show that the belfry was let for sightseers of this tournament. They also record that the queen's alms at the coronation was £10 13s 4d.[48]

A house called Ormond's Inn[49] was granted to the newly crowned queen, and there she soon set up an elaborate ménage. At the head of her household was placed her chamberlain, Lord Berners, who was paid £40 a year and a reward of 40 marks; but to judge from their salaries, the Master of the Horse, John Woodville, and the two carvers, Sir Humphrey Bourchier and James Harte, who also got £40 each, were equally important. There were five ladies-in-waiting; Anne, Lady Bourchier, and Elizabeth, Lady Scales, who, like the chamberlain and the Master of the Horse, received £40 each, and Lady Alice Fogge, Lady Joanna Norreis, and Lady Elizabeth Ovedale, who received £20 each; moreover, besides these ladies, there were seven damsels and two other women attendants, whose salaries ranged from £10 to 5 marks. The queen also had three minstrels who, for £10 divided between them, 'made sweet music for her pleasure'. She also had her confessor, Edward Story, Chancellor of Cambridge University, and later Bishop of Carlisle, to whom she paid £10 a year 'for shriving her', and her physician, Domenico de Sirego, who got £40 'for physicking her', her chancellor, Roger Radcliff, her clerk of the signet, John Aleyn, her receiver-general, John Forster, her attorney-general and solicitor, John Dyve and Robert Isham, and, finally, her own council chamber in the New Tower next to the Exchequer. It is of some interest to know that the young Duke of Buckingham and his brother, Humphrey Stafford, also lived under the queen's roof, and that she hired one John Giles, master scholar, to teach them grammar. Poor Master John received a mere pittance for his labours; for while the king allowed the queen 500 marks a year for the expenses of the two boys,[50] £6 was all that their tutor received for nearly two years' services.[51]

# 4

# THE BIRTH OF PRINCESS ELIZABETH & THE DISAFFECTION OF WARWICK

Elizabeth Woodville was now fully installed as Queen of England, but during all the ceremonies connected with her coronation one person had been conspicuously absent. The Earl of Warwick, probably to Edward's relief as well as his own, was abroad on an embassy to the Duke of Burgundy.[1] As Warwick had shunned the queen's coronation, so in September (1465), when the earl's brother, George Neville, the Chancellor, was enthroned Archbishop of York, it was noticed that the king and queen were the only notable absentees.[2] Thus only a few months after Elizabeth's coronation were the seeds of discord already sown.

However, in the summer of 1465 Warwick had returned home just in time to hear of a new stroke of fortune which had been experienced by Edward. On 13 July, Henry VI, after being surprised at Waddington Hall, was captured at Bungerly Hippingstones, in Lancashire.[3] On the day of Henry's capture, Edward and Elizabeth had arrived at Canterbury, where they were received with great pomp by the archbishop and the prior.[4] Yet even a pilgrimage had to give place to such important news, with the result that the announcement was made to the royal couple about five days later. Edward and Elizabeth, accompanied by Archbishop Bourchier, thereupon proceeded to the cathedral to inform the people, a

*Te Deum* was sung, after which there followed a procession to Becket's tomb.

A few days later, on 24 July, the royal captive was brought to London, and Warwick, who had just returned from Calais, rode out to Islington to meet him, and conducted him to the Tower in a most unnecessarily ignominious fashion. On the following day the king and queen returned themselves to Westminster Palace, in all probability to take their part in the public rejoicings at the unfortunate Henry's capture.[5]

Edward's queen bore him his first child on 11 February 1466.[6] There is a story that the royal physicians, by means of their studies of astrology, had solemnly assured the king, who was a keen astrologist, that the queen would most certainly bear him an heir. One of these physicians, a certain Master Dominic, seems to have been more than usually positive of this fact, and doubtless hoping to be the first to inform the king that his forecast had been correct, he gained admission to an outer chamber, when the queen's hour of travail came, and as soon as he heard the child cry, called to one of the queen's ladies and asked 'what Her Grace had'. The ladies about Queen Elizabeth not wishing to answer, 'Only a girl,' one of them replied, 'Whatsoever the queen's grace hath here within, sure it is a fool that standeth there without.' Whereupon Master Dominic, being much distressed by this sharp answer, and having no news to report, stole away 'without seeing of the king for that time'.

Even if the sex of the queen's first child was disappointing, there was nothing lacking in the reception given to the little princess. Almost a month before the queen's confinement the Archbishop of Canterbury and nine other bishops had been summoned to assist at the baptism of the child 'which the queen shall bring forth'.[7]

The subsequent enmity between Elizabeth and Warwick had not at this time amounted to anything serious, for the earl stood godfather to the little princess, who was baptised by George

Neville, Archbishop of York, when she received her mother's name of Elizabeth.[8]

The churching of the queen was made an occasion for as much pomp and ceremony as the baptism, and most fortunately Gabriel Tetzel of Nuremberg, who had arrived in England about three weeks after Princess Elizabeth's birth, with Leo, Lord of Rozmital, brother of the Queen of Bohemia, has left us a full account of this ceremony.[9]

First in the procession to the abbey, Tetzel relates, came ecclesiastics with sacred relics, then scholars bearing lighted candles and singing as they walked, then noble matrons and maidens from all parts of the kingdom, then trumpeters, pipers, and players of stringed instruments, then forty-two of the king's minstrels, followed by twenty-four heralds and pursuivants, sixty lords and knights, and finally, under a canopy, the queen herself, supported by two dukes and followed by her mother and about sixty other ladies. Tetzel does not describe the actual service in the abbey, but, he tells us, when it was over the same stately procession accompanied the queen back to the palace, and there all remained to dine. So numerous were the guests that they filled four large halls, where 'the king's greatest earl' – very probably Warwick – who, as etiquette did not permit the king himself to be present, occupied the royal seat and, as the king's representative, received all the honours of royalty. During the dinner a largess was distributed among the heralds and musicians, and as the happy recipients went through the hall announcing in loud voices the amount of gifts received, Tetzel was able to learn that to the heralds alone as much as 400 nobles had been given. But at length Warwick rose from the table, and knowing that the strangers were anxious to see all there was to be seen, he led Tetzel and his friends into another hall, most lavishly decorated, where the queen sat at table in solitary grandeur upon a golden chair. Even the queen's mother and the king's sister were required to keep at a deferential distance and kneel if spoken to. Not until the first course had been served and the queen had drunk some water were her mother and sister-in-law allowed to sit down, and even then the other ladies remained on their knees. All through dinner (three long hours) the ladies knelt, and never a word did the queen utter;[10] when at long last the tables were removed and the dancing began, the queen, still sitting in her golden chair, looked on, while her mother knelt before her, standing up from time to time, and then only to rest her tired muscles. The dancing lasted some time, and among the many noble ladies who took part in it was the king's sister, who danced with a couple of dukes, making many curtsies before the queen. At last everybody was tired, and then the king's minstrels were called upon to close the festivities with their music.[11]

Meanwhile Edward, probably with an eye to his family alliance against the Nevilles, continued to shower favours on the rest of Elizabeth's family. It was not enough that Margaret Woodville had already been betrothed to the heir of the Earldom of Arundel. At the christening of the baby Princess Elizabeth three more of the queen's sisters, Catherine, Anne and Joan, were married to Henry, Duke of Buckingham,[12] the grandson of the duke slain at Northampton; William, Lord Bourchier, son and heir of the Earl of Essex;[13] and Anthony Grey de Ruthyn, son of the Earl of Kent.[14] Later on another sister, Jacquetta, was married to Lord Strange of Knockyn,[15] while in September Mary was betrothed to Lord Herbert's son, William, the future Earl of Pembroke, after he had been created Lord Dunster, the marriage being solemnised at Windsor Castle on the following 20 January,[16] and finally her youngest sister Martha married Sir John Bromley of Bartomley and Hextall, Shropshire.[17]

Nor was it on behalf of her sisters alone that Elizabeth sought to derive profit from her influence over the king's mind. On 4 March (1466) Walter Blount, Lord Mountjoy, Treasurer of England, who had served Edward faithfully from the day he first aspired to the

Crown, was given 1,000 marks for his services at the time of the queen's coronation and of the baptism of Princess Elizabeth, and was then required to resign his office in favour of the queen's father, Lord Rivers.[18] A few weeks later, on Whit Sunday, 25 May, the king promoted his new Treasurer to the rank of Earl Rivers,[19] and on 24 August the next year created him Lord High Constable.[20]

Edward, whether he wished to please Elizabeth or not, would have been far wiser had he sought the advancement of her relations another way. For much as Warwick had been vexed both by the removal of his uncle by marriage, Lord Mountjoy, from office,[21] and by the marriages arranged for the queen's sisters, he was even more annoyed by the marriage of her son, Sir Thomas Grey. Warwick had set his heart on marrying Anne, heiress of the exiled Duke of Exeter, to George Neville, the heir of his brother John, and so far had his plans succeeded that the young couple had already been betrothed. However, nothing daunted, Elizabeth, who appears to have been directly responsible for this arrangement, actually paid the Duchess of Exeter 4,000 marks to break off the match,[22] with the result that on 1 October 1466, the lady Anne was duly wedded at Greenwich Palace to the queen's eldest son by her first marriage.[23] This was a bitter blow to Warwick, who now realised, if he had not already suspected it, that even the marriages which had been arranged for his relations were in future to be broken by a word from Elizabeth.

It is difficult not to sympathise with Warwick at this stage. Not only had he exerted himself to the utmost to raise Edward to the kingship, but since the Battle of Towton he had used every means in his power to consolidate the position of the House of York on the throne, with the result that nearly everyone in England had come to look on him as the real ruler of the kingdom. Then suddenly, when the real hard work was over and his services were no longer so urgently required, not only did Edward, without so much as asking his advice, marry Elizabeth Woodville and make him, and his proposed embassy to France, the laughing-stock of both nations, but the earl found himself and his friends pushed to one side in favour of the queen's relations, the Woodvilles, whom he regarded as mere upstarts who had been partisans of the House of Lancaster till the very last minute. However, there is also much to be said in Edward's favour. Doubtless Warwick was inclined to presume farther than any loyal subject should, and if his queen and her relations whispered in the king's ear that the Nevilles enjoyed too much authority,[24] perhaps they were not altogether wrong. Warwick's influence did indeed pass the bounds of safety; he held too many important posts; his wealth was too vast, his friends and followers among all classes were too numerous. In London especially the earl had gained a dangerous amount of popularity, largely by means of lavish hospitality.[25]

But while it might be as well to curb the wealth and power of the Nevilles, the undertaking was a very delicate one, more especially since Edward was so greatly indebted to them. Vaguely resentful because Warwick seemed to overshadow him, and probably only half aware of what he was doing, Edward allowed himself to be drawn away from the earl more and more every day, until the wound which his secret marriage had made in the earl's pride festered beyond hopes of healing.

Nevertheless, the Woodvilles, although they may have done everything in their power to thwart Warwick's plans, cannot be held directly responsible for the open breach that finally came about between Edward and Warwick. Despite the fact that Edward's secret marriage had certainly been the first step towards the breaking up of the friendship between the two men,[26] it was Warwick's determination to shape England's foreign policy, as he, not the king, saw fit, that was the real cause of all the trouble. Indeed, the choice of friendship between France and Burgundy was soon to lead to open war between king and kingmaker.[27]

The next slight that Warwick received from Edward touched him even more closely. The earl wished to marry his eldest daughter, Isabel, now in her sixteenth year, to the king's brother George, Duke of Clarence, who was equally in favour of the match, since Isabel was not only rich, but pretty. Edward, however, did not in any way approve of this proposal, and following a long visit which Clarence and his younger brother Richard, Duke of Gloucester, had paid to Warwick at Cambridge towards the end of 1466, Edward summoned them to his presence on their return and asked why they had left London, and by whose advice they had visited the earl. They replied that 'none had been the cause save they themselves.[28] When asked whether there had been any talk of a marriage, they replied that there had not. But the king, who had been fully informed of all, waxed worth, and sent them from his presence.'[29] Edward strictly forbade the marriage, and for the moment there was no more talk of it; however, Clarence and Warwick always kept in touch with one another, much to Edward's annoyance. It was not at all pleasing to him to find his heir presumptive and his most powerful subject on such apparently good terms.

A few months later Edward insulted Warwick even more by thwarting his foreign policy. The king sent the earl on an embassy to France in the spring of 1467, ordering him to visit Louis XI and turn the eighteen-month truce made in 1465 into a permanent peace on the best possible terms. It soon became obvious, however, that Edward, probably encouraged by the queen,[30] had devised this commission simply in order to get the earl out of the kingdom, at a time when his presence there was most undesirable.

Once Warwick was safely out of the way in France,[31] Edward proceeded to work out his own plans for an alliance with Burgundy. Despite the fact that its primary object had been non-political,[32] the famous tournament, which took place in Smithfield in June 1467 between Anthony, Lord Scales, the queen's brother, and the Bastard of Burgundy,[33] did much to strengthen the ties of friendship between England and Burgundy, and helped to a considerable extent in furthering the project of an English alliance with Burgundy by means of a marriage between the king's sister, Margaret, and Charles the Bold, son of Philip, Duke of Burgundy.

That Edward favoured this policy was, however, due in no small degree to the queen and her relations, who had Burgundian connections,[34] and moreover understood how popular the Burgundian alliance would be among the English trading classes.[35] Thus, like *la Pompadour* after her, Elizabeth made her influence felt even in the foreign policy of the time, and it would appear that more credit should be given to her for the Burgundian alliance and all that it entailed than has hitherto been the case.

As was only to be expected, Elizabeth and her relations played a leading part in the festivities which came after the tournament, whereas not one single member of the Nevilles is noted as having been present.

As for the king and queen, they had caused a supper to be prepared on the second day of the tournament (12 June) in the Grocer's Hall;[36] and thither came the ladies sixty of four-score, of such noble houses that the least was the daughter of a baron. And the supper was great and plentiful; and Mons. the Bastard and his people feasted greatly and honourably.[37]

And Mons. the Bastard prayed the ladies to dine on the next Sunday, and especially the queen and her sisters: and he made great preparations.[38]

Suddenly, however, all this festivity was turned into mourning. On 15 June Philip, Duke of Burgundy, died; his son, Charles the Bold, becoming duke in his place.[39] On receiving the news of Philip's death, the Bastard, whose mission to England had been highly successful, left England as soon as possible (21 June).

On 1 July[40] Warwick returned to England, bringing with him an embassy from Louis XI. On his arrival he soon discovered that the queen had once again made full use of her influence over the king to deal another shattering blow at him and the whole House of Neville. The earl immediately realised the cool astuteness of his greatest enemy, when he heard that on 8 June his brother, George Neville, Archbishop of York, had been deprived of the Great Seal,[41] and he must have been even further convinced of her powers of intrigue on hearing that Edward was less inclined than ever before to favour a French alliance. In fact, during Warwick's absence the king had been seeking alliances all over Europe, with the exception of the traditional enemy, France.

There can no longer have been in Warwick's mind the slightest shadow of a doubt that the queen was bringing her influence to bear, and that in no uncertain fashion, in the political as well as the domestic field. During his enforced absence she had contrived, and that successfully, to upset all his carefully laid plans. Not only had she persuaded the king to take the Great Seal from his (Warwick's) brother, and by so doing greatly weakened the position held by the Nevilles, but, more mortifying still, she had apparently gone a long way towards persuading the king to decide in favour of a Burgundian alliance in preference to an alliance with France, and that when he had just returned from the latter country bringing with him an embassy. If Warwick disliked Elizabeth prior to his departure, that dislike must from that moment on have turned to a hatred so intense that it was, before very long, destined to lead to open hostilities, and end with the death of Warwick himself on Barnet Field.[42]

# 5

# ELIZABETH & THE BURGUNDIAN ALLIANCE

Meanwhile George, Duke of Clarence, was on very bad terms with the king, his brother, and on equally good terms with Warwick. Their common hatred of the Woodvilles[1] and the king's refusal to allow the marriage with Isabel were sufficient to bring them together. They became still further attached to each other as the result of Edward's incivility to Warwick and the embassy that came with him from Louis XI. It was noted that Clarence alone went to meet the ambassadors on their arrival; and when Edward, after admitting them to one formal interview, withdrew on 6 July with the queen to Windsor to avoid seeing them again,[2] Clarence and Warwick were the only persons with whom they had opportunity to negotiate. Warwick accordingly showed the Frenchmen that the king was governed by 'traitors', who not only were opposed to the interests of France, but also had persuaded the king to deprive his brother of the Great Seal, and that they must concert measures of vengeance together against him.[3] From this time onwards, Clarence and Warwick began to entertain the designs which eventually led to armed insurrection against the king.

In the midst of all this political discord Elizabeth was residing at Windsor, quietly awaiting her second confinement. On 16 July her mother, the Dowager Duchess of Bedford, also arrived at Windsor in order to be with her daughter at so critical a time.[4] Early in August Elizabeth gave birth to a second daughter, who received at her baptism on 12 August the name of Princess Mary,[5] on which auspicious occasion the French ambassadors would appear to have honoured her with their presence.[6] On 9 October the queen was granted £400 a year for the expenses of her two daughters, who resided, during their early years, at the Place of Sheen under the care of their governess, Margaret, Lady Berners.[7]

Two days after the christening of the little princess (14 August) the French embassy left England, having, as was in the circumstances only to be expected, accomplished little or nothing. On their departure Warwick retired in exasperation to his castle at Middleham.[8] Advantage was taken of his voluntary absence to resume the suspended negotiations for the marriage of Edward's sister Margaret and Charles the Bold; another embassy, in which figured the queen's brother, Anthony, Lord Scales, being sent to Burgundy on 20 September.[9] On 1 October Princess Margaret, in a Grand Council of peers held at Kingston-on-Thames,[10] gave her formal consent to the marriage.

While Warwick was absent from Court he received a visit from the Duke of Clarence, with the result that Edward soon became aware that the marriage, which he had already strictly forbidden, between the duke and Isabel Neville, the earl's eldest daughter, was being pressed forward. As both parties were within the prohibited degrees of relationship,[11] a dispensation from Pope Pius II was necessary, and Edward is reported to have made representations to His Holiness in order to prevent its being granted.[12]

When at Christmas the king summoned Warwick to Court, the earl sent back the somewhat haughty reply that 'never would he come again to the council while all his mortal enemies, who were about the king's person, namely Lord Rivers the Treasurer, and Lord Scales and Lord Herbert and Sir John Woodville, remained there present'.[13]

Everything seemed to be heading for an open rupture when their common friends interfered, by whose means the Archbishop of York and Earl Rivers met at Nottingham and settled the terms of reconciliation. Thanks to their perseverance, Warwick saw fit to appear at Court once more.[14]

When on 18 June 1468 Edward, accompanied by his queen, conducted his sister Margaret to the Court on her way to Flanders for her marriage with Charles the Bold, Warwick had so far recovered from his former annoyance that he rode 'before hur on hur horse'.[15]

The first stage of this journey ended at the monastery of Stratford Langthorne, where the king and queen and the future Duchess of Burgundy spent several days.[16] On 23 June the royal party journeyed from Canterbury to Margate, where, on the 24th, Margaret embarked for Sluys with a large retinue.[17]

Here also Elizabeth had secured positions of honour for her relations to the exclusion of the Nevilles. Her brother, Lord Scales, who was to act as her 'presenter', and another brother, Sir John Woodville, also accompanied their sister-in-law. It was indeed a great moment for Elizabeth. As the *New Ellen*[18] sailed gracefully away, the queen must have regarded that stately vessel with a gleam of triumph in her eye. Did it not bear the fruits of yet another great triumph over Warwick and the Nevilles?

Thus escorted, Margaret landed at Sluys on 25 June, and on 3 July the marriage duly took place at Damme. The splendour of the festivities, which lasted for nine days, taxed even the power of the heralds to describe. There were many tournaments, in some of which Elizabeth's brothers took part, Sir John Woodville having the satisfaction of carrying off one of the chief prizes.[19] In such a way was celebrated this marriage, destined to be a turning-point in the history of Europe.[20]

No sooner had Margaret sailed away than the king and queen hastened back to London, where a very important trial was due to begin. Early in June 1468 a man named Cornelius,[21] an emissary from Margaret of Anjou, had been captured at Queenborough by Elizabeth's younger brother, Sir Richard Woodville,[22] bearing letters from a Lancastrian exile to friends in London. This unfortunate man was brought before the king at Stratford, where, under torture, he accused several prominent Londoners, among whom was John Hawkins, a servant of Lord Wenlock, of complicity in correspondence with Margaret.[23] Hawkins was then arrested, and on being questioned, he in his turn accused, among others, Sir Thomas Cooke, who was not only an alderman but high in the king's favour.[24] Cooke was immediately arrested.[25] It then came to light that Hawkings had attempted to borrow 1,000 marks from him on behalf of Margaret of Anjou, but when Cooke had discovered for whom the money was meant, he had refused to lend even £100. Princess Margaret, on the point of setting out for Burgundy, went bail for Cooke,[26] but no sooner than had she left England than he was again arrested. He was then brought with others to the Guildhall, where, possibly because Edward wished them to think that he still had cause to regard their loyalty as above suspicion, both Clarence and Warwick took their place among the Justices, as did Elizabeth's father, Earl Rivers.[27] From a judge like Markham, who was popularly known as 'the upright judge',[28] the prisoners might well have hoped for a fair trial, and presumably they would have received one, had not an unfortunate incident occurred to prejudice the king's mind against them. At this very moment there came news from Wales, which seemed to confirm the stories of Cornelius and Hawkins – namely, the arrival of Jasper Tudor near Harlech.[29]

Although this small attempt at insurrection was doomed to end in failure almost before it had begun[30] it was to cause the unfortunate Thomas Cooke the greatest imaginable hardship.

The moment Edward was told of Jasper Tudor's landing in Wales, he jumped to the conclusion that all Cornelius had confessed was true; he thereupon decided to make a special example of Sir Thomas Cooke, who was still confined in the Tower, his wife being committed to the custody of the mayor.[31] Thereupon the Treasurer of England, Earl Rivers, Elizabeth's father, who 'to the said Sir Thomas was a great enemy', and Sir John Fogge,[32] the treasurer of the king's household, ransacked both Cooke's town house and his country house at Gidea Hall, Essex; though they pretended to be searching for proof of his guilt, they carried off not only his papers but his most valuable belongings.[33] £1,600 worth of woollen cloth was also seized, and ultimately found its way into the hands of the king's creditor, Gerard Caniziani.[34]

In the excitement of the moment Cooke's guilt had been taken for granted, yet early in July the jury found him guilty only of misprision of treason,[35] and on 26 July he was granted a pardon.[36] This, however, did not mean that the unfortunate Sir Thomas either recovered his property or escaped other penalties. From the Tower he was sent to Bread Street Compter, thence to the King's Bench prison, and on 21 November he was deprived of his aldermanry by the king's command.[37] Not until he had paid a fine of £8,000 was he set at liberty, and even then, Queen Elizabeth, who also wished to have her share of the spoils, came forward with a demand, based on the ancient and almost obsolete custom of *aurum reginae* ('queen-gold'), that for every £1,000 he paid to the king by way of fine he must pay her 100 marks.[38] Cooke did not submit to this further fleecing without a struggle, but finally he had to give the queen all she wanted, and 'many good fits' to her counsel besides.[39]

Cooke's sufferings appear to have been entirely undeserved. Hawkins, his sole accuser, made on the day of his execution a declaration in which he stated that Cooke was innocent of everything of which he had been accused.

The truth of the whole story seems to be that the Earl and Lady Rivers and quite possibly the queen, probably because they coveted his great wealth, wished to get rid of Cooke, and took advantage of the king's need of money in order to carry out their purpose. Moreover, it was Rivers who, because Chief Justice Markham had circumvented his designs by directing the jury to return a verdict of misprision only, succeeded – presumably owing to Elizabeth's influence of the king – in having Markham removed from office.[40]

Thus once again did Queen Elizabeth cause the name of Woodville to be hated not only by her ancient enemy Warwick and the old nobility but – and this was a far more serious matter – by a large section of the people as well. This demand for *aurum reginae*, following so soon after Desmond's death, must have had a great effect on public opinion. Little did she suspect that the people were soon to show, in no uncertain fashion, that they were prepared to take extreme measures in aiding Warwick in his attempt to check once and for all her family's seemingly insatiable ambition.[41]

According to some accounts, Elizabeth visited Cambridge sometime during 1468:[42] probably with a view to inspecting her recent foundation, Queens' College, of which, as early as 1465, she had, 'as the true foundress by right of succession', become patroness.[43]

# 6

# THE REBELLION OF 1469

Throughout the length and breadth of England storm-clouds were now gathering. Fully aware that he dared attempt nothing without Clarence's help, Warwick appears to have promised to make him king, or at least ruler of all England.[1] Once the earl saw that Clarence was eager to fall in with his plan, he conspired with his brother, George Neville, the Archbishop of York, to raise up insurrections in the North when he gave word for action.

During May 1469 the Court had been at Windsor, where, on the 21st, the king had elevated Lord Stafford of Southwick to the Earldom of Devon.[2] Edward then decided to make his long-planned tour through East Anglia. Accompanied by Rivers, Scales, and Sir John Woodville, he was on 15 and 16 June at Bury St Edmunds, whence he continued his journey, visiting Norwich, Walsingham, King's Lynn and Wisbech. At Norwich the king had 'right good cheer and great gifts, wherewith he holdeth himself so well content that he will hastily be here again, and the queen also'.[3]

A revolt had meanwhile broken out in Yorkshire, which is generally referred to as Robin of Redesdale's[4] insurrection, from the name assumed by its leader Robert Hilyard.[5] The insurgents published manifestos everywhere, complaining of the too-great influence enjoyed by the queen's relations, whom they considered the authors of the taxes that impoverished them and of the calamities that oppressed the nation.[6] The insurgents further demanded the restoration of the Earldom of Northumberland to the heir of the Percies, whose title had been granted by Edward to Warwick's brother, John, Lord Montagu, in recognition of his services at Hedgeley Moor and Hexham. This latter demand proved fatal to their cause, since, at the first sign of danger to his earldom, Montagu marched against the insurgents, defeated them, and beheaded their leader.[7]

But this engagement was far from checking the rising. In a week the whole of Yorkshire was in arms, and it soon became evident in whose interest the movement was working.[8] Sir John Conyers replaced Hilyard, and assumed his name of Robin of Redesdale, advancing southwards with a large army.[9]

By this time London was feeling so troubled about the state of the kingdom that, on 20 June, the master and wardens of the armourers' company were forbidden to send any arms out of the city without a licence from the mayor;[10] but the king, seemingly quite unconcerned, made his pilgrimage to Walsingham, then to Croyland, whence he took ship to Fotheringay, where he fixed his headquarters;[11] Elizabeth was awaiting him at Fotheringay, and there he spent a week, during which time more troops joined him.[12] But by 5 July he had arrived at Stamford, and by the 7th Grantham, whence he appears to have pushed on at once to Newark. On his arrival at Newark, Edward realised for the first time the seriousness of this insurrection, and finding his forces totally insufficient to face the rebels, immediately turned back to Nottingham,[13] where news reached him which suddenly revealed the whole scope of the insurrection.

The moment that Edward's attention had been distracted by the Northern rising, Warwick and Clarence had, on 6 July, quietly slipped over to Calais, being accompanied by George Neville, Archbishop of York.[14] This began to look suspicious, and on 9 July

Edward wrote to Clarence, Warwick and the archbishop bidding them all to come to him without delay.[15] Long before his orders can have reached them, the full tale of treason was out. Within a few days after his departure, on 11 July,[16] Clarence was married at Calais to Warwick's elder daughter, Isabel, thanks to the efforts of James Goldwell, the future Bishop of Norwich, who, apparently encouraged by bribes from Clarence,[17] had for a long time been attempting to obtain the necessary dispensation from Pius II.[18] By this act Warwick had openly defied the king.

On the next day, 12 July, Warwick issued a manifesto stating that he, Clarence and the archbishop considered the articles of Robin of Redesdale just and salutary, and that they were coming to lay a petition before the king.[19] On 18 July they duly reached Canterbury, where thousands of his Kentish supporters rallied to his banner.[20] From Canterbury the rebels advanced on London, which promptly threw open its gates. Having obtained a loan of £1,000 from the mayor, the earl left the city to meet Robin of Redesdale, who was already marching south to join him.[21] The king thus found himself caught between two armies – Robin's in the North, and Warwick's in the South.

Even before Edward was fully aware of Warwick's treason he had begun to recognise the danger of the Northern rising. Two considerable forces under the leadership of the earls of Pembroke and Devon were now in arms on his behalf. The king remained at Nottingham with Hastings, Mountjoy and the Woodvilles, but the general dislike of the latter was once again to prove fatal to his cause.

When the king expressed the desire to fight in order that he should not be surprised by Warwick's forces, Lord Mountjoy is stated to have said to him, 'Sire, no one wishes your person ill, but it would be well to send away my Lord Rivers and his children when they have done speaking with you.'[22]

When Lord Rivers heard this he said to the king, 'Sire, I am ready to do your will; for I do not wish that, on my account, there should be any discord between you and those of your blood.'[23] Edward deemed it prudent to take his father-in-law's advice. Rivers and Sir John Woodville thereupon retired to Grafton,[24] while Scales joined Elizabeth at Norwich.[25]

During the time that the rebels under Robin of Redesdale were marching to join Warwick, the Earls of Pembroke and Devon were hastening to the king's aid. The two armies met on 26 July at Edgecote, just at the time when Devon, having quarrelled with Pembroke about lodgings, had withdrawn all his archers from the army. The battle resulted in the complete defeat of Royalist forces, Pembroke himself being captured.[26]

This defeat left the king entirely at Warwick's mercy. A few days later he was captured by the Archbishop of York at Olney, near Coventry,[27] whence he was conducted first to the town of Warwick, and afterwards to Middleham.[28] The queen's father, and brother, Sir John Woodville, were also captured by the rebels at Grafton, and put to death at Northampton on 12 August.[29] This act must almost certainly have been Warwick's own deed, as the Earl Rivers and Sir John Woodville had always been his pet aversions.

During the events which led to the deaths of her father and brother, Elizabeth had been in comparative safety in East Anglia. At the time of the king's departure from Fotheringay, Elizabeth had been preparing to accompany him on a progress into Norfolk;[30] since, however, Edward was prevented by force of circumstance from accompanying her, she seems to have had both the courage and the presence of mind to undertake the proposed journey to Norwich alone.

Thus, on 6 July, while Edward was on his way from Stamford to Grantham, John Aubrey, then Mayor of Norwich, addressed a letter to Sir Henry Spelman, the Recorder, informing him that the Sheriff of Norfolk himself[31] had told him the queen should be at Norwich 'up on Tuysday[32] cometh the sevenyght suyrly'. Furthermore 'by cause of this shuld be hir first comyng hedir … he let [him] to wete that she well desire to ben resseyved and attendid as wurshepfully as evir was quene a fore hir'.[33]

As soon as the Corporation were informed of the queen's intention to visit the city, they began their preparations to receive her, and hastened to make themselves acquainted with her movements.

One Lyntok went to Windsor, by order of the mayor, to bring certain intelligence of the queen's coming. Subsequently he rode to Bury St Edmunds on a similar errand; and then another man rode to diverse parts of Norfolk to gain intelligence of the queen's progress. After this, Robert Horgoner went to ascertain the road the queen intended to take; finally John Sadler rode to tell the queen's servants to enter the city by Westwyk Gate.

Meanwhile preparations for the queen's reception were going on within the town. A Committee of the Council was appointed; it inaugurated its proceedings with a feast at Henry Bradfield's hostelry. Indeed, such extreme care was taken that everything should be in order throughout her progress through the city that a Freemason was actually paid sixpence for mending the crest of the conduit on the north side of St Andrew's churchyard.

When the queen eventually arrived, with her daughters and suite, at the Westwyk Gate, she was received by the mayor and Corporation. At these gates, under the direction of one Parnell of Ipswich, a stage had been constructed covered with red and green worsted, adorned with figures of angels, and with scutcheons and banners of the king's and queen's arms, and fourteen square scutcheons powdered with crowns, roses, and *fleurs-de-lys*. Here were also two giants made of wool and *hungry* (Hungary) leather, their bodies stuffed with hay, and their crests glittering all the grandeur of gold and silver lead. There were also two patriarchs, twelve apostles, and sixteen virgins in mantles with hoods. A certain friar played Gabriel. John Mumford's son assisted in this performance; and Gilbert Spirling exhibited a pageant of the Salutation of Mary and Elizabeth, which required a speech from him in explanation. There were many clerks singing finely, accompanied upon the organs. Thence the queen proceeded to the gates of the Friars Preachers, and here, under Thomas Cambridge's house, another stage had been erected, similarly decorated: the stairs leading up to it covered with 'Tapser work', lent by the Friars Minors, who also contributed a number of their vestments for the pageant; and here had been brought from the cathedral, for the accommodation of the queen, the great chair of St Luke's Guild, which seems, by the money expended in treating the fraternity for lending it, and the care and labour bestowed upon its protection from injury, to have been a fabric of great magnificence. The entertainment offered to the queen at this point was limited to a vocal performance by one 'Fakke' and his boys. It seems probably that yet more pageantry would have been provided, had the shows and pageants not been terminated abruptly on account of the heavy and continuous rain.

The queen and her suite retired to her lodgings at the Friars Preachers, and the Corporation and performers rushed to the Guildhall, where numerous men carried dry clothes for them. A house was taken close by Westwyk Gate, into which the covering and ornaments of the stage were quickly placed; Stephen Skinner and others found coats and hoods for the many other performers. Very considerable damage was done to the decorations by the rain, for every bill paid had extra allowance made for the damage to articles caused by it or by the haste with which they had been removed; and thus ominously did the reception, which was to rival that of 'any queen that was afore her', end.[34]

The actual date of the queen's arrival in Norwich is not named, nor is it certain how long she remained there.

We are aware that the king, after his progress through East Anglia, spent a week with the queen at Fotheringay Castle. It seems probably that on Edward's departure, about 4 July, Elizabeth returned to Windsor, as the Mayor of Norwich sent Lyntok to that place to inquire about the queen's coming journey to Norwich. Possibly as a result of Lyntok's journey the Mayor of Norwich wrote to the Recorder stating that the queen was expecting to arrive in Norwich 'up on Tuysday cometh sevenyght' – namely, 18 July.

If, as seems likely, the queen arrived before Westwyk Gate on that day, she was probably joined a few days later by her brother, Lord Scales, whom Edward had sent to Norfolk for safety.[35]

Elizabeth does not appear to have remained in Norwich for any great length of time, for by 21 July she was certainly back in London.[36] From the absence of all notice of processions and pageants on her leaving Norwich, one may conclude that the report of the defeat of the Royalist forces at Edgecote on 26 July, followed by the yet more serious and distressing news of the king's capture by Warwick, about four days later,[37] caused her to depart without any further displays, and to make for London as fast as ever she could. It was there that a few days later she first heard the terrible news of the execution of her father and younger brother, and the attempted indictment of her mother for sorcery.[38] This must indeed have been a bitter blow to one whose family affections were so strong. This, however, was but the first of the many cruel blows that the unfortunate Elizabeth was to be called upon to endure; with her father's death began that long period of doubt and uncertainty, victory and defeat, joy, sadness, and suffering which was to last to the end of her life. She was permitted to remain in London during Edward's captivity, keeping 'scant state' but safe and unmolested.[39] Nevertheless she seems to have been well looked after, as, on 31 July, the mayor and aldermen had voted to make her a gift of wine.[40]

Edward was over a month in Warwick's hands.[41] The earl then began to realise that his troubles were only just beginning. Edward was certainly in his power, but he was far too brave a man to be frightened into acquiescing to his captor's demands by mere captivity. And what of the queen? Warwick was perhaps even more afraid of her than he was of the king. If Edward was once set at liberty, she was not likely to let him forget that Warwick had caused her father and brother to be beheaded. He may even have pictured her in his mind's eye, lying awake at night, weeping for her loved ones and planning some deep revenge on their executioner, now her husband's jailer.

Such a state of affairs could not go on indefinitely. There had already been riots in London, where Edward was always exceedingly popular, and the Duke of Burgundy had actually gone so far as to write to the Lord Mayor to promise the city aid, should this prove necessary.[42] Moreover, when Warwick found himself unable to raise any forces in Yorkshire to suppress a Lancastrian rising under Sir Humphrey Neville as long as he continued to hold the king a prisoner,[43] he considered it would be greatly to his advantage if he released the king,[44] whom he had never kept in very strict confinement, allowing him, through accompanied by keepers, to hunt in the castle grounds. Consequently after Edward had given 'fair speech and promise', he was conducted back to London by the Archbishop of York.[45]

Before Christmas Warwick and Clarence received a general pardon for all their past offences,[46] and, on 6 November, Edward agreed to the betrothal of his eldest daughter, Princess Elizabeth, to George Neville, Warwick's nephew and nearest male heir,[47] who, in honour of the alliance, received the title of Duke of Bedford.[48] It is possible that Edward hoped by this means to draw Montagu apart from his brothers by giving him this special interest in the royal prosperity.[49] Whatever the king's intentions may have been, Elizabeth cannot have regarded the prospect of her eldest daughter's betrothal to so close a relation of him whom she considered as her father's murderer with anything but mixed feelings. She may even have had some suspicions that Warwick was planning to join the houses of York and Neville in order to overthrow her own relations and deprive them of the influence which they held at Court; however, like the king himself, she was forced to keep silent and await future developments. If only she could give the kingdom an heir, her anxiety would be greatly diminished. She seemed fated to bring nothing but daughters into the world. A few months before her husband's captivity, on 20 March, she had given birth at Westminster to 'a very handsome daughter, which rejoiced the king and all the nobles exceedingly, though they would have preferred a son'. Two barrels of hippocras and a pipe of Gascon wine were 'delivered into the king's cellar' for the christening, when the baby princess received the name of Cecily.[50]

As this eventful year drew slowly towards its close, it must have seemed to Elizabeth that she had just awoken from some ghastly nightmare. As the vision of the past events slowly glided before her eyes – her father's death, her husband's captivity, her own deep humiliation – she needs must have realised that everything pointed to the fact that Warwick alone was responsible for all the sorrow and suffering which she had experienced in the last twelve months. He had won this time. Let him be on his guard! Should an opportunity for revenge one day occur, she would not hesitate to make full use of it.

# 7

# WARWICK'S FLEETING TRIUMPH

After the general pardon accorded to Warwick and Clarence, Edward's confidence in his brother, at least, appears to have returned; this impression was confirmed when, early in March 1470, on the outbreak of a fresh insurrection in Lincolnshire, Clarence offered his services and those of Warwick to help subdue the rebels. This new outbreak was admittedly a movement in favour of Henry VI, headed by Sir Robert Welles, the eldest son of Lord Welles. This insurrection, very carefully organised by Warwick and Clarence, had been purposely deferred till they left the king and retired into Warwickshire. They then informed the rebels that they would come from the west and join them;[1] Edward, although unwilling to believe their treason, nevertheless saw fit to advance as far as Stamford. On his arrival the king learned that Sir Robert Welles was but 5 miles away, at Empingham, where he was preparing for battle. The next day, 12 March, Edward made a surprise attack on the rebels at Empingham, before Warwick and Clarence had time to join them. In a few moments it was all over, the king remaining the undisputed victor of Losecoat Field.[2]

Two days after this battle the Earl of Worcester, despite his great unpopularity and well-known brutality, was appointed Constable of England.[3] This appointment would seem to provide yet further evidence of Elizabeth's influence over Edward. It appears almost inconceivable that anyone else could have persuaded Edward to take this step. Furthermore, the Earl of Worcester, taking advantage of the queen's friendship, was daily obtaining more and more influence over the king. Not content with the many offices which she had already procured for him, Elizabeth succeeded, on 10 July, in having Worcester created Treasurer of England.[4] Small wonder that Worcester had been willing to help her against Desmond two years back. By persuading the king to shower honours on a man who was openly referred to as the 'Butcher' of England,[5] Elizabeth not only made herself thoroughly unpopular, but contributed to Worcester's being sent to the scaffold during Edward's temporary exile. Worcester's friendship with the queen had, however, at least one very important result, in that the earl probably succeeded in interesting Elizabeth and her brother in literature, thus preparing the way for the royal patronage of Caxton's printing press.[6]

Following the Battle of Losecoat Field, Sir Robert Welles was captured, and before suffering the extreme penalty, made a full confession, with the result that Edward immediately realised that Welles was merely the instrument of Warwick's and Clarence's extreme treachery; he also learned one more thing – namely, that their object was nothing less than to kill him and set Clarence on the throne.[7]

On this amazing revelation Edward sent a summons by Garter King of Arms to the treacherous earl and duke, charging them to come to him and clear themselves, but they only withdrew to Lancashire, attempting as they went to raise the North of England against the king. Edward thereupon advanced to York, and on 24 March issued a proclamation summoning the earl and duke to his presence within four days.[8] The four days having duly expired, Edward returned south to Nottingham, where on the 31st he declared them traitors. They now prepared for flight, and, taking their wives with them, embarked at Dartmouth on the west coast for Calais,[9] which they hoped to secure.

Edward had, however, anticipated this movement, and had already sent Galliard de Duras and other officers to warn Lord Wenlock, who was in command at Calais, that he was on no account to permit them to enter the town.[10] Thus on his arrival at Calais the earl was duly refused admittance, and after vainly attempting to negotiate with Wenlock, and having cruised about the Channel for a few days, the fugitives finally decided to go to France and solicit aid from Louis XI. They therefore set sail for Normandy, landing on about 1 May at Hornfleur,[11] where, at Louis XI's command, they were warmly received by Louis, Bastard of Bourbon.[12] They then repaired to Louis XI at Angers, where there occurred one of the strangest negotiations in all history.

On the flight of their enemies, Warwick and Elizabeth evidently decided to return thanks for their almost bloodless victory by celebrating the Feast of Pentecost at Canterbury.

No effort would seem to have been spared in order to make this festival as gorgeous as possible. The king arrived at Canterbury on 6 June, while the queen and Princess Elizabeth came two days later, being received at the cathedral door by the prior, John Oxney, and the monks wearing white copes. The next day arrived the bishops of Ely, Durham, Bangor and Carlisle, together with many of the nobility, including the queen's brother, Lord Rivers, and her friend, the Earl of Worcester. The next day, being Whit Sunday, the king and queen took part in the procession at High Mass, which was celebrated by Thomas Rotherham, Bishop of Rochester, while they attended both High Mass and Vespers on the following day.[13]

On 13 June Elizabeth finally left Canterbury for London, with Edward, who had visited Dover and Sandwich the day before, following her on 15 June.[14]

In such a way did the king and queen render thanks for their latest triumph over their enemies, seemingly unaware of the sinister plot that was already being hatched for their overthrow.[15]

Warwick and Clarence were far from being the only persons opposed to Edward IV. Margaret of Anjou and her son Prince Edward must have hated him even more bitterly than the treacherous pair who had just succeeded in making their escape from his thoroughly justifiable anger. In spite of this fact, it hardly seemed possible that Margaret, who undoubtedly looked upon Warwick as the chief cause of all her misfortune, would ever wish to hear even his name again. Nevertheless, Louis contrived not only to bring them together at Angers, on 4 August, but to reconcile them with a view to united action against their common enemy. Eventually Margaret was persuaded not only to pardon Warwick, but to seal the matter with a contract for the marriage of her son Edward to the earl's second daughter, Anne, on condition that Warwick should in the first place invade England, and recover the kingdom for Henry VI.[16]

One person alone was thoroughly vexed at the success of Louis's scheme.[17] The Duke of Clarence had no wish to see Warwick reconciled to the House of Lancaster, since he had already entertained serious thoughts of himself becoming king. He had now to be contented with Margaret's promise that his name should be inserted in the succession after that of her son, should the latter have no issue. Since, however, Prince Edward of Lancaster was a healthy, promising young man, even this prospect seemed extremely remote; Clarence, indeed, began to regret that he had ever placed himself under Warwick's guidance.

Just at this critical moment Edward sent his brother a message from England, through a lady attending on his wife the Duchess Isabel, praying him not to wreck the fortunes of his own family by adhering to the House of Lancaster, and bidding him remember the hereditary hatred that lay between them. Edward ended by offering his brother a free pardon. Clarence replied by promising to come over to Edward's side as soon as he should reach England.[18] Furthermore, their mother, Cecily, Duchess of York, their sisters,

Anne, Duchess of Exeter, Elizabeth, Duchess of Suffolk, and Margaret, Duchess of Burgundy, together with Cardinal Bourchier, Stillington, Bishop of Bath, the Earl of Essex, William Lord Hastings, and many others, were using every means in their power to bring Clarence over to Edward's side.[19] Of all these negotiations Warwick appears to have been totally unaware.[20]

Thus it was that, assisted by Louis, Warwick and Clarence crosed to England, landing in the ports of Plymouth and Dartmouth on 13 September.[21] Yet another step had been taken in the now bitter struggle between king and kingmaker.

Following the flight of Warwick and Clarence, Edward had returned early in June in triumph to Canterbury, where he was met by Elizabeth and his eldest daughter. Yet not even with the help of Worcester's brutal hand could Edward keep his kingdom under control. About the end of July rumours reached him of a fresh rebellion in the North under the leadership of Henry, Lord Fitzhugh.[22] Fearful as to what the outcome of this event might be, Edward placed the queen, who was expecting another child in a few months, and his daughters safely in the Tower of London,[23] and then hastened north to meet the rebels. While he was at York the news reached him on 25 September that Warwick and Clarence had landed unopposed at Dartmouth.[24]

Now, among those ordered by Edward to raise troops to quell this open rebellion was Warwick's brother Montagu, who had been created Earl of Northumberland in 1464. This nobleman, who was at Pontefract, only a few miles from York, had hitherto remained most loyal to Edward. Unfortunately Edward had just recently persuaded him to resign the Earldom of Northumberland in favour of the heir of the Percys, and had promoted him instead to the dignity of a marquis with his old title Montagu.[25] This was really more of a burden than a compensation, for, as he himself said, the king had given him but 'a pye's nest to maintain his estate with'. Thus, having raised 6,000 men, as if for Edward's service, and advanced to within 6 or 7 miles of the king, he informed his followers that he had now changed masters, and a cry of 'King Henry' rose from all his army.[26]

Edward was spending the night at Doncaster when Alexander Carlile, the sergeant of his minstrels, burst into his bedroom with the news that his enemies were 'coming for to take him',[27] and soon afterwards he received confirmation of his faithful servant's message from a few loyal men who had managed to escape from Montagu's army.[28] Unwilling to be captured by Warwick a second time, Edward resolved to escape as quickly as possible. He waited for no further warnings and fled, not only from Doncaster, but from England. After narrowly escaping death by drowning in the Wash, the fugitive king, accompanied by his brother Gloucester, the queen's brother Rivers, Lord Hastings and about 800 followers, succeeded, on Michaelmas Day, in reaching King's Lynn, whence, on 2 October, they set sail with all speed for Burgundy.[29] So precipitate had been their flight that they had no clothes save those they wore, and they landed at Alkmaar in a state of great destitution, after narrowly escaping capture by the Easterlings, who were then at war with both England and France. Edward had so little money that the only reward he could give to the master of the ship was the rich gown lined with marten's fur that he had worn during his flight.[30] Most fortunately, Louis de Gruthuyse, the Duke of Burgundy's governor in Holland, who had, during a visit to England in 1467, formed a personal friendship with Edward[31] was at Alkmaar. He immediately sent help to his exiled friend, and paid his expenses and those of his companions, until he had conducted him to the Hague, where he arrived on 12 October.[32]

So precipitate had been Edward's flight that he had been forced to leave his wife and children behind him. Elizabeth thus found herself left alone with her mother to face the storm. At the time of Edward's flight she was at the Tower, where her party still held Henry VI a prisoner. While danger was yet at a distance, Elizabeth showed remarkable courage and resolution; she actually went so far as to provision and prepare her dwelling-place for siege.[33] When, however, she received the news that Warwick and Clarence were approaching London, in a truly feminine panic Elizabeth, with her children, secretly left the Tower at night and came by water to Westminster. Here, on 1 October[34] she registered herself, her mother and her three young daughters as sanctuary-women.[35]

From her place of refuge Elizabeth then sent the Abbot of Westminster to Richard Lee, the Mayor of London, to inform him and the aldermen that 'the men of Kent and many others from divers parts of England in great numbers were purposing to enter the city and lay siege to the Tower and the men at arms whom the queen had left behind'[36] there. Furthermore, the queen bade the abbot say that she desired the Tower to be surrendered to the mayor and aldermen because she was afraid that should this not be done 'the said Kentishmen and others would invade the sanctuary of Wesminster to despoil and kill her'.[37]

Thus it was that on Wednesday 3 October, the Tower was duly surrendered to the mayor and to Sir Geoffrey Gate and other members of Warwick's council,[38] on condition that all who were then in the Tower 'should remain safe and secure with their goods and be conducted in the City of London either to the sanctuary at Westminster or Saint Martin according as they might wish'.[39]

Elizabeth's request was evidently acceded to, for soon after a proclamation from King Henry strictly forbade any man on pain of death to 'defoul or distrouble' the churches or sanctuaries, or to vex, rob or injure any person in them 'for any manner cause or quarrel, old or new'.[40] No one derived more benefit from this proclamation than Elizabeth, who, much as Warwick hated her and all her relations, was permitted to remain, safe and undisturbed, in the Westminster sanctuary. Here, separated from her husband and brother, of whose fate she was as yet unaware, she, a queen, awaited with a heavy heart the hour in which her fourth child was first to see the light.

As the queen's confinement was known to be near at hand, Elizabeth, Lady Scrope, was appointed by Henry's council to wait on her, and was given a reward of £10 for doing so.[41] On 2 November 1470,[42] during this dark eclipse of the fortunes of that house, the long-awaited heir to the House of York was born. Elizabeth was in an almost destitute state, but her friends did not desert her. Thomas Millyng, Abbot of Westminster, sent various gifts,[43] while Marjory Cobb, Elizabeth's midwife, was evidently permitted to come to the sanctuary in order to assist the unhappy queen in that dread hour of anguish and maternal peril.[44] She was also attended by her physician, Master Serigo, and furthermore received from a friendly London butcher, John Gould, 'half a beef and two muttons a week for the sustentation of her household'.[45]

The little prince was baptised soon after his birth, in Westminster Abbey, with no more ceremony than if he had been a poor man's son, Thomas Millyng, the Abbot of Westminster and the prior John Esteney[46] being his godfathers, and Lady Scrope his godmother.[47] The sub-prior performed the ceremony, the child receiving the name of his exiled father. The advent of Edward IV's son and heir into the world was treated as a matter of little importance by Warwick and his party, but to those whose sympathies were with the absent father it was hailed as a happy omen.[48]

# 8

# THE DEATH OF WARWICK

On 6 October Warwick and Clarence entered London.[1] Within eleven days after his landing at Dartmouth the earl was master of all England.[2] One of the first things Warwick did on entering London was to visit Henry VI in the Tower, to which place he himself had conducted the unhappy king with so much unnecessary ignominy five years before. Finding that Henry was 'not worshipfully arrayed as a prince, and not so cleanly kept as should beseem his state', Warwick first removed him to another room in the Tower which Elizabeth had fitted up very handsomely for her approaching confinement.[3] Henry was then arrayed in royal robes and brought in state to St Paul's, where, after returning thanks for his deliverance, he took up his residence in the Bishop of London's palace.

Warwick, besides being named the king's lieutenant, took again the captaincy of Calais and the great chamberlainship for himself, and later,[4] the title of Lord High Admiral. Henry VI now reigned, but it needed no great stretch of the imagination to see that it was Warwick who ruled. Clarence, however, was already getting jealous of the power enjoyed by Warwick, and insisted on having some share in the supreme authority: he was, however, not permitted to share in the title of lieutenant to Henry VI, and, needless to say, this was a cause of friction between him and Warwick from the very start.[5]

Despite the fact that he had played a prominent part in Henry VI's restoration, Clarence was thoroughly dissatisfied with his position.[6] He was now further removed from the throne than ever. It seems likely that, had he been given the chance, he would have joined Edward's party immediately after he and Warwick had landed in England. Events had, however, moved too swiftly for him, and Edward had been forced to fly from the country before Clarence could strike a blow on his behalf. During the winter of 1470–71, while Elizabeth lay in sanctuary, Clarence was once again in communication with his brother, the correspondence being carried out through their sisters, Anne, Duchess of Exeter, from England, and Margaret, Duchess of Burgundy, from abroad.[7] By this means Clarence renewed his promises of help to Edward, and swore to join his brother the moment that he should set foot in England.

Warwick does not appear to have been aware of his son-in-law's treachery. In a short time Margaret of Anjou and her son Edward were expected to join him in England. In the meantime Warwick was doing his utmost to bring about the French alliance, which Edward IV, on the advice of Elizabeth and her relations, had rejected in favour of an alliance with Burgundy. An embassy headed by the Bishop of Bayeux came to London early in January (1471) to conclude a peace for twelve years and a treaty of alliance against Burgundy.[8]

Although Charles, Duke of Burgundy, did not at first receive the exiled Edward with any particular show of friendship, as soon as he heard that Louis XI had sent an embassy to England,[9] he let it be known that he was ready to receive Edward, and on 2 January (1471), they met at Aire,[10] and on the 7th at St Pol, where Edward was the guest of his wife's uncle, Jacques de Luxembourg.[11] Charles, although he made a public announcement that no aid was to be given to Edward, yielded secretly to his request for help, sending him a sum of 50,000 florins, and placing at his disposal three or four large ships which were equipped at Veere, besides hiring fourteen Easterling vessels to transport his followers to England.[12]

Thus it was that early in March 1471 Elizabeth was cheered by the news that her husband had landed at Ravenspur.[13] Exhibiting letters under Northumberland's seal inviting him to return,[14] stating that he had come only to claim his dukedom of York and not the Crown, and actually going so far as to wear the Lancastrian prince's badge of the ostrich feather, the former exile succeeded, on 18 March, in entering York.[15] Edward, after slipping past Montagu (to whom Clarence, as co-protector of the realm, had apparently written telling him not to fight till he came) at Pontefract,[16] marched swiftly to Nottingham, where he threw off his mask, openly declaring himself as king.[17]

Clarence's ruse was the greatest help to Edward, who from Nottingham suddenly turned on the Earl of Oxford at Newark, where on 29 March,[18] barely a fortnight after his landing at Ravenspur, he hastened to meet Warwick at Coventry. So swiftly had Edward moved that Warwick did not dare attack him; all he could do was to glare sullenly at his enemy's soldiers from the castle walls. Warwick decided to wait for reinforcements, as he probably realised that if only he could keep Edward idle at Coventry, the latter would then be caught like a rat in a trap. Edward was, however, far too good a general to be caught thus simply.

Meanwhile the reinforcements for which Warwick was so anxiously waiting appeared to be well on the way. Clarence was reported to be coming with troops from the west, but Warwick did not even suspect that the duke was bringing them, not to help him, but the brother whom the Kingmaker had tempted him into betraying. Indeed, so hastily had Clarence caused his men to change sides that their coats still had the Lancastrian collar with the Yorkist rose over it.[19] On 3 April the two brothers met near Banbury,[20] where a personal reconciliation took place within sight of their two armies. Clarence called on his men to shout for King Edward, 'and with that the kynge browght his brother Clarence, and sucheas were there with hym, to his felowshipe, whom the sayd duke welcomyd into the land in his best manner, and they thanked God, and hym, and honoryd hym as it apparteygned'.[21] The two armies then joined and went together to the town of Warwick. Clarence then tried unsuccessfully to get Warwick to come to terms with Edward. The earl had gone too far to recede; he was now joined by the Duke of Exeter, Montagu, the Earl of Oxford, and hosts of followers.

Realising the vital importance of gaining possession of London, Edward started for that city on 5 April. When the king drew near to the capital, he sent from Dunstable on 9 April 'very comfortable messages to his queen, and to his true lords, servants and lovers, who advised and practised secretly how he might be received and welcomed in his City of London'.[22] He arrived before London on 11 April, and during the dinner hour, while the guards were off duty, the recorder, Thomas Urswick,[23] and aldermen opened the gates to Edward, who promptly entered the city.[24] Thereupon the Archbishop of York, 'having small confidence in the citizens that they would resist King Edward or his people, shifted for himself, and left King Henry in the palace all alone'.[25]

After entering the city Edward hurried, as soon as ever he could, to the sanctuary 'and comforted the queen, that had a long time abided there … in right great trouble, sorrow and heaviness, which she sustained with all manner patience that belonged to any creature, and as constantly as hath been seen at any time so high estate to endure'.[26] But above all Edward must have wished to see the son and heir born to him in his absence, whom the queen, to his 'greatest joy', presented to him on his arrival 'to his heart's singular comfort and gladness, and to all them that him truly loved and would serve'.[27]

Probably considering that Elizabeth would be safer inside the walls of London than at Westminster, Edward took her that same day to the city, where he lodged her and her children in Baynard's Castle, his mother's palace. Here Edward and his queen heard divine service that night and kept the next day, Good Friday, together.[28] The next day, 13 April, Elizabeth had once again to bid her husband farewell. Soon after noon he marched out of London with his army and the captive King Henry to Barnet to meet the Earl of Warwick, who, doubtless hoping to take Edward by surprise during the Easter Festival, was now approaching to contest the possession of the capital. On the next day, Easter Sunday, took place the Battle of Barnet, in which Edward gained a great victory, Warwick and his brother Montagu being left dead on the field.[29]

> By ten of the clock came tidings to London that King Edward had won the field, but yet was no credence given, till one came riding through the city towards Westminster in all haste possible with one of the king's gauntlets, which the king sent unto the queen for a token.[30]

After the battle, in order to forestall 'feigned seditious tales' that Warwick was 'yet on life', Edward commanded the earl's body and that of Montagu to be 'putt in a cart' and brought back from Barnet to London, and 'there commaundede the seide ij bodyes to be layede in the chyrche of Paulis, one the pavement, that every manne myghte see them; and so they lay three or four days' naked save for a loincloth.[31] Thus was Elizabeth avenged on Warwick for the death of her father and brother John in 1469. One may well wonder whether her desire for vengeance was such that it prompted her to take her place among that vast crowd of gaping and incredulous people who came to gaze on the ghastly face of her bitterest enemy, the man who had made and unmade kings.

Bishop Stubbs[32] has written so admirable an appreciation of Warwick that we cannot do better than reproduce it here.

Warwick has always occupied a great place in the view of history; and his character, although in some respects only an exaggeration of the common baronial type, certainly contained some elements of greatness. He was greedy of power, wealth and influence; jealous of all competitors, and unscrupulous in the measures he took to gain these ends. He was magnificent in his expenditure and popular in consequence. He was a skilful warrior both by land and sea, and good fortune in battle gave him another claim to be a national favourite. He was a far-seeing politician too, and probably if Edward had suffered him, would have secured a settlement of the foreign relations of England as might have anticipated the period of national recovery of which Henry VII obtained the credit. He was unrelenting in his enmities, but not wantonly bloodthirsty or faithless: from the beginning of the struggle, when he was a very young man and altogether under his father's influence, he had taken up with ardour the cause of Duke Richard, and his final defection was the result of a profound conviction that Edward, influenced by the Wydevilles, was bent on his ruin. He filled however for many years, and not together unworthily, a place which never before or after was filled by a subject, and his title of Kingmaker was not given without reason. But it is his own singular force of character, decision and energy, that mark him off from the men of his time. He had in him the makings of a great king.[33]

# 9

# THE DEATH OF HENRY VI &
# THE RECEPTION OF LOUIS DE
# GRUTHUYSE

Edward returned in triumph to London, but he was not given much time in which to rest upon his laurels. Two days later (16 April) news reached him of the arrival of Margaret and her son at Weymouth.[1] After placing Elizabeth in the Tower, for her greater security, Edward left London three days later in search of his new enemy. On 4 May the two armies met at Tewskebury,[2] where Edward gained a complete victory, Henry VI's son being slain,[3] and Margaret of Anjou herself captured three days later.[4]

The news of her husband's victory had scarcely reached Elizabeth before the Tower, her temporary dwelling-place, was threatened with an attack from Thomas Neville, the Bastard of Fauconberg, who was attempting to capture London and restore Henry VI. Edward was then at Coventry, where, on 14 May, he received 'tydyngs from the lords and citizens [of London], which, with great instance, moved him, in all possible haste, to approche and com to the citie, to the defence of the qwene, than being in the Tower of London, my lord prince, and my ladies his doghtars ... whiche, as they all wrote, was likely to stand in the grettest ioperdy that evar they stode'.[5]

Greatly disturbed by this alarming news, Edward prepared to march to the relief of London. He immediately sent forward 1,500 picked men 'for the comforte of the quene, the lords, and the citizens',[6] and on 16 May, he left Coventry in person. Meanwhile Fauconberg, after having, on 12 May, attacked and burnt London Bridge, was finally repulsed by Elizabeth's brother, Anthony, Lord Rivers, who suddenly attacked the enemy from a postern in the Tower.[7] Presumably Elizabeth aided and encouraged her brother before the attack, and she may even have watched, with a beating heart, the outcome of that short but sharp encounter. A few days later, observing that he could make no impression on London's defences, Fauconberg withdrew into Kent, and almost immediately after, on 21 May,[8] for the second time within little more than a month, Edward entered his capital in triumph.[9] Elizabeth must have been overjoyed to see her husband again, and he must have heard many glowing accounts of her fortitude and courage. Edward was probably clever enough to realise that the interesting situation in which the queen had placed herself during his exile had played no small part in his ultimate success. Indeed, the feminine helplessness of Elizabeth and the passive resignation with which she had endured all the inconveniences of the sanctuary in her hour of childbirth, had created for her, throughout the kingdom, a tender regard that was possibly as beneficial to the House of York as the indomitable spirit of Margaret of Anjou was harmful. Wonder and affection were awakened for Elizabeth, as is illustrated by the fact that, some time after Edward's restoration, on the same day that Louis de Gruthuyse was created Earl of Winchester,[10] she was praised by the Speaker of the House of Commons, William Alynton, 'the whiche declared before the kinge and his noble and sadde counsell, thentente and desyre of his Comyns, specially in the comendacion of the womanly behaveur and the greate constance of the quene, he beinge beyonde the see'.[11] Edward also bestowed large rewards on those who had aided 'his Elizabeth' in that fearful crisis;[12] while Elizabeth, in gratitude for the hospitality extended to her at Westminster, founded the chantry and chapel of St Erasmus,[13] which was attached to the old Lady chapel.[14]

Edward's triumph, although a source of great joy to Elizabeth, was fatal to his rival, the unhappy Henry VI. Fauconberg's attempt to capture London finally sealed his doom. With the death of the young Prince Edward of Lancaster at Tewkesbury, no further object would be served by keeping his father alive. Thus on the very night of Edward's triumphant return to London, the unfortunate Henry VI was murdered.[15] The most circumstantial account of this tragedy is given by Warkworth,[16] who thus describes the old king's death:

> And the same nyghte that Kynge Edwarde came to Londone, Kynge Henry, beynge inwarde in presone in the Toure of Londone, was putt to detehe, the xxj day of May, on a tywesday nyght, betwyx xj and xij of the cloke, beynge thenne at the Toure the Duke of Gloucetre,[17] brothere to Kynge Edwarde, and many other...

Edward had now triumped so decisively over all his enemies that the remaining years of his reign were passed in comparative quietness, and he was thus able to spend a great deal more time in the company of his wife and family.

The most pleasing task that Edward was called upon to perform after his two great victories was to make suitable provision for his son and heir born to him during his enforced absence. On 26 June 1471, the prince being then seven months old, he was by charter created Prince of Wales; and the king, by letters patent, dated on 8 July following, ordained the queen, the Archbishop of Canterbury, George, Duke of Clarence, Richard, Duke of Gloucester, Robert Stillington, Bishop of Bath and Wells, Anthony, Earl Rivers, Thomas Millyng, Abbot of Westminster, chancellor to the prince,[18] and many others to be of council unto the said prince, 'giving unto them, and every four of them, *with the advice and express consent of the queen*, large power to advise and counsel the said prince ... the said authority to continue until the prince should accomplish his age of fourteen years'.[19]

In September 1471 the king and queen went on a pilgrimage together to Canterbury.[20] With what feelings of thankfulness and relief must this pilgrimage have been undertaken! The last time they had gone on such a journey together, a bare fifteen months previously, they had been to rejoice over Warwick's flight from England. Since then many stirring events had taken place. Elizabeth herself had spent several months in sanctuary, Edward had been driven out of the kingdom, and two decisive battles had been fought and won. Now all was over, their enemies were vanquished, and they were reunited, and going to Canterbury together once again. Small wonder that they wished to lay their offerings and prayers at the ancient martyr's shrine. 'Never,' so we are told, 'so moche peple [had been] seyn in Pylgrymage heretofor at ones.'[21]

Edward and Elizabeth spent the whole winter of 1471–72 at Westminster Palace,[22] advantage being taken of the midwinter festivals to remind his subjects that he was king again. On Christmas Day both the king and Queen Elizabeth were crowned at Westminster, while on New Year's Day, as also on Twelfth Day, the king and queen 'went in procession', the king again wearing his crown on the latter day, though Elizabeth did not wear hers 'because she was grete with childe'.[23]

All this pomp and pageantry must have given as much pleasure to the king and queen as to their subjects, for it helped to blot out the memory of unhappy events. Moreover, towards the end of the winter Edward had the extreme satisfaction of getting rid of one of the most unpleasant survivals of the recent rebellions by settling a bitter quarrel between his two brothers.[24] On 17 February Paston wrote that the king and queen and the dukes of Clarence and Gloucester had gone 'to Sheen to pardon, men say not all in charity', that the king 'entreateth my Lord of Clarence for my Lord of Gloucester, and, as it is said, he answereth that he will have my lady his sister-in-law but they shall part no livelihood, as he saith'.[25]

In April Edward and Elizabeth were staying at Windsor, where, on the 19th, the queen gave birth to another daughter, Princess Margaret, who, however, lived only for a few months. Shortly before Christmas she was laid to rest in Westminster Abbey, 'at the altar end before St Edward's shrine'.[26]

Nor was this the only sorrow Elizabeth was to experience in that year. On 30 May her mother, the old Duchess of Bedford, to whose diplomacy she owed so much, died.[27] This must have been a terrible blow to Elizabeth, because she was deeply attached to all her relationships. However, her duties as queen did not long allow her to mourn even for the death of one whose memory was so precious. Four months later, in September 1472, Edward, calling to mind the help given him by Louis de Gruthuyse during his exile,[28] invited his former benefactor to England in order to prove his gratitude by creating him Earl of Winchester, and at the same time to introduce him to the queen. Bluemantle Pursuivant, who accompanied the future Earl of Winchester on his visit, has given a very interesting description of the splendour and luxury of the queen's Court at Windsor and Westminster at that time. Upon Gruthuyse's arrival at Windsor, Bluemantle relates,[29] Lord Hastings, Sir John Parr, Sir Jon Don 'with divers other lords and nobles' took him at once to speak with the king and queen 'on the far side of the quadrant', where they received him in 'three chambers richly hanged with clothes of Arras, and with Beddes of astate, and when he had spoked with the king's grace and the queen', he was escorted to his apartments by the Lord Chamberlain, and Sir John Parr, 'with divers more', who had supper with him in his room.

After supper, the Lord Chamberlain conducted him once more to the king's apartments.

Then incontinent the king had time to the queen's chamber, where she had there her ladies playing at the morteaulx,[30] and some of her ladies were playing at Closheys of yuery,[31] and Daunsinge. And sum at divers other games according.

*Above*: 1. Portrait of Elizabeth Woodville, see appendix 1.
*Below*: 2. Signature of Elizabeth Woodville.

*Left*: 3. Elizabeth Woodville in her coronation robes. *Below*: 4. Letter written by Elizabeth Woodville to Sir William Stonor.

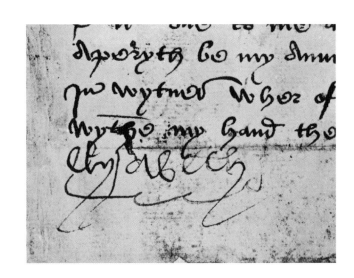

*Right*: 5.
Signature
of Elizabeth
Woodville in
1491.
*Below*: 6.
Elizabeth
Woodville,
portrait in the
window of the
Martyrdom
Chapel in
Canterbury
Cathedral, see
appendix 1.

*Above left*: 7. Edward IV, Elizabeth Woodville's second husband. (Courtesy of David Baldwin)
*Above right*: 8. Richard, Duke of York, father of Edward IV and Richard III and Elizabeth Woodville's father-in-law. (Courtesy of David Baldwin)

9. Surrounded by his courtiers including Richard, Duke of Gloucester (the future Richard III), Edward IV receives a book (*Dictes of the Philosophers* printed by William Caxton) by the author, Elizabeth Woodville's brother, Anthony Woodville, Earl Rivers. The earl's ward, the future Edward V, is the child. Elizabeth Woodville is on the right of the illustration next to the king. (Courtesy of Jonathan Reeve JR1580b4p582 14501500)

*Above left*: 10. Edward V, Elizabeth Woodville's eldest son and one of the Princes in the Tower. (Courtesy of David Baldwin) *Above right*: 11. Richard III. (Courtesy of Jonathan Reeve JR1564b13fp717 14501500) *Below*: 12. Margaret of York, Duchess of Burgundy, Richard III's sister. (Courtesy of Jonathan Reeve JR1565b13p704 14501500)

*Opposite*: 13. The White Tower. This late fifteenth-century manuscript illumination shows the Tower of London much as it was in 1483. (Courtesy of Jonathan Reeve JR992b4p640 14501550) *Above left*: 14. Elizabeth of York, Elizabeth Woodville's eldest daughter. (Courtesy of Amy Licence) *Above right*: 15. Henry VI. (Courtesy of Jonathan Reeve JR1561folio6 14001450) *Below left*: 16. Henry VII by Hans Holbein. Elizabeth of York married Henry in 1486. (Courtesy of Elizabeth Norton) *Below right*: 17. Margaret Beaufort, mother of Henry VII. (Courtesy of Elizabeth Norton)

*Above*: 18. Richard Neville, Earl of Warwick, the 'Kingmaker'. (Courtesy of David Baldwin) *Below*: 19. Anne Neville, daughter of Richard Neville, the 'Kingmaker'. On the left of the illustration is her first husband, Prince Edward of Lancaster, Henry VI's son who was killed at the Battle of Tewkesbury on 4 May 1471. On the right of the illustration is Richard III, her second husband. (Courtesy of Jonathan Reeve JR1731b90fp109c 14001500)

The whiche sight was full pleasant to them. Also the king danced with my lady Elizabeth, his eldest daughter. That done, the night passed over, they went to his chamber. And in the morning, when Mattins was done, the king heard in his own chapel our Lady Mass, which was melodiously sung. When the Mass was done, the king gave the said Lord Grautehuse a cup of gold, garnished with pearl. In the midst of the cup was a great piece of a unicorn's horn,[32] to my estimation, 7 inches [in] compass. And on the cover was a great sapphire. Then he went to his chamber, where he had his breakfast. And when he had broken his fast, the king came into the quadrant. My lord prince also, borne by his chamberlain, called Master Vaughan, which bade the Lord Grautehuse welcome. Then the king had him and all his company into the little park, wheer he made him to have great sport. And there the king made him ride on his own horse, on a right hobby,[33] the which the king gave him. The king's dinner was ordained [ordered] in the lodge.[34]

After dinner 'it was near night, yet the king shewd him his garden, and vineyard of pleasure, and so turned into the castle again, where they heard evensong in their chambers'.

The queen did to be ordained a great banquet in her own chamber. At the whiche banquet were the king, the queen, my lady Elizabeth the king's eldest daughter, the Duchess of Exeter, the lady Rivers, [and] the Lord Grautehuse, sitting at one mess, and at the same table sat the Duke of Buckingham, my lady his wife,[35] with divers other ladies, my lord Hastings, chamberlain to the king ... also certain nobles of the king's own court. There was a side table, at the which sat a great vue [number] of ladies, all on the one side. Also in the outer chamber sat the queen's gentlewomen all on one side. And when they had supped, my lady Elizabeth, the king's eldest daughter, dancied with the Duke of Buckingham, and divers other ladies also. Then, about nine of the clock, the king and queen, with her ladies and gentlewomen, brought the said Lord Grateuhuse to three chambers of Pleasance all hanged with white silk and linen cloth, and all the floors covered with carpets. There was ordained a bed for him 'selve' [alone], of as good down as could be gotten, the sheets of Raynys [Rennes] and also fine fystans [festoons];[36] the counterpane cloth of gold, furred with ermine, the tester and the *celer* also shining cloth of gold, the curtains of white sarcenet; as for his head suit and pillows [they] were of the queen's own ordonnance. [In] the second chamber another state-bed,[37] the which was all white. Also in the same chamber was made a couch with feather beds, hanged with a tent, knit like a net, and there was a cupboard. In the third chamber was ordained a bayne [bath] or two, which were covered with tents of white cloth. And when the king and queen with all her ladies and gentlewomen had showed him these chambers, they turned again to their own chambers and left the said Lord Grauthuse there, accompanied with my lord chamberlain, which dispoyled him [disrobed him], and went both together to the bath. And when they had been in their baths as long as was their pleasure, they had been ginger, divers syrups, comfits and ipocras, and then they went to bed. And on the morn [morrow] he took his cuppe[38] [leave] of the king and queen, and turned to Westminster again, accompanied with certain knights, esquires, and other of the king's servants, home to his lodging. And on St Edward's Day[39] openly in the parliament chamber was created Earl of Winchester.[40]

This done, the king went into the White Hall, whither came the queen, crowned, also the prince, in his robes of state, which was borne after the king by his chamberlain, called Master Vaughan. And so proceeded forth into the abbey church, and so up to the shrine of St Edward, where they offered.

Then the king turned down into the choir, where he sat in his throne to the procession time. The Earl of Winchester bare his sword all the procession, and so forth unto the time that they went to dinner ... That done the king went to his chamber, accompanied with his lords, where the Earl of Winchester took his *congy* [leave].[41]

In the meantime there had been serious unrest in the west, with the result that in February 1473 Elizabeth accompanied the Prince of Wales to Hereford[42] in the hopes that the presence of the heir to the throne, to whom the king had now granted a separate household, would serve as a restraining influence, should there be any danger of a plot against the king.

It was only to be expected that the influence of Elizabeth would once again be seen in the appointment of the officials charged with the care of the young prince.[43] When, therefore, about the time of his third birthday, he took up his residence in Ludlow Castle, it was not surprising that Earl Rivers should be appointed his governor.[44] Whether, as Lingard suggests,[45] this was done with a view to surrounding the prince with his maternal relatives in order that, by growing up under their tuition, he might become more attached to them, is correct or not, one must bear in mind that at this time nobody could have foreseen that Edward IV would be dead before ten years had gone by. That Elizabeth asked for her brother to be made governor to the prince, and that Edward was very willing to accede to her request, is by no means unlikely. It is, indeed, absurd to believe that in obtaining this post for her brother Elizabeth had any thoughts or designs against the king's relations.

During the next few months the king and queen were a good deal apart, Edward spending the whole summer moving from place to place. In June 1473 he visited his son and heir, for whom he always had a special affection, at Ludlow, and from here he travelled to Coventry, Kenilworth and Leicester. In August he went to Shrewsbury,[46] to be with the queen, who was expecting another child. On 17 August[47] his heart was made glad by the birth of his second son, Richard of Shrewsbury.[48]

In 1474 Elizabeth was once again on the lookout for an advantageous match, on this occasion for her eldest son Thomas, of whom she was very fond. A few years previously she had been bitterly disappointed in that his first wife, Anne, daughter of the Duchess of Exeter, whose marriage with her son she had strained every nerve to bring about in 1466,[49] had died a little over a year afterwards.[50] Thus it came about that during the summer session of the 1474 Parliament,[51] arrangements were made for marrying her son to Cecille Bonville, in her own right Baroness Bonville and Harington.[52] Elizabeth must have been delighted with this arrangement, for not only had she succeeded in providing her son with a title, money and numerous estates, but the settlement drawn up in Parliament contained two very important clauses, in which Elizabeth's influence over the king can be clearly seen. In the first of these clauses it was stipulated that on the death of the queen's eldest son, Thomas, all the estates were to be transferred to his younger brother, Richard,[53] while the second clause stated that 'the quene, hir executours and assignees' should 'take the issues and profittes of all the seid maners, lordships, londes and tenementes for terme of II yere next' after Cecille, who was then but twelve years old, should attain the age of fourteen.[54]

Nor did the favours secured by Elizabeth for her eldest son end here. He had about two years previously been created Earl of Huntingdon,[55] and now, a few months after the agreement of 1474, he was, on 18 April 1475, created Marquis of Dorset.[56]

Thus once again did Elizabeth obtain her son's advancement, but at the same time she drew upon herself and her relations yet more hatred and jealousy, which, on the death of the king, were destined to cause not only the death of her brother and two younger sons, but the fall of the House of York itself.

# 10

# THE DEATH OF CLARENCE

Early in 1475 Edward began making preparations for his long-awaited invasion of France. At the beginning of May all was ready, and the king left London for Canterbury on 30 May. After some delay he eventually left Canterbury for Sandwich on 20 June.[1] Before crossing the Channel Edward signed his Will, by which he appointed Elizabeth to be principal executrix, but made no special provision for her beyond her dower, except securing to her some household goods as private property and ordaining that the marriage portions which he bequeathed to his daughters should be conditional on her approval of the marriages contracted by them. Finally he wished that if the unborn child the queen was then carrying should prove to be a daughter, that daughter was to have 10,000 marks towards her marriage on the same conditions.[2]

Thus Elizabeth was once again separated from her husband. The month of July 1475 must have been a miserable one for this wife, who knew not whether her husband would ever return to fondle the child which she was then carrying. However, her sorrow was soon to be turned into joy, for on 28 September Edward returned to London without, however, having conquered an inch of French territory.[3]

By the scandalous Treaty of Picquigny (29 August), the two kings arranged, among other things, for the marriage between Charles, the Dauphin of France, and Elizabeth, 'the daughter of the most victorious King of England', when they should reach marriageable age, and if Princess Elizabeth should die before the marriage took place, then the Dauphin was to marry her sister Mary instead. Queen Elizabeth was extremely proud of this engagement, and 'positively degraded her young princess by the impolitic parade she made regarding these expectations, always referring to her daughter as "her dauphiness".'[6]

Few events of interest occurred in England during the months immediately following the king's return from France. The child for whom Edward had provided at the time of his departure for France was born at Westminster on 2 November, receiving the name of Anne.[7] Edward, who had been at Westminster during his wife's confinement, left on 28 November to 'minister justice' in Hampshire and Wiltshire.[8]

Edward appears to have wished to atone for his lack of success in France by many gorgeous displays of pageantry. Thus on 28 April 1476, on the Sunday following St George's Day, Elizabeth took part in a most picturesque ceremony, when she attended Mass in St George's chapel, Windsor, to which 'she came on horseback in a murrey gowne of Garters', accompanied by the Lady Elizabeth, the king's eldest daughter, in a gown of the same livery.[9] This seems to have been the Annual Garter Service, as the king and all the Knights of the Garter are reported as having attended, 'every manne to hys owne Stalle'.[10]

In July of the same year there took place at Fotheringay the re-interment of the remains of the king's father and his brother, Edmund, Earl of Rutland. The coffins, 'covered with black velvet', were brought in solemn procession from Pontefract, where they had been interred since 1461, to Fotheringay, where, on 29 July, they were met by the king, the Duke of Clarence, Dorset, Rivers,

Hastings, and many other noblemen. The next day, 30 July, with the queen and princesses Elizabeth and Mary, the king attended the Mass of Requiem, at which they offered the Mass-penny.[11]

Soon after this began the series of events which were destined to terminate with the death of the Duke of Clarence. The past offences of Clarence had been such as 'could be forgiven but not forgotten'.[12] Elizabeth had lost her father and younger brother in the rebellion of 1469, when Clarence made his first essay in treason; this neither she nor her relatives could ever forget.[13] It was, therefore, by no means surprising that from that moment on he had been the queen's most bitter enemy. In view of the fact that mischief-makers carried what each of them said, or was reported to have said, to the other,[14] it was only to be expected that relations between the two were strained almost to breaking point, and that it needed but a very tiny spark to kindle the flame.

That spark was not long in coming. On 21 December 1476,[15] Isabel Neville, Clarence's wife, died, and the death of Charles the Bold at Nancy about a fortnight later (5 January 1477) left his daughter, Mary of Burgundy, whose hand had once been sought for Clarence, mistress of all Charles's domains. Clarence immediately offered himself as a suitor, but on political as well as personal grounds,[16] Edward strictly forbade the match. The king's refusal seems to have roused Clarence to fury, more especially as the queen took advantage of her influence over the king to put forward as a candidate in his place her own brother, Earl Rivers,[17] actually going so far as to offer the widowed Duchess Margaret an English army if she would favour his suit.

Clarence's disappointment, when he saw his briefly entertained hope fade so quickly away, was so intense that he made not the slightest effort to conceal it. He seems to have lost all control of himself and to have sought revenge in a most unnecessarily vindictive manner. On 12 April he had one of his late wife's attendants, Ankarette, widow of Roger Twynyho of Cayford,

Somerset, through whom he doubtless wished to strike at the queen,[18] arrested without the formality of a warrant, on a charge of having caused her mistress's death by a 'venomous drunke of ale myxt with poison'. She was hurried off to Warwick, her native county, and summarily tried, condemned and executed by the justices in petty sessions, apparently in Clarence's presence. Nor was she the only victim of Clarence's wrath, as one John Thuresby of Warwick, accused of having poisoned the infant son of the Duke and Duchess of Clarence, who lived but a few weeks and whose birth was without doubt the true cause of the duchess's death, was executed at the same time.[19]

Clarence's weapon was, however, turned against himself. On hearing this disgraceful procedure, Edward endeavoured to convey an unmistakable warning to Clarence by arresting and placing on trial for 'constructive treason' and sorcery, Thomas Burdett of Arrow, a friend of Clarence's John Stacey, his household chaplain, and Thomas Blake of Oxford, a clerk in holy orders.[20] They were accused of 'treasonably imagining and compassing the death of the king', and having been found guilty were, on 19 May, formally executed, Blake alone being pardoned.

Furious at his friends' deaths, Clarence 'muttered imputations of sorcery against the queen,[21] in which he implicated King Edward'.[22] Elizabeth was at Windsor with the king when the news was brought to them not only that Clarence had forced his way into the council chamber, bringing with him Dr William Goddard, who had read the dying protestations of innocence made by Burdett and Stacey,[23] but that at the same time the duke had uttered most disrespectful words against the queen and his royal person concerning their deaths. This very bold act was the more unfortunate for Clarence, in that he had chosen for his spokesman the very man who had preached the restoration of Henry VI in 1470. It is hardly likely that the queen's comments contributed to any large extent in softening Edward's heart, for he hurried to

Westminster and gave orders that Clarence be committed to the Tower,[24] from whose dark and gloomy precincts he was never again to come forth alive.

While Clarence was lying in the Tower awaiting his fate, great festivities were going on at the Court. On 15 January took place the marriage of Edward's second son, Richard, Duke of York, then only in his fifth year, with Anne De Mowbray, aged five, daughter and heiress of John de Mowbray, 4th Duke of Norfolk,[25] who had died without male issue. With the earls of Lincoln and Rivers supporting her on either side, the little bride was conducted from the queen's chamber to St Stephen's chapel, where the walls had been hung with carpets of azure besprinkled with golden *fleurs-de-lys*, and where the king and queen, the Prince of Wales and the young bridegroom were awaiting her under a canopy of cloth of gold. The marriage ceremony was performed by the Bishop of Norwich, the king himself giving away the bride. After the ceremony the dukes of Gloucester and Buckingham led the little bride back to the king's great chamber, where the wedding banquet was spread and where 'the press was so great that [one] might not see to write the names of them that served, the abundance of the noble people were so innumerable'.[26]

It is difficult to determine whether this match was due to the queen's influence or to Edward's own policy; but it certainly seems to have much in common with the many alliances, some of them quite extraordinary, procured by Elizabeth for her own relations. On the other hand, it must not be forgotten that Edward was pursuing a deliberate policy, by which he was striving to strengthen and dignify the Crown and the royal family. Elizabeth cannot, therefore, be held solely responsible for this union.

To the ordinary observer nothing could have appeared more bright and happy than the English Court on the Duke of York's wedding day. Yet everybody was aware that Clarence lay in the Tower awaiting his fate, and many an anxious glance must have been cast at the king and queen during the wedding festivities. Would Elizabeth make use of her undoubted influence over Edward to save Clarence, or would she rather take advantage of this opportunity of avenging on him her father's death and the many insults with which she had had to bear for so long?

They were soon to know. The day after the wedding (16 January), in a Parliament summoned for that purpose, Edward brought in against his brother a Bill of attainder,[27] in which, justly furious at Clarence's insults to the queen, he accused him among other things of spreading a report that the king 'wrought by necromancy and used craft to poison his subjects such as him pleased', and of circulating reports that the king was a bastard, and had no right to the throne.[28]

Edward ended his accusation by declaring his brother guilty of high treason,[29] sentence of death being passed in a Court of Chivalry presided over by the Duke of Buckingham on 8 February.[30] Ten days later Clarence was reported dead.[31]

The Woodvilles, even if they had urged the king to put Clarence to death, did not derive any great material profit from their action. Some of Clarence's confiscated estates, together with the wardship and marriage of his heir, were indeed granted to the queen's son, Dorset,[32] while her brother Rivers received estates to the value of £100 a year for six years in satisfaction of a sum of £666 13s 4d alleged to be owing to him from Clarence.[33] Thus was Elizabeth avenged on yet another of her bitterest enemies,[34] while the whole kingdom was now more at Edward's command than ever it had been during his brother's lifetime.

# I I

# THE LAST YEARS OF EDWARD IV

Sometime before 15 November, most probably in March 1477, Elizabeth had given birth to a third son, George of Windsor,[1] on whom the king conferred Clarence's old office, the lieutenancy of Ireland, on 6 July 1478.[2]

Meanwhile James III of Scotland had in June of that same year proposed a marriage between his sister Margaret and the queen's brother, Earl Rivers.[3] Once again Elizabeth appears in the role of matchmaker with a view to the advancement of yet another of her relations. Although arrangements had progressed so far that Edward had begun to make plans to attend the wedding, and a safe conduct had actually been sent to the proposed bride on 22 August 1479,[4] the queen's plans were nevertheless destined to end in failure. For some reason, possibly owing to the discovery of Edward's intrigues with her brother's subjects,[5] Margaret never arrived, with the result that the whole ambitious scheme had to be abandoned. Rivers may have been disappointed, Elizabeth almost certainly was, but to Edward himself the marriage was a matter of no very great importance.[6]

It seems to have been in the early part of the year in which she incurred this great disappointment that Elizabeth gave birth, at

Eltham, to her sixth daughter, Catherine.[7] About March this same year the royal couple had the misfortune to lose their third son, George.[8] However, the birth of a seventh princess, which also took place at Eltham on 10 November 1480,[9] may have afforded them some consolation. There was all the usual pomp and display at the christening, at which the little princess received the name of Bridget, with a stately procession composed of knights, squires, and 'other honest persons' to the number of 100, all carrying lighted torches, and, following after, Lord Maltravers with the basin in his hands and 'a towel about his neck', and finally Lady Maltravers[10] with 'a rich chrison pinned over her left breast', and the Countess of Richmond, now Lady Stanley, who, with the assistance of the Marquis of Dorset, carried the child. The Bishop of Chichester officiated at the font, the baby's grandmother, the Duchess of York, her eldest sister, Princess Elizabeth and the Bishop of Winchester were her sponsors, and when she was taken back to her mother's chamber, the 'great gifts' her godparents had given her were carried before her.[11]

In the autumn of 1481 Elizabeth accompanied the king on a visit to Oxford. On 22 September, following a visit from William Waynflete, the founder of Magdalen College, the king promised him that 'he would come to see his college and lodge therein'.[12] That same evening the royal party arrived from Woodstock shortly after sunset, and entered Oxford with a great crowd of people running before the royal carriages bearing torches. Elizabeth's brother, Lionel Woodville, the newly elected Chancellor,[13] received them at Magdalen College with an oration. With them also came the queen's sister-in-law, Elizabeth, Duchess of Suffolk,[14]

with a considerable retinue after her, to whom the university fave wine and gloves, and the next day, being 23 September, between Mattins and Procession, the president of the college delivered by command of the founder a short congratulatory speech before the king, desiring him that he would be favourable to the university and college; to which the king gave satisfactory answers, and professed himself ready to do those things that were fit. Afterwards he with his lords followed the procession within the limits and cloister of the college. The next day he was pleased to be present at public disputations, and to hear the divinity lecture (later founded by him at the university) read by Lionel Woodville, the Chancellor: to the hearing of which he about this time had sent his nephew Edmund de la Pole (whom the university in their letters do highly commend)[15] and other young men of his blood. After the king had visited several parts of the university and heard scholastical exercises he departed with great content.[16]

Edward was now wealthy, corpulent, and fond of ease.[17] His foreign policy had, since the Treaty of Picquigny, undergone a complete change, for he had accepted a French alliance instead of a Burgundian, and when, after the death of Charles the Bold, Louis XI overran Burgundy and Picardy, depriving the young Duchess Mary of her inheritance, she appealed in vain to Edward for assistance.

To scorn such an appeal was little short of madness, for the success of France imperilled English commerce with the Low Countries. However, Edward was more afraid of losing both his pension and the stipulated marriage of Princess Elizabeth to the Dauphin, and he was even base enough to offer to side with Louis, if the latter would share with him his conquests on the Somme.[18] The queen, on the other hand, ever a supporter of the Burgundian alliance, would have engaged him the other way if the Council of Flanders would have allowed the marriage, to which reference has already been made,[19] between Mary and her brother, Anthony, Earl Rivers; since, however, this match was considered too unequal in point of rank,[20] Mary, for her own protection, was driven to marry Maximilian of Austria.

Nor was this Elizabeth's only disappointment. Not only had she failed to obtain the greatest heiress in Christendom for her brother,[21] and by that failure the alliance with Burgundy, but a few months later she experienced a yet more bitter disappointment when, less than four years after her marriage with the Duke of York, the young duchess died.[22] Elizabeth had every reason to grieve at the death of her little daughter-in-law, as the great estates she had inherited now passed out of the royal control into that of the Howard and Berkeley families. It must indeed have seemed to Elizabeth that all her carefully laid plans had been made in vain. However, she did not long remain idle. Probably observing that the king's health was beginning to fail, and sensing that he had not much longer to live, she resolved to do everything in her power to provide for yet more of her many relations.[23] Thus during the Parliament held in the last month of Edward's reign[24] there was effected with the Berkeley family a compromise by which William, Viscount Berkeley, released his claims on the Mowbray estates in favour of the queen's young son, Richard, Duke of York.[25] Not content with having regained the Mowbray inheritance, the queen next brought her influence to bear on the king with a view to making a yet more advantageous marriage for another of her relations. During the session of the same Parliament a marriage was arranged between Anne,[26] daughter and heiress of the king's late sister, the Duchess of Exeter, and her grandson, Thomas Grey, son of the Marquis of Dorset. The scheme was so worked as, in effect, to make provision for both the queen's sons by her first marriage out of the Exeter estates.[27] The king, moreover, received a *douceur* of 7,000 marks (£4,666 13s 4d) from the queen and her sons for his help in this transaction.[28]

On 27 March 1482, Mary of Burgundy was killed by a fall from her horse;[29] she left two small children, Philip and Margaret.

The Flemings, who refused to acknowledge any authority on the part of Maximilian, wished for peace and friendship with France. The men of Ghent, supported by France, controlled everything, and compelled him to conclude with Louis the Treaty of Arras (23 December 1482), by which it was arranged that Margaret should be married to the Dauphin, and have as her dower the country of Artois and some of the best lands in Burgundy taken from her brother Philip's inheritance. Thus the compact, so dear to Elizabeth's heart, for the marriage of the Dauphin and Princess Elizabeth's was deliberately and boldly violated, with a view to a future annexation of those provinces to the Crown of France.

Edward and Elizabeth celebrated Christmas that year with particular magnificence at Eltham Palace, where the king 'kept his estate all the whole feast in his great chamber, and the queen in her chamber, where as daily more than 2,000 persons served'.[30] A striking description of the splendour of the Court has been handed down by a contemporary writer. 'You might have seen in those days the royal Court presenting no other appearance than such as fully befits a most mighty kingdom, filled with riches and with people of almost all nations, and boasting of those most sweet and beautiful children.'[31] The king appeared 'clad in a great variety of most costly garments, of quite a different cut to those which had been usually seen hitherto in our kingdom. The sleeves of the robes were very full and hanging, greatly resembling a monk's frock and so lined within with the most costly furs and rolled over the shoulders as to give that prince a new and distinguished air to beholders.'[32]

However, the king does not appear to have thought only of himself, but of the queen and his eldest daughter as well. A few months earlier he had 'by vertue of a warrant undre his signet and signe manuelle bering date the vij day of August in the XXth yere of his moost noble reigne' given 'unto oure souverayn lady the quene and to Lady Elizabeth his doughter for ij gownes for them, XV yerdes of grene tisshue clothe of gold'.[33]

On Candlemas Day (2 February) the king went in procession with the queen from St Stephen's chapel to Westminster Hall, when, 'at his proceeding out of his chamber', he made Sir Richard Wood, and Sir William Catesby, one of the Justices of the Common Place, knights.[34]

Nevertheless, there was behind this outward appearance of festivity and prosperity, plenty to trouble the mind of the king. The news of the Treaty of Arras had sunk deep into his heart. At the end of March he took to his bed at Westminster, where he died on 9 April 1483,[35] in his forty-first year, leaving Elizabeth far more desolate and unprotected than in her first widowhood.

By his Will, similar in many ways to that drawn up by him prior to his departure for France, in 1475,[36] Edward left to each of his daughters 10,000 marks chargeable on the revenues of the Duchy of Lancaster, 'so that they be governed and ruled in their marriage by our dearest wife the queen and by our son the Prince of Wales if God fortune him to come to age of direction'.[37]

The care of the future Edward V and the kingdom seems to have been bequeathed to the late king's brother, Richard, Duke of Gloucester, as the man most likely to be able to keep the peace between the two opposite factions at the Court.[38] Edward IV had needed all his powers of strength and persuasion to keep the peace in his Court, where ineradicable dissensions prevailed. Indeed, the whole Court was animated with a spirit of intrigue which the animosity of the different factions had fomented to a degree hitherto unknown in any former reign. Elizabeth and her relations were exceedingly unpopular, not only with the old nobility, whom they had supplanted, but also with the common people, who attributed everything that was in any way oppressive or irritating to the grasping Woodville faction.[39]

This party was far from being a numerous one: the queen's three brothers, Anthony, Earl Rivers,[40] Lionel Woodville, Bishop of Salisbury,[41] and Sir Edward Woodville,[42] the Marquis of Dorset, her eldest son by her first marriage, and his brother, Sir Richard Grey, could not of themselves have had unlimited power, and the various lords who had been given Woodville wives do not appear to have become greatly attached to the queen's party.[43] The king's policy in promoting and favouring them must be judged from its political effects in the weakening of the older baronage, not for its immediate effect in strengthening his own position, which, indeed, it did not do. There seems to have been something in the ill-fated Elizabeth and, indeed, in all the family, which made them incapable of conciliating their enemies – an insolence or falseness which made them objects of continual suspicion. Thus, despite the fact that Elizabeth constantly strove to form and create a party, so great was the jealousy with which she was regarded that she never succeeded in gaining either confidence or respect.

Opposed to the Woodvilles was the party led by William, Lord Hastings, who, like them, owed everything to the late king. Ever since, in 1471, Edward had deprived her brother, Lord Rivers, of the lieutenancy of Calais, and had conferred it on Hastings,[44] Elizabeth's chagrin had been very deep, and it led to an enmity between Hastings and the Woodvilles which was scarcely less bitter or less disastrous to the House of York than the enmity which had previously existed between Warwick and the queen's family.[45] Elizabeth's dislike for Hastings was particularly intense, in that it was based not only on the slight that had been put on her brother, but on a suspicion that he was 'secretly familiar with the king in wanton company'.[46] Furthermore, she and her relatives probably had cause to hate him in that they saw in him the only obstacle between them and their complete dominion over Edward.

It was, therefore, not altogether surprising that soon after Edward's death strong evidence appeared of the jealousy with which Elizabeth and her relations were regarded. Although Edward had on his deathbed actually made an attempt to end this hostility between Hastings and the Woodvilles,[47] which, he feared, might prove a great danger when his restraining hand was removed and the sceptre passed to his young and inexperienced son, suspicion at once revived when the queen proposed in council that her son, Edward V, should come up from Ludlow, where he was residing at the time of his father's death, with a strong escort.

It is evident that Elizabeth and her relations were expected to make a great effort to preserve by force the authority they had hitherto exercised by their influence over the late king. The wiser members of the Council, therefore, considered it expedient to remove the young king entirely from the hands of his maternal relations, more especially as the queen 'naturally but unwisely'[48] claimed the regency for herself. Moreover, the Woodvilles, presumably bearing in mind the enforced end of Humphrey, Duke of Gloucester's protectorate in 1429, almost certainly aimed at crowning the young king prior to the arrival of the future Protector, Richard, in the capital, in which case the protectorate would automatically have ceased, giving place to a Council of Regency in which the Woodvilles would have had the majority.[49]

It was, therefore, only to be expected that the queen's proposals met with the most bitter opposition. Hastings, possibly calling to mind his short period of detention in the Tower, asked her insolently, 'Against whom was the young sovereign to be defended? Who were his foes? Not Richard, Duke of Gloucester?' He ended by threatening that he would retire to Calais, of which place he was governor,[50] if the king were to enter London surrounded by soldiers. Thus, in view of the decisive part that Calais had played in Warwick's days, Elizabeth found herself forced to promise that the young king's escort should not exceed 2,000 horse.[51]

# I2

# THE USURPATION OF RICHARD III

So far the more prudent counsels had prevailed; but this state of affairs did not last very much longer. Sunday 4 May was the date fixed for the coronation, and it seemed to indicate a definite desire to set aside the late king's will as soon as possible.[1] The queen and her friends thoroughly distrusted the dukes of Gloucester and Buckingham, and taking advantage of their absence from London, sought to exclude them from every position of authority.[2]

Richard, Duke of Gloucester, was in Yorkshire, probably at his castle of Middleham,[3] when news reached him of his brother's death. After writing affectionately to the queen,[4] Richard immediately started for London, but did not reach Northampton till 29 April.[5] The young king, who had left Ludlow on the 24th, had arrived there that same day and passed on to Stony Stratford. His uncle, Lord Rivers, and his half-brother, Sir Richard Grey, who had accompanied him, rode back to Northampton to salute Gloucester, and they, with the Duke of Buckingham, who arrived about the same time from London, sat down to supper together.

After supper Richard and Buckingham had a private conversation together, and it seems probable that Buckingham, who also hated the Woodvilles,[6] informed Gloucester of all that had been taking place in London since the late king's death.

The news Gloucester heard must indeed have surprised him, for the things that had been going on in London were certainly most suspicious. Apart from the early day fixed for the coronation and the attempt to bring the young king to London with a formidable escort under his uncle Rivers, the Marquis of Dorset (Constable of the Tower) had so far abused his office as to obtain from thence supplies of arms and money,[7] with which he and Sir Edward Woodville had fitted out some vessels in order to command the Channel.[8] Everything pointed to the fact that the Woodville party had determined to keep the government in their own hands by main force until their ascendancy had been secured on a proper constitutional basis by the coronation, following which event the services of a Protector would be no longer required. Thus the fortune of the two parties depended on a race to London; but the 2,000 men composing the young king's escort were now rather more of a handicap than an advantage, with the result that Rivers must have begun to doubt the success of the the queen's plans, when he found Gloucester advancing so close upon him at Northampton.

He was soon to discover that his suspicions were correct. Early next morning (30 April), having secured the keys of the inn where Rivers and Grey were spending the night, Gloucester and Buckingham arrested them with some others.[9] They then proceeded to Stony Stratford, whence they brought the young king back to Northampton, telling him that his maternal relatives were plotting to seize the Government by force. The poor young king burst into tears; nevertheless this tale was very generally believed when the dukes, on their way to London, exhibited the 'barrels of harness' which, it was said, had been 'privily conveyed' in the baggage of 'those traitors' from Ludlow, the populace expressing the opinion that 'it were alms to hang them'.[10]

After these somewhat startling developments the king resumed his journey in the company of his uncle, Gloucester; the news of the arrest of Rivers and Grey preceded them, and threw the capital into the greatest confusion. Elizabeth herself received the news on 30 April at midnight.[11] In that moment of anguish the widowed queen either remembered or, as seems more likely, was reminded by the Chancellor, Archbishop Rotherham,[12] one of her staunchest friends, for whose advancement she was to a great extent responsible, and whose fidelity to her was later to cause him to be imprisoned by Richard, that as long as she could keep her second son in safety, the life of the young king was secure. 'Therefore, she took her young son, the Duke of York, and her daughters, and went out of the palace of Westminster into the sanctuary, and there lodged in the abbot's place; and she and all her children and company, were registered as sanctuary persons.'[13] Her apprehensions for her personal safety were perhaps not unreasonable; she had indeed played for big stakes, and been well and truly beaten. She seems, however, to have been hardly less anxious about her property. For that night her servants conveyed to the Westminster sanctuary a large amount of personal property and furniture, to make easy entrance for which they actually broke down the walls which separated the palace from the sanctuary. While all this was going on 'before the day broke, the Chancellor, having received the news of the Duke of Gloucester's proceedings', despite the fact that Hastings had assured him that

> there was no danger to the young king or his mother, called up his servants, and took with him the Great Seal and went to the queen, about whom he found much heaviness, rumble, haste, and business with conveyance of her [household] stuff into sanctuary. Every man was busy to carry, bear, and convey household stuffs, chests, and fardels; no man was unoccupied, and some walked off, with more than they were directed, to other places. The queen sat alone alow [below] on the rushes in dismay, her long fair hair, so renowned for

its beauty, escaped from its confinement, and streaming over her person, swept on the ground.[14]

The archbishop tried to reassure the sorrowing queen with the message

sent him by Lord Hastings in the night. 'Ah, woe worth him!' replied Elizabeth, 'for it is he that goeth about to destroy me and my blood.' 'Madame,' said the archbishop, 'be of good comfort; I assure you, if they crown any other king than your eldest son, whom they have with them, we will on the morrow crown his brother, whom you have with you here. And here is the Great Seal, which in like wise as your noble husband gave it to me, so I deliver it to you for the use of your son.' And therewith he delivered to the queen the Great Seal, and departed from her in the dawning of the day; and when he opened his window and looked forth on the Thames, he saw the river covered with boats full of the Duke of Gloucester's servants, watching that no one might go to the queen's asylum.[15]

Therefore it was not long before he realised that he had been guilty of a very serious violation of the trust imposed upon him, whereupon he secretly sent for the Seal again.[16]

Meanwhile the whole of London was in a panic. While Gloucester's supporters occupied the Thames in boats to prevent any communication with the queen at Westminster, the queen's party rose in arms, many of the citizens joining it.[17] But Hastings, ever the greatest enemy of the Woodvilles, succeeded in persuading the lords in council that Gloucester's action was in no way directed against the king, and would prove justifiable when legally examined.[18]

The enforced interruption of the king's progress had rendered it impossible for the coronation to take place on the day originally appointed. As it was, he only reached London on that very day (4 May),[19] accompanied by the dukes of Gloucester and Buckingham. A council was hastily summoned, by which Gloucester was recognised as Protector of the King and Realm.[20]

The king, who was at first lodged in the Bishop of London's palace near St Paul's, was soon transferred to the royal apartments in the Tower.[21] A new day – 22 June[22] – was fixed for the coronation, and Parliament was summoned to meet three days later.[23] Archbishop Rotherham having been deprived of the Great Seal, Dr Russell, Bishop of Lincoln, was made chancellor in his place.[24] Thus the Woodville influence was completely subverted. The queen's brother, Lionel, Bishop of Salisbury, was in sanctuary with her, while the property of her son, the Marquis of Dorset, was confiscated.[25] Since, however, some of this property was in the custody of the Abbot of Westminster, it may have been among the many things the queen had so hastily taken with her to the sanctuary on the night she sought refuge there.[26]

On 9 June the Protector held a council, which sat from 10 till 2 o'clock, and it was significantly noted that no communication was held with the queen.[27] Next day Richard wrote to the Mayor and Corporation of York, requesting them to send up at once as many armed men as they could get together, to protect him and the Duke of Buckingham against an alleged conspiracy of the queen's adherents. The letter is in these words:

> The Duke of Gloucester, brother and uncle of kings, Protector, Defender, etc., of England. Right trusty and well-beloved, we greet you well. And as you love the weal of us and the weal and surety of your own self, we heartily pray you come unto us to London in all the diligence ye can possible, after the sight hereof, with as many as ye can make defensibly arrayed, there to aid and assist us against the queen, her bloody adherents and affinity, which have intended and daily

doth intend to murder and destroy us and our cousin the Duke of Buckingham and the old royal blood of this realm, and (as is now openly known) by their subtle and damnable ways forecasted the same, and also the final destruction and disherison of you and all other the inheritors and men of honour as well of the north parts as of other countries that belongen us, as our trusty servant,[28] this bearer, shall more at large show you, to whom we pray you give credence. And as ever we may do for you in time coming, fail not, but haste you to us hither. Given under our signet at London the 10th day at June.[29]

It would appear, then, that on 10 June Richard professed to be seriously alarmed at a conspiracy by the queen and her supporters, the existence of which had just been divulged and was then notorious.

The Woodvilles were accused of conspiring to destroy himself and the Duke of Buckingham 'and the old royal blood of the realm'. Nevertheless it would appear that the Protector could not rely on the power at his command in London to put down this conspiracy, and therefore demanded aid from his dependants in the North.

In point of fact, the alleged discovery of this conspiracy was by no means so 'sudden' as the Protector made out.

It was just the day before (9 June) Richard wrote to York that Stallworth had written to Sir William Stonor that 'ther wass none that spake with the quene'.[30] It is now certain that before that day, there had been several efforts made by the Council to come to some understanding with Elizabeth and induce her to leave sanctuary.[31] On 9 June, however, this policy was abandoned. Though the council had sat from 10 o'clock till 2, none of its members spoke to her. On the very next day Richard wrote to the North for assistance against her and her supporters.

It must not, however, be too readily presumed that Richard's charge of conspiracy against the queen and her relations was entirely without foundation. According to Polydore Vergil,[32] an act of sudden violence to liberate the young king from Richard's control had already been contemplated. Richard would appear to have been well aware of this intention, and to have been by no means so alarmed as he pretended. Two whole days passed by after he had written to York, and nothing more was heard in London of the plot which he had declared to be so notorious. On the third day it was proclaimed through the city by the Protector himself; but it would seem to have been proclaimed merely as the justification of an act of tyranny.[33]

The truth of the matter appears to lie in the fact that the conspiracy, however much the queen and her relationships may have advanced and seconded it, did not originate with them.

Some of the Council, especially Hastings, who had hitherto opposed the Woodvilles, and even boasted that he had defeated their designs and created a complete revolution 'without shedding so much blood as would have flowed from a cut finger',[34] were beginning to be more apprehensive of Richard's ambition than that of the queen's party. Much as Hastings disliked Elizabeth and her whole family, he now positively regretted the change that he had so recently gloried in having effected. He made overtures of reconciliation, with the result that conferences took place at St Paul's and elsewhere as to the best means of getting the king out of his uncle's power; the Protector himself held private consultations with his more confidential friends at Crosby's Place in Bishopsgate Street, and for a time deserted the regular Council in the Tower.

It would appear that Richard's ambition was now beginning to soar beyond a Protectorate which, at the most, could last for only four or five years: he must have realised that his nephew would be almost bound to share his mother's dislike of him. He had, indeed, begun to contemplate a usurpation. It is, however, most improbable that he entertained any such idea prior to his triumph over the Woodvilles. The Tudor chroniclers would have us believe that he had always been a schemer[35] and that he had been solely responsible for his brother Clarence's death.[36] All this seems most improbable since no one could have foreseen that Edward IV would have died at the comparatively early age of forty-one; had he lived but nine years longer, the possibility of any attempt at usurpation would have been extremely remote.[37]

According to More,[38] the object of the Protector's meetings was to procure his own elevation to the throne. It is, however, extremely doubtful whether he at this stage revealed his whole plan even to his staunchest supporters. There were many outstanding points on which to take counsel with his friends without showing them the full scope of his ambition. His power as Protector was in a most critical state, one party in the Council being clearly opposed to its continuance, added to which fact the coronation day was fast approaching, when, according to the precedent of Henry VI's time, his tenure of office would automatically end. Since, however, his Parliament was to meet immediately after, Richard proposed to obtain from the lords there assembled a confirmation of his authority until such time as the young king should be considered fit to rule in person.[39]

It would seem, therefore, that there were two separate councils, neither of which was quite aware of what was going on in the other. Lord Stanley is said to have warned Hastings that he did not like the two separate councils,[40] but Hastings was apparently lulled into a false sense of security owing to the presence in Richard's council of his protégé, William Catesby,[41] who kept him well informed of everything that was going on there.

This Catesby was endeavouring to serve two masters. With his help Richard attempted to ascertain whether Hastings would agree in his intended usurpation of the crown, Catesby going so far as to broach the subject to him; but Hastings answered with such 'terrible words',[42] that Catesby not only realised it was hopeless, but feared a diminution of his own credit with Hastings, for having dared to mention it. He, therefore, decided to betray Hastings, and secretly informed Richard of all that his old benefactor had told him.[43]

The crisis came quite suddenly on 13 June. The Protector came to the Tower, entering the council chamber about 9 o'clock. He was very cheerful, asked Bishop Morton for some strawberries from his garden at Holborn,[44] and, after opening the business, begged leave of temporary absence. An hour later he returned with a strangely altered manner, and inquired what punishment those who had conspired against his life deserved. He then accused Elizabeth as a sorceress who, with Jane Shore as her accomplice, had wasted his body 'by their sorcery and witchcraft', in proof of which he bared his left arm to the council, shrunk and withered, as, to judge by Sir Thomas More, 'it was ever such since his birth'.[45]

Hastings answered that if they had done so they deserved heinous punishment. 'What!' quoth the Protector, 'dost thou serve me with ifs and ands? I tell thee they have so done, and that I will make good on thy body, traitor!' He then struck his fist violently on the council table. Whereupon armed men rushed in and arrested Hastings, Lord Stanley, Bishop Morton, and Elizabeth's great friend and supporter., Archbishop Rotherham. Hastings was borne off to immediate execution, the Protector swearing that he would not dine till he had seen his head off.[46] With Hastings's death the last faint hope of the Woodvilles disappeared.

Richard then sent for some of the leading citizens, before whom he and Buckingham appeared in rusty armour which they had hastily put on, and told them they had just escaped a plot to assassinate them in the council chamber. A proclamation was also published to that effect, rather too neatly written, as some observed, to give it much credit, for it seemed to have been prepared beforehand.[47]

Another person who was made to feel like the Protector's displeasure at this time was Edward IV's former mistress, Jane Shore, who, following on the execution of Hastings, was imprisoned in the Tower.[48]

Doctor James Gairdner's theory[49] that Jane was employed as a political agent and go-between by Hastings and the queen is very reasonable, when one takes into consideration the great influence she had enjoyed at the Court of Edward IV, and her relations with Dorset since that king's death.[50] Although it was certainly a very frivolous charge that Richard brought against her of conspiring with Elizabeth to do him personal injury, it must not be forgotten that the most doubtful assertions are frequently founded on something plausible. In all probability we are not fully aware of the whole extent of the accusation against either the queen or Jane Shore; the very fact that they were accused of acting in concert at all seems in itself to imply a better understanding between the two women than has generally been believed. When, however, one considers the desperate plight of Elizabeth together with the fact that Jane Shore was at that time the mistress of her eldest son, Dorset,[51] such a state of affairs is by no means improbable. Living as she was under Hastings's protection, nothing could have been easier for her than to take messages from one party to the other. This would appear to be Richard's reason for imprisoning her, rather than the explanation given by More, that the Protector wished to obtain possession of her goods. Had Richard desired to enrich himself at someone else's expense, there must have been many other persons in London far richer than his late brother's unfortunate mistress. Nevertheless this unhappy woman's penance, if it did nothing else, served to draw the attention of the public to the late king's dissolute character, thus preparing them, in some measure, for the remarkable events which were about to take place.

The death of Hastings was unlikely to remove those suspicions which had caused Elizabeth to seek refuge in the sanctuary at

Westminster. Moreover, there was no longer even one member of the Woodville family in the Council. The queen's friends were either dead or imprisoned. Westminster was full of armed men,[52] and the forces, for which Richard had written to his friends at York, were expected to arrive in London any day.[53] Yet Gloucester seems to have got his own way as much by persuasion as by force, and he certainly received active support from such impartial persons as Cardinal Bourchier, whose position rendered them less apprehensive of personal violence than men like the ill-fated Hastings. Be that as it may, Richard was supported with the greatest cordiality when, at the meeting of the Council on the Monday following Hastings's death (16 June),[54] it was proposed that the young Duke of York should be sent for out of sanctuary to keep the king, his brother, company in the Tower. It was unanimously resolved that Queen Elizabeth should be requested to deliver him up, and there was, according to More,[55] even some discussion whether, in the event of the queen's anticipated refusal, he should not be taken from her by force. The Council apparently considered that even if there was no fear for his safety in the Tower, there was a real danger of renewed intrigues so long as he remained with the queen in sanctuary. Finally an agreement was reached that if the queen would not deliver up the duke by persuasions, 'he should be fetched'.[56] Since, however, it was considered preferable 'that all fair means should be first tried', Cardinal Bourchier, with several lords to accompany him, was sent into the sanctuary to the queen; the Protector and the rest of the Council going into the Star Chamber at Westminster to await the result.[57]

When the cardinal was come into the queen's presence, after all dutiful salutations, he delivered to her the cause of his coming, saying: 'That he was with those other lords, sent by the Protector and the Privy Council to her Majesty, to let her know how much her detaining of the Duke of York in that place was scandalous to the public, and disliked by the king his brother ... that it would be a very great comfort to his majesty to have his natural brother in company with him; nor would it be of less advantage to the young duke himself, because it would confirm and strengthen their loves to be brought up together, as well at their books as sports ... upon which accounts, as he was sent by his majesty and the council ... he could not but earnestly entreat her to comply with a thing so very reasonable, and every way convenient.'

The queen, who was of sharp wit and graceful speech, answered the cardinal, and said, 'My Lord, I cannot deny, but it is very convenient that my son, the duke, should be in the company of his brother the king, as well for society, as love's sake but since they are both so young, as that it is the most suitable for them to be under the government of their mother, it is better for the king to be with me here, than that I should send the duke to him; though was it really otherwise, that duty obliged the duke to go to him, yet necessity, in this case, creates a dispensation, because he hath been of late so sorely afflicted with diseases, and being not perfectly recovered, is in so great a danger of relapse (which generally physicians say is more fatal than the first sickness) that I dare trust no earthly person as yet with the care of him. For though I doubt not but that he might have such about him as would do their best to preserve his health, yet since I have ordered him all along and am hos mother, it must be allowed by all men, that as I am the most able, so shall I be the most affectionately careful and tender of him. And, for these reasons, I hope both the king and his council will dispense with his absence awhile, till he is perfectly recovered and in health; before that I cannot endure to hear of parting with him.'

The cardinal, hearing this reply, answered, 'No man, good madam, doth deny, but that your majesty is the fittest person to take care of all your children, and I am sure the council will be very pleased to hear that it is your pleasure so to do; yea, they would beg it of you, provided you would be contented to do it in such a place as is consistent with their and your own honour; whereas, if you resolve to tarry in this place, then they judge it is more convenient that the duke should be with the king at liberty ... than to remain in sanctuary ... for it is not always so necessary that the child should be with the mother, but there may be reasons sometimes of taking him from her, and that for the best; as your majesty knows there was, when your eldest son, then Prince of Wales, and now king, was sent to keep his Court at Ludlow for his own honour and the good of the country, of which your majesty was so well convinced, that you seemed contented with it.'

The queen grew a little warm, and smartly retorted, 'Not so very well contented neither at that separation! Though the case is much different now: for the prince was in good health, the duke is now sick; for though the height of the distemper is past, yet he is weak; in which condition, while he remains, I wonder that the Protector and council should be so earnest to have him from me, since, if the child should grow sick and miscarry, they would incur the censures of some ill dealings with him. And whereas you say that it is dishonourable to my child, and to them, that he remain in this place, I think the contrary; for certainly it is most for their honour to let him abide, where no man can doubt he will remain safest, and that is here, so long as I continue here; and I do not intend to leave this place and endanger my life with my friends who, I would to God, were rather in safety here with me, than I were in hazard with them.'

'Why, Madam,' saith the Lord Howard, 'do you know any reason that they are in danger?' 'No truly,' said she roundly, 'nor why they should be in prison neither, as they now be; but

I have great cause to fear, lest those, who have not scrupled to put them in prison without cause, will as little value to destroy them without law or right.'

Upon these words the cardinal winked upon the lord to put an end to that discourse; and then added himself, 'That he did not doubt but that those lords, who, being of her kindred, remained under arrest, would, upon a due examination of matters, discharge themselves well enough of any accusation alleged against them: and as to her own royal person, there neither was, nor could be, any kind of danger.'

'How shall I be certain of that?' said the queen. 'Is it that I am innocent? It doth not appear that they are guilty. Is it that I am better beloved of their enemies? No; but rather they are hated for my sake. Is it that I am so neatly related to the king? They are not much further off. And therefore since it seems to me, that as I am in the same cause, so I am in like danger; I do not intend to part out this place. And as for my son, the Duke of York, I purpose to keep him with me till I see how business will go; for the more greedy and earnest some men are to have him into their hands without any substantial cause, the more fearful and scrupulous am I to deliver him.'

'And the more suspicious you are, Madam,' answered the cardinal, 'the more jealous are others of you; lest, under a causeless pretence of danger, you should convey him out of the nation; and so if they permit him to remain with you now, it shall not be in their power to have him for the future. Wherefore it is the opinion of many of the council, that there is a necessity of taking the Duke of York immediately into their care and government; and since he can enjoy no privilege by sanctuary, who has neither will to require it, nor malice or offence to need it, they judge it no breach of sanctuary, if you finally refuse to deliver him by fair means, to fetch him out of it; and I assure you, madam, that the Protector, who bears a most tender love to his nephews, and the council, who have an equal care and respect for your children, will certainly set him at liberty, unless you resign him to us, lest you should send him away.'

'Ay,' says the queen, 'hath the Protector, his uncle, such a love for him, that he fears nothing more than that he should escape his hands? I unfeignedly declare, that it never so much as entered into my thoughts to send him out of this place into any foreign parts; partly because his health will not bear any journies, and partly because, though I should not scruple to send him into any part of the world, where I knew him out of all danger; yet I do not think any place more secure than this sanctuary, which there never was any tyrant so devilish, who dare violate; and I trust that the Almighty God will so awe the minds of his and my enemies, as to restrain them from offering violence to this holy place. But you tell me, that the lord Protector and the council are of opinion that my son cannot deserve a sanctuary, and therefore may not be allowed the privileges of it. He hath found out a goodly person, is not of greater force to defend the innocent, because he is in no danger, and therefore can have no need of it; which is an opinion as erroneous as hellish. But the child, you say, cannot require the privilege of a sanctuary and therefore since he has no will to choose it, he ought not to have it. Who told the Protector so? Ask him, and you shall hear him require it. But suppose it were really so that he could not ask it, or if he could, would not, but would rather choose to go out; I think it is sufficient that I do require it, and am registered a sanctuary-person, to make any man guilty of breaking sanctuary to take my son out of it by force and against my will. For is not the sanctuary a protection in that case as well for my goods as myself? No man can lawfully take my horse from me, if I stole him not, or owe nothing; and surely much less my child. Besides, by law, as my learned council sheweth me, he is my ward, because he hath no lands by descent holden by knights service, but only by soccage; and then I being the guardian of my son by law, no man can take him by force from me, without injustice, in any place, and without sacrilege from hence.

'And, upon this right, I do insist and require the privilege of sanctuary for him, as my pupil and infant, to whom alone by law the care of him belongs; and if this triple cord may be broken; I mean, the right which I have to keep him with me by the law of man, as his guardian; by the law of nature, as his mother, and by the law of God, as being in Sanctuary with him – if all this be not enough to secure him from any human force, I think nothing under heaven can. But I do not despair of safety, where I have always found so much. Here was I brought to be of my son, who is now king; and though his enemy reigned, and might have used the same or like pretences to have us taken from sanctuary, yet he did not: and I hope no man will have the boldness to act contrary to all former precedents, but the place that protected one son will be as great a security to the other; for to be plain with you, my lord, I fear to put him into the Protector's hands, because he hath his brother already; and since he pretends to be the next heir to the crown after them, notwithstanding his sisters, if they any ways miscarry, his way to the throne lies plain and easy to him. Now, this is so just a cause of fear, that even the laws of the land teach me it, which, as learned men tell me, forbids every man the guardianship of them, by whose death they become heirs to their inheritance: and if the law is so careful of such as have the least inheritance, how much more ought I to be fearful that my children come not into his power, who, by their death, will have the kingdom for his inheritance. For these reasons I am confirmed in my resolutions of keeping my son in sanctuary with me, and my right so to do; and think them so far to outbalance the Protector's frivolous reasons, of keeping his brother company, and being dishonourable to him, that I cannot alter my mind: for I have reason to think that whoever he proves a protector to, he will prove a destroyer to them, if they be once in his hands and power. I know the Protector and council have power enough, if they will, to take him and me from this place; but whosoever he be that shall dare to do it, I pray God send him shortly need of a sanctuary, but no possibility to come to it!'

The cardinal, seeing the queen grow more and more passionate by discoursing ... thought it time to break off arguing with her, and therefore to bring things to a conclusion, said unto her:

'Madam, I will not dispute the matter longer with you: it is equal to me whether you deliver him or not. I am, with these lords, but the messenger to know your resolution, and beg you to tell us plainly, whether you will, or will not, deliver him to us. For though, if you resign him to us, I durst pawn my own body and soul to you for his safety, yet, if you deny it, I will immediately depart, and finish my trust, resolving never to engage in the matter again, since I see you so resolute in your own judgement, as if you thought both me, and all others, lacked either wit or honesty; wit, in that we, not perceiving the Protector's ill designs, were made the tools of his wicked craft; honesty, in that, knowing his intentions, we have laboured to bring your son into the Protector's hands to destroy him; an execrable treason, which, as ourselves abhor so, we dare boldly say, was far from the Protector's thoughts, and cannot be imputed to any in this case: but you must brand the whole council with short-sighted advice and disloyalty to their prince.'

These words of the cardinal being peremptory and short, much bemused the queen being put to it on a sudden to resolve whether she would send him or no. The cardinal she saw ready to depart, and the Protector and council were near, she knew; what to do she could not tell. She feared that, by delivering him, she cast into the mouth of ruin, and by keeping him, she did but provoke the Protector and council to be more rough and severe with them both. She saw there was no way to save him from the Protector's hands, but by conveying him out of his knowledge of power, which, though she wished, yet she had no way to effect it; wherefore she resolved to make the best use of necessity, and since the Protector must have him, take the best way to secure him in his hands. She considered that her fears were but grounded on vehement presumptions, and therefore hoped things might not prove so bad as she imagined. She could not doubt of the cardinal's sincerity and loyalty to her son; and though she indeed feared he might be deceived, yet she did not believe either he, or the lords present, would be in any way accessory to his destruction: and for these reasons she thought it better to deliver him to them, who were ready to pawn their honour and lives for his security, and would therefore look upon themselves engaged for his safety, than suffer him to be taken from her. And thereupon taking her son, the Duke of York, in her hand, she led him to the cardinal and lords, and with great earnestness said to them: 'My lord cardinal, and you my lords, I am not so opinionated of myself, or ill-advised concerning you, as to mistrust either your wisdom or fidelity, as I shall prove to you by reposing such trust in you, as, if either of them be wanting in you, will redound to my inexpressible grief, the damage of the whole realm, and your eternal shame and disgrace: for, lo! Here is my son, the person whom you desire; and though I doubt not but that I could keep him safe in this sanctuary from all violence, yet here I resign him into your hands. I am sensible that I run great hazards in so doing; no whit less than my fears suggest;

for I have some so great enemies to my blood that if they knew where any of it lay in their own veins, they would presently let it out; and much more in others, and the nearer to me the more zealously. Experience also convinces us all, that the desire of a kingdom knows no kindred. The brother in that case hath been the destruction of the brother, and the son of his father, and have we cause to think the uncle will be more tender of his nephews? Each of these children are the other's defence, while they are asunder; if one be safe they are both secure; but being both together they are in great danger, and, therefore, as a wise merchant will never adventure all his goods in one ship, so it looks not so politically in me to put them both under the same hazards. But notwithstanding all this, (whether rightly foreseen or no, I leave you to think on, and prevent) I do here deliver him, and his brother in him, to your keeping, of whom I shall ask him again at all times before God and the world. I am confident of your fidelity, and have no reason to distrust your wisdom, power or ability to keep him, if you will make use of your resolution when it is required; and if you are unwilling to do that, then I pray you leave him here with me: and that you may not meet with more than you did expect, let me beg of you, for the trust which his father ever reposed in you, and for the confidence I now put in you, that as you think I fear too much, for you would be cautious that in this weighty case you fear not too little, because your credulity here may make an irrecoverable mistake.' Having thus spoken, she turned to the child and said to him, 'Farewell, mine own sweet son! The Almighty be thy protector! Let me kiss thee once more before we part, for God knows when we shall kiss again.' And then, having kissed him, she blessed him, and turned from him and wept, and so went her way, leaving the child with the lords weeping also for her departure.[58]

Thus three days after the death of her ancient enemy, Hastings, the unhappy Elizabeth, feeling that all further resistance would be useless, surrendered her child to the Protector. Meanwhile the little prince, leaving his mother and sisters behind him in the sanctuary, was conducted by Archbishop Bourchier and the other lords of the deputation to Westminster Hall, where he was met by the Duke of Buckingham. At the door of the Star Chamber he was received by the Protector himself, who embraced his nephew affectionately, and conducted him to the Tower,[59] which neither he nor the young king his brother were to leave again.

On the Saturday after the Duke of York's surrender, Elizabeth found herself completely deserted by her friends. A letter, dated 21 June 1483, written by Simon Stallworth to Sir William Stonor, mentions the fact that her brother-in-law, Lord Lisle,[60] had gone over to the Protector's side.[61]

The next day, Sunday 22 June, had long been appointed for the coronation, which was now deferred until 2 November.[62] On the very day it should have taken place, Dr Ralph Shaw preached a sermon, at St Paul's Cross, in which he intimated that the children of Edward IV and Elizabeth Woodville were illegitimate, and that the crown belonged by right to the Protector, Richard, Duke of Gloucester.[63] Nor did the preacher end there. He continued by insinuating that Edward IV himself was a bastard,[64] which insinuation he must have been authorised by Richard to make, to the dishonour of his own mother, who was still living. Further, it had been arranged that Richard was to pass by during the sermon, but he arrived rather late, with the result that when the preacher, returning to the subject said, 'This is his father's own figure,'[65] the crowd, already deeply shocked and not a little puzzled, 'stood as they had been turned into stones, for wonder of this shameful sermon'.[66]

On the Tuesday following, 24 June, the Duke of Buckingham, with some other lords and knights, addressed the citizens at the Guildhall in an eloquent speech in favour of Richard's claims.[67] The citizens remaining speechless, the Recorder was instructed to ask whether they would have Richard for their king, and a few at the far end of the hall cried, 'Long live King Richard!'

On the next day, 25 June, took place at Pontefract[68] the execution, apparently by command of the Earl of Northumberland, but without any legal trial,[69] of Earl Rivers, and possibly Sir Thomas Vaughan and Sir Richard Haute, Sir Richard Grey having been executed a few days previously.[70]

Parliament had been summoned to meet on this same day, and, although a *supersedeas* had been received at York three days earlier (21 June)[71] to countermand the sending up of the representatives, something closely resembling a Parliamentary assembly seems to have taken place in London on that day.[72] A roll was brought in declaring Richard to be the rightful king, and stating that the marriage of Edward IV with Elizabeth Woodville had led to 'great misgovernment, tyranny and civil war'; it further stated that the marriage had been 'made of great presumption, without the knowing and assent of the lords of this land, and also by sorcery and witchcraft committed by the said Elizabeth, and her mother, Jacquetta, Duchess of Bedford – as the common opinion of the people and the public voice and fame is, through all this land'. This roll also asserted that Edward's marriage with Elizabeth was invalid, since 'the said Edward stood married and troth-plight to one Dame Eleanor Butler, daughter of the old Earl of Shrewsbury'.[73] Moreover, it was insisted that Edward IV has been born abroad at Rouen, and Clarence at Dublin. Richard alone of the three brothers was the true-born Englishman. On these grounds a deputation was sent to the Protector at Baynard's Castle, asking him to assume the crown. Buckingham was spokesman, and Richard, with feigned reluctance, accepted the honour.[74] On the next day, accompanied by a number of nobles, he went to Westminster and seated himself in the marble chair.[75] From that day, 26 June, he dated the beginning of his reign.

# 13

# THE MURDER OF THE PRINCES IN THE TOWER & REBELLION OF THE DUKE OF BUCKINGHAM

The state in which the unhappy Elizabeth now found herself was destitute in the extreme. With the death of Edward IV her honours and happiness had come to an abrupt end. How often must she, while languishing in sanctuary, have looked back on her former widowhood, and grieved to think that in proportion to her rise in life, her sorrows had increased. At that time, though deprived of a beloved husband and though she had seen 'his fair fame tainted', she had an affectionate family to whom she might flee for refuge, and who were anxious to soothe her grief and offer her assistance. Her marriage with the king, which had raised her from obscurity, and which they had hailed as the harbinger of their own elevation, had but hastened their destruction.

Her father and one of her brothers had fallen early victims to the jealousy of their contemporaries: to her mother alone was it granted to die a natural death, and to be spared the horror of witnessing the destruction of her family. To whom could Elizabeth now turn for support? Her sons by the king were in their uncle's power, and too young to assert their rights. Of those by her former husband, whom in their infancy she had fondly clasped to her breast as the sole consolation of her declining years, one had already been sacrificed with her other brother to the jealousy of their rivals, and the other obliged to flee with her to sanctuary, her only remaining place of refuge. Here also Elizabeth's situation was changed: during her former stay in this retreat she had never given up hope of being restored to her husband and the throne; she had then been surrounded by friends and followers by whom her expectations were shared; they had loved her as their queen, and their kind attentions had alleviated her sorrows. But now her influence was waning! Her son, Edward V, had been deposed, and his uncle, under the usurped title of Richard III, held the crown.

Sir Richard Ratcliffe now came from the North with the troops that had been levied in Yorkshire, as the result of Richard's letter of 10 June, to protect him against the dowager queen. This force, which was joined by other troops from Wales, was sufficient to keep London quiet till the coronation, which duly took place with great splendour on 6 July.[1]

The success of the usurpation, however, immediately produced a changed feeling among the nobility, and the newly crowned king lost the hearts of many who 'would have jeopardised life and goods with him if he had remained still as protector'.[2]

On 23 July,[3] soon after his coronation, King Richard started on a royal progress through his kingdom. The secret order for the death of the two young princes seems to have been given by Richard some time between 7 and 15 August[4] while on this journey. During this progress the princes were at first kept in close custody within the Tower, with the result that little was known about them, and conspiracies began to be formed for their liberation. There was also a project for conveying some of their sisters in disguise to the Continent, but, to defeat any such project, Richard set a guard about the sanctuary under the command of John Nesfield, without whose permission no one was able either to enter or leave the place.[5]

With what misgivings must their unhappy mother have looked on her daughters and trembled for their fate. If her sons were held prisoners, what might not the usurper attempt against them? She had already been disappointed in her hopes for one of them, and could hardly have anticipated the possibility of a brighter prospect for the others, any more than for herself.

Risings against Richard in favour of Edward V now spread all over the southern counties, and it was given out by proclamation on 15 October that Buckingham would lead the movement.[6] Then came the news that the two young princes were dead.[7] How they had met their fate no one knew; however, few persons doubted that they had been murdered.[8]

Elizabeth must have heard of Richard's coronation, and trembled for the lives of her sons, rightly suspecting that the usurper would not suffer them to live long, even if they were kept in close confinement. Nevertheless the news of their death must have come as a terrible shock to her.

When these newes wer first brought to her it strake to her harte like the sharp darte of death; for when she was first enformed of the murther of her ii sones she was so sodinly amasyd, that she swooned and fell to the ground, and there lay in great agony, like a dead corpse. And after she was revived and came to her memory again, she wept and sobbed, and with pitiful screeches filled the whole mansion. Her breast she punched, her fair hair she tare and pulled in pieces, and being overcome with sorrow and pensiveness rather desired death than life, calling by name divers times her sweet babes, accounting herself more than mad that she deluded by vile and fraudulent promises had delivered her younger son out of sanctuary to his enemy to be put to death ... after long lamentation, she kneeled down and cried on God to take vengeance, who she nothing doubted would remember it.[9]

Every mother's heart beat in sympathy with the once unpopular Elizabeth, and when, in April the following year, Richard lost his only son, Englishmen declared that the imprecations of the agonised mother had been heard.

It seems probable that the Duke of Buckingham's certain knowledge that the two princes had been murdered was the determining cause of the first and most startling rebellion that Richard was called upon to put down. The position Buckingham held in the country at this time was unique. Indeed, no subject since the Kingmaker had been so liberally treated by his sovereign.[10] Not only was he Lord High Constable,[11] but a host of minor offices had been showered upon him.[12]

No adequate explanation of Buckingham's conduct can be possible, other than that, having obtained early knowledge of the princes' murder,[13] he was disgusted to discover the full infamy of the situation into which his alliance with Richard had led him. The rebellion does not, however, appear to have originated with Buckingham. On the contrary, the rising represented a coalition of all the parties hostile to Richard, and was supported among others by Elizabeth's three brothers, Sir Edward and Sir Richard and Lionel Woodville, and by her son Dorset.[14]

The original object of this rising had been to replace Edward V on the throne, a plan for which Buckingham would have had no sympathy whatsoever. And when he became aware of the young king's death, he lost all the respect he had ever felt for Richard, and began to seek means whereby to dethrone him.[15] Buckingham had, indeed, accompanied Richard on his progress as far as Gloucester, where, on 2 August,[16] he had taken his leave of the king to retire to his castle of Brecon. A little over two months later (15 October) Buckingham was in open revolt. Although he seems, at first, himself to have aspired to the crown,[17] he was soon convinced by Bishop Morton, his prisoner,[18] that the claim of his (Buckingham's) cousin, Henry, Earl of Richmond, was far superior to his own.[19]

Buckingham was finally persuaded by Morton, the probable originator of this design,[20] to join the conspiracy already on foot in favour of Henry, who was to marry Elizabeth, eldest daughter of Edward IV and Elizabeth Woodville, and thus unite on the throne the rival houses of York and Lancaster.[21]

Richard's absence from London favouring their design, by Morton's advice, one Reginald Bray[22] was deputed to inform Henry's mother, Margaret, Countess of Richmond,[23] of Buckingham's plans. The first thing the countess had to do was to communicate with Queen Elizabeth, who was still in sanctuary surrounded by armed men, but, ever a schemer, she accomplished this seemingly impossible task in a most ingenious way. She was aware that the unhappy Elizabeth's health had sunk under the burden of intense anguish inflicted by the murder of her two sons, and that no suspicion would be aroused should the queen receive a visit from a doctor. Thus she sent her own physician, 'one Lewis a Welshman, and break the matter to her'. As the countess had foreseen, Lewis's visit was not in the least suspected. 'When he was admitted into her presence, and everybody was withdrawn, he gave her to understand what errand he was sent upon.'[24]

The unfortunate Elizabeth received with joy a proposal so advantageous to herself and daughters, and once more indulged in the hope of seeing better days. She

heard him with attention, agreed to his proposals, and bade him tell his lady, that all King Edward's friends and dependants should join with her for the Earl of Richmond, on condition he took his corporal oath to marry Lady Elizabeth, her eldest daughter, or, in case she were not living, her second daughter. Dr Lewis carried this pleasing answer to his mistress, from whom he went frequently to the queen as physician, and from her to the countess, till matters were fully concluded between them.[25]

It was finally arranged that, in October, Buckingham should lead a rebellion, which was to be aided by the landing of Richmond with troops from Brittany. A simultaneous rising did actually take place, as agreed, on 18 October 1483, all over the South of England, Buckingham raising his standard at Brecknock; the Marquis of Dorset, who had escaped out of sanctuary,[26] raised the signal of revolt at Exeter, and Elizabeth's brother Lionel raised the men of Salisbury,[27] while at Maidstone many relations or connections by marriage of the Woodvilles, among whom figured Sir John and Sir Richard Guildford, John and Reginald Pympe, Sir John Cheyney, Sir John Fogge, and finally Sir William and Richard Haute,[28] also appeared in open revolt.

Despite the fact that the secret had leaked out, and Richard was already making plans to crush the traitors, the rebellion was defeated not so much by force of arms as by the extraordinarily bad weather. An usually large flood, long referred to as 'the Duke of Buckingham's water', swelled the Severn, with the result that Buckingham was unable to get out of Wales. Provisions ran short, and his followers deserted. Finally the duke himself fled north to Shropshire, where he was betrayed by one of his retainers, named Ralph Banastre or Bannister of Lacon Hall, near Wem.[29] Buckingham was brought to Salisbury, whither Richard had come with his army, on 1 November, by Thomas Mytton, Sheriff of Shropshire.[30] Richard refused to see him, and on the next day (2 November), though a Sunday, he was sent to summary execution upon a new scaffold purposely erected in the marketplace.[31] Meanwhile the storms had also dispersed Richmond's expedition, and the whole rebellion collapsed. Richard was received in triumph at Exeter, and returned to London before the end of November.

# 14

# THE DESPERATE PLIGHT OF
# ELIZABETH & THE DEATH OF
# RICHARD III

As a result of this abortive rising Richard pursued with relentless cruelty all whom he considered friendly to Richmond's cause; the hapless Elizabeth, confined with her children in sancutary, heard with a sickening dread of the many executions of her adherents. Well indeed did Shakespeare describe to what pitiful straits of sorrow the former queen was now reduced:

One heav'd a-high, to be hurl'd down below;
A mother only mock'd with two sweet babies…
A queen in jest, only to fill the scene.[1]

Meanwhile the Earl of Richmond had recrossed the Channel to Normandy, and after three days returned by land to Brittany, which he reached before 30 October.[2] He could hardly have known at this time how complete had been the failure of the rebellion in England. Later on, however, he heard that Dorset and other friends had escaped like himself to Brittany, and were at Vannes. He summoned them to a council at Rennes, where it was decided to make another attempt when there arose a more favourable opportunity, and on Christmas Day they all bound themselves to each other and to Henry at Rennes Cathedral, where the latter made a solemn oath to marry Princess Elizabeth after obtaining the crown.

In England, Parliament, which met on 3 January 1484, confirmed the king's title and declared his son, Prince Edward, heir-apparent to the crown,[3] the leading lords and gentlemen of the household being called to swear to the succession.

Richard, 'who by spies had a full account of all their proceedings',[4] knew that the hopes of Richmond and his whole party were founded on the earl's promise to marry Princess Elizabeth, and this he resolved by some means or other to prevent; and to that end he did his utmost to ingratiate himself with her mother, Queen Elizabeth, and to draw her and her daughters out of sanctuary.[5] Before the lords who had attended Parliament had left London, he called upon them and the lord mayor and aldermen of the City, to witness a very solemn promise that if his brother's wife and daughters would come out of sanctuary, he would protect their persons, give them a sufficient maintenance, and find suitable husbands and marriage portions for the princesses. The terms of his offer were as follows:

I, Richard, by the grace of God, etc., in presence of you, my lords spiritual and temporal, and you, my lord mayor and aldermen of London, promise and swear, *verbo regio*, that if the daughters of Elizabeth Grey, late calling herself Queen of England, that is to wit, Elizabeth, Cecily, Anne, Catherine, and Bridget, will come to me out of the sanctuary of Westminster, and be guided, ruled, and demeaned after me, then I shall see that they shall be in surety of their lives, and also not suffer any manner hurt by any manner person or persons to them or any of them in their bodies and persons to be done, by way of ravishing or defiling contrary to their wills, nor them nor any of them imprison in the Tower of London or any other prison; but I shall put them into honest places of good name and fame, and them honestly and courteously shall see to be founden and entreated, and to have all things requisite and necessary for their exhibitions and findings as my kinswomen; and that I shall do marry (cause to be married) such of them as be marriageable to gentlemen born, and every of them give in marriage lands and tenements to the yearly value of 200 marks for term of their lives, and in like wise to the other daughters when they shall come to lawful age of marriage, if they live. And such gentlemen as shall hap to marry with them I shall straitly charge lovingly of love and entreat them, as wives, and my kinswomen, as they will avoid and eschew my displeasure.

And over this, that I shall yaerly content and pay, or cause to be contented and paid, for the exhibition and finding of the said Dame Elizabeth Grey, during her natural life, at four terms of the year, that is to wit, as Pasche (Easter), Midsummer, Michaelmas, and Christmas, to John Nesfeld, one of the esquires of my body, for his finding to attend upon her, the sum of 700 marks of lawful money of England, by even portions; and moreover I promise to them that if any surmise or evil report be made to me of them by any person or persons, that then I shall not give thereunto faith nor credence, nor therefor put them to any manner punishment, before that they or any of them so accused may be at their lawful defence and answer. In witness whereof to this writing of my oath and promise aforesaid in your said presence made, I have set my sign manual, the first day of March, in the first year of my reign.[6]

Very strong assurances were certainly necessary to warrant reliance upon the king's good faith; but nothing could well have been stronger than a promise like the above, witnessed as it was by 'the lords spiritual and temporal', and the lord mayor and aldermen of

London. Still, there had been strong assurances before, when, for example, the Duke of York had been given up, and it seems almost inconceivable that, in light of previous events, even the most solemn promises could have induced the dowager queen to throw herself and her remaining children on the protection of one who had already shown her – and that in so terrible a fashion – exactly how much his promises of protection were worth. However, 'messengers being men of gravity, handled the queen so craftily'[7] that she and her daughters were finally persuaded to leave the sanctuary, and 'yield themselves unto the king',[8] thus apparently casting aside all thoughts of aiding Henry Tudor.

For this step Elizabeth Woodville has been severely blamed by those who have not taken into consideration the extreme difficulties of her situation. She had probably, in the course of ten months, not only exhausted her own means – a fact which seems distinctly possible when one considers that not only had the letters patent, by which she had been entitled to her dower as queen,[9] been annulled, but Richard's servant had even to 'find her with food, clothes and attendance' – she may also have grown somewhat weary of the hospitality of the monks. Moreover, though Richard could not lawfully violate the liberties of sanctuary, there was nothing to prevent his cutting off supplies and starving out the inmates; he had, indeed, already caused the sanctuary to be surrounded by a guard.[10]

The conditions of Elizabeth's surrender were bitter in the extreme; for it is evident from the terms of Richard's offer that she – who but a short time before had been acknowledged as queen of all England – and her daughters were not only relegated to the rank of mere private gentlewomen, but Elizabeth herself seems to have been held in personal restraint, since the annuity of 700 marks allotted by Act of Parliament for her subsistence was to be paid, not to her direct, but to John Nesfield 'for the exhibition and finding of the said Dame Elizabeth Grey, *late calling herself* Queen of England'.[11] It is thus clear that her situation was a forlorn and comfortless one; and it was impossible to know how long even the right of sanctuary would be respected, if she refused to accept the offer made her by the king. It was, therefore, not altogether surprising that she and her daughters, probably bearing in mind the fate of the Duke of York, their son and brother, ventured forth from the quiet serenity of sanctuary to face once more the unknown evils of the world outside.

Meanwhile the danger of invasion was so great that commissions of muster and array were issued on that same day for most of the counties of England,[12] and Richard established himself at Nottingham as a central position, where he might the more easily receive news of invasion from any quarter.

In order to defeat his rivals' designs, Richard certainly could not have done anything more shrewd than to immediately redeem his promise touching his brother Edward IV's children, so far as to provide a husband for the eldest daughter. For as the Earl of Richmond had received the support of many partisans of the House of York only on the condition of his undertaking to marry Princess Elizabeth whenever he should succeed in obtaining the crown, that support must necessarily have failed him if once the lady were married to somebody else. It was, therefore, only to be expected that Richard had given most serious thought to this matter, and that he had spoken to the dowager queen about it, and even with Princess Elizabeth herself. For, since venturing forth from sanctuary, the dowager queen had apparently been completely won over by Richard, with the result that she not only forgot her promise to the Countess of Richmond, but even wrote, at the king's suggestion, to her son, the Marquis of Dorset, at Paris, to abandon the Earl of Richmond's party and come to England. This was an amazing thing; but it seems still more extraordinary that she could have received with any degree of complacency Richard's proposition that he should marry that princess himself. All who had planned the marriage between Henry and Princess Elizabeth were struck with the deepest consternation, and greatly incensed at the unfortunate Elizabeth's conduct, but these steps seem to be the evident result of the personal restraint she was then enduring.[13]

In the light of subsequent events, it seems almost certain that Richard so threatened the dowager queen as to compel her to write to her son, Dorset, advising him to abandon Henry's party. This policy of Richard's was very near being successful, and at one time threatened the invaders' schemes with serious disaster. While Henry was at Paris, Dorset received his mother's letters advising him to desert his party. Dorset acted on her advice, and secretly left Paris, doubtless intending to reach England by way of Flanders; but Henry, on discovering his departure, applied to the French king, Charles VIII, who gave orders that his flight be intercepted. Dorset was overtaken at Compiègne by Humphrey Cheyney and brought back to Paris.[14] This was a very serious alarm indeed, for had Richard succeeded in getting Dorset back into his power, not only would all Henry's carefully laid plans of invasion have been instantly divulged, but Richard would, in the person of her son, have had an even stronger weapon to use against Elizabeth's rebellious relations than even he could have hoped for.

The defection of Dorset would have been mischievous enough, but it was not the only way in which Henry's prospects were endangered by Richard's control of the wretched Elizabeth. The king's pledge to provide husbands for her daughters seems to have been given with the deliberate intention of marrying them as bastard children, considerably below their rank. If, therefore, he chose to court her daughter as his wife, then Elizabeth ought to be acquitted of all blame; for it is evident that had she been so ready to yield to Richard's plans she would not then have been under the control of John Nesfield.[15]

Whatever Richard's designs with regard to Princess Elizabeth may have been, his wife, Queen Anne, who had been ill for some considerable time, died on 16 March,[16] and soon after her death the rumour became general that Richard intended to marry his niece himself.[17] Although this news dismayed the Earl of Richmond to such an extent that he began seriously to think of another marriage for himself, it was so badly received in England that Richard's leading councillors, William Catesby and Sir Richard Ratcliffe, declared to him very strongly that if he did not deny it publicly before the mayor and aldermen of London, he could no longer expect any sympathy or help from his friends in the North. The excitement, indeed, reached such a pitch that Ratcliffe is said to have declared to him that if it were once believed that he seriously intended to marry his niece, then the suspicion, which was already entertained by many, that he had poisoned his queen to make way for his marriage with his rival's intended wife,[18] would be greatly strengthened.

Yet it is to be presumed that Ratcliffe and Catesby opposed this revolting marriage not only from the desire to protect the king from the righteous indignation of others, but also owing to their own personal fears. For they suspected, and probably quite correctly, that if Princess Elizabeth became queen, her mother would almost certainly recover a large amount of influence, with the result that the deaths of Rivers and Lord Richard Grey, the latter's brother and son, would be speedily avenged on those who had counselled them.

Be that as it may, the king, feeling that he could not well withstand so serious an opposition, shortly before Easter called a meeting of the mayor and citizens of London at Clerkenwell. Here he protested that the design imputed to him was a fiction, and that he had never entertained any such idea.[19] But in order to remove Princess Elizabeth as far out of harm's way as possible, since he was not going to marry her himself, he sent her to Sheriff Hutton Castle, where the young Earl of Warwick,[20] looked upon by the more ardent Yorkists as heir-apparent, was also confined.

Meanwhile Henry was busy preparing to invade England. Although he had at one time been so sadly disconcerted by the news of Princess Elizabeth's proposed marriage to his rival, no thought of abandoning his purpose had ever entered Henry's head. He had even entertained the idea of marrying a sister of Sir William (II) Herbert,[21] who was very powerful in Wales, and with this in view had sent secret messages to the Earl of Northumberland, who had married Maud, one of Sir William's sisters,[22] to request his support in this scheme, which would have secured him not only the power of Wales, but that of the North of England as well. However, the coast and all the roads were so carefully watched that the message could not be conveyed, and it must, therefore, have been with feelings of considerable relief that Henry heard soon afterwards of the declaration made by Richard at Clerkenwell.[23]

Time was, however, drawing on, and by the end of July Henry's plans for the invasion of England were complete. With the aid of the English refugees, together with the fleet and about 2,000 troops given him by the *Régente*, Anne de Beaujeu, in the name of Charles VIII, King of France,[24] Henry finally embarked at Harfleur on 1 August 1485, and on the 7th landed unopposed at Milford Haven.[25] His company numbered only about 2,000 men, but he relied to a large extent on his Welsh countrymen, many of whom joined him on his way to Shrewsbury. Henry also summoned to his aid Lord Stanley, and his brother Sir William, who were powerful in Cheshire and Lancashire. Lord Stanley was the invader's stepfather, as he had recently married his mother, Lady Margaret Beaufort.[26] The latter, though deprived of her lands by Richard for conspiring in her son's favour, was permitted to live in seclusion, her husband being security for her good behaviour. Lord Stanley was afraid to join Henry, as he had received a similar summons from Richard, and had been obliged to leave his son, Lord Strange, in Richard's hands. Sir William Stanley also temporised. Many others, however, came over to Richmond, who, on the night of 21 August, took up a position near Market

Bosworth in Leicestershire, where, with 5,000 men, protected by a rivulet on the left and a morass on the right and in front of him, he awaited the attack of King Richard, who was advancing against him from Nottingham. The next day (22 August) took place at Bosworth[27] the battle on which the destiny of England depended. After about two hours' fighting Richard endeavoured to single out his enemy, when Sir William Stanley, who until then had viewed the action from a neighbouring hill, brought his men into the field to Henry's aid. Richard was surrounded, and 'met a more glorious fate than he deserved'.[28] He had gone into battle wearing his crown. This was afterwards found by Reginald Bray, who brought it to Lord Stanley, and the latter placed it on the victor's head, while his followers hailed him as 'King Henry'.[29]

# 15

# THE ACCESSION OF HENRY VII
# & THE RESTITUTION & DEATH
# OF ELIZABETH

One of Henry's first acts after his victory was to send Sir Robert Willoughby to Sheriff Hutton to bring Princess Elizabeth and the young Earl of Warwick to London.[1] Henry probably felt that it was just as well to make sure of the person of this unfortunate boy, whose title to the crown in the direct male line might be preferred by some ardent Yorkists to that of Princess Elizabeth herself.[2] As for Princess Elizabeth, 'she received also a direction to repair with all convenient speed to London, and there to remain with the dowager queen her mother; which accordingly she soon after did, accompanied with many noblemen and ladies of honour'.[3]

With what joy must Elizabeth Woodville have received her daughter, from whom she had been separated while their fate and that of England trembled in the balance! Now at last was the widowed queen avenged of all the restraint in which Richard had kept her, and of the odious proposition of marrying her daughter to her most bitter enemy.[4] Now, instead of being under the despotic control of John Nesfield, Elizabeth was restored to liberty. For the first time for many long years her life was no longer in imminent danger.

Meanwhile Henry himself slowly advanced to London, which he entered on 3 September,[5] a Saturday, 'which day of the week, first upon an observation, and after upon memory and fancy, he accounted and chose as a day prosperous unto him'.[6] A severe plague, known as the sweating sickness, delayed Henry's coronation for some weeks. However, he was eventually crowned at Westminster on 30 October as King Henry VII.[7]

A few days later, on 7 November, the newly crowned king met his first parliament, which duly confirmed his title to the crown. One of the first acts of this Parliament was to restore to Elizabeth Woodville the title and dignity of dowager queen, and this was done by enacting that she should have the same rank and station as she would have had if the statute of Richard III, by which she was degraded, had never been passed.[8] This restitution was immediately followed by the repeal of the Act by which her marriage with Edward IV had been declared invalid and their children illegitimate.[9] Out of respect for her who was to be queen, neither the title nor the body of the Act was read in either house. By the advice of the judges it was merely designated by the first words, 'that the matter might be and remain in perpetual oblivion for the falseness and shamefulness of it'.[10] The original was then ordered to be burnt; and all persons who possessed copies were commanded to deliver them to the Chancellor before Easter, under the penalty of fine or imprisonment.[11]

The whole nation now eagerly awaited the moment when Henry would fulfil his promise to marry the Princess Elizabeth. It was, therefore, only to be expected that when, on 10 December, Parliament presented to the king the usual grant of tonnage and poundage for life, they coupled with it a petition that he would be pleased to 'take to wife and consort the Princess Elizabeth', which marriage 'they hoped God would bless with a progeny of the race of kings';[12] and Henry graciously answered that he was willing to comply with their request.[13]

With what mixed feelings of joy and anxiety must the dowager queen and her daughter have looked forward to this event, on which all their future happiness depended. Moreover, it was also about this time that Elizabeth had the further joy of witnessing the return of her eldest son, Dorset, for whom Henry had sent at the beginning of December.[14]

The long and eagerly awaited marriage took place on 18 January 1486. It was believed that the delay arose from a desire to prevent his queen's name from being inserted in the Act of Settlement.[15] Once that point had been obtained, the king hastened to gratify the wishes of his people and Parliament.

Many historians are of the opinion that even if the ambition of Princess Elizabeth was flattered by this union, she had little reason to congratulate herself on the score of domestic happiness.[16] Lodge,[17] indeed, goes so far as to say that 'if the queen loved her mother with that feminine filial tenderness which is heightened by participation in calamity, she could not possibly have cherished much affection for her husband'. To judge, however, by Henry's treatment of his mother-in-law, the dowager queen, this would hardly seem to have been the case. As the Act by which he had restored Elizabeth to the dignity of dowager queen did not vest her in any of the lands which were forfeited by the statute that degraded her, the king, by letters patent, dated 4 March 1486, granted her various lordships for life – namely Waltham, Badowe Magna, Masshebury, Dunmore, Lieghes, and Farnham, in Essex[18] – as part of the dower belonging to her after the death of Edward IV; while the very next day he granted her, in full satisfaction of the residue of her dower, £102 per annum out of the fee farm of the town of Bristol.[19] This was hardly treatment that would be likely to cause the young queen any undue sorrow.

It would appear that Elizabeth Woodville now wished to retire from the Court, for on 10 July she obtained a lease of the Abbot's House at Westminster,[20] where she probably lived until her final withdrawal to Bermondsey Abbey early in the following year.

On 20 September the young queen gave birth to a son, and 'on the Sunday following, her mother, the queen-dowager, stood godmother to him in Winchester Cathedral'. After describing the procession, in which Queen Elizabeth's sister, Princess Cecily, attended by her sister Anne, carried the infant, the commentator adds, 'Queen Elizabeth [Woodville] was in the cathedral, abiding the coming of the prince; she gave a rich cup of gold, covered, which was borne by Sir Davy Owen. The Earl of Derby gave a gold salt, and the Lord Maltravers gave a coffer of gold; these standing with the queen as sponsors.'[21] The little prince received the name of Arthur.

Next year (1487) took place that 'strange accident of state',[22] a rebellion in favour of Lambert Simnel, who impersonated the young Edward, Earl of Warwick. Simnel met with quite extraordinary success in Ireland, where he was actually crowned as Edward VI, and invaded England with the earls of Lincoln and Kildare, and a number of Irish followers, together with a band of Germans supplied and financed by Henry's bitter enemy, that most ardent of all Yorkists, Margaret, Duchess of Burgundy.[23]

On the first news of the conspiracy, on 2 February, Henry called a council at Sheen and caused the real Warwick to be taken out of the Tower and paraded before the people in the streets. He is also reported to have deprived Elizabeth (Woodville) of all her lands and estates; to have conferred them on her daughter, the queen; and, finally, to have induced her to spend the rest of her life in seclusion in Bermondsey Abbey.[24]

The only support for this statement appears to be founded on mere assertion. On his accession Henry VII found Elizabeth Woodville one of the most pitiable objects in the whole of his dominions. Stripped of her dignity and estates, her honour and virtue impeached, her children declared illegitimate, her kindred banished and attainted, and herself destitute of any other means of support than the annuity of £233 granted her by Richard III. It seems scarcely possible for Henry to have increased the misery of her situation by depriving her of her liberty; but if most historians are to be believed, having once granted her some estates and money, he seized on them all again, and from a suspicion of her having countenanced Lambert Simnel's rebellion, imprisoned her for life in the monastery of Bermondsey, the pretext being that, having consented to her daughter's marriage with him, she had delivered her into the hands of Richard III.

Nothing, however, appears to be more erroneous than these statements. As we have already observed, one of the earliest Acts of Henry's reign consisted in restoring the greatly maligned Elizabeth to her fame as a woman, and to her dignity as dowager queen, this Act being followed as early as 4 March 1486 by another granting her various lordships for life.[25] Furthermore, far from being exiled from her daughter's Court, she was, in that same year, chosen as Prince Arthur's godmother, and attended at the font.[26]

If, as some authorities state,[27] the king, on the rebellion of Simnel, deprived her of all her lands and estates, then it would appear that they are once again in error. If, however, these authorities, when writing of her lands and estates, refer to her dower as queen, the only property she had, then they have been greatly mistaken, since she had already been deprived of that by Richard III; nor was it restored to her by Henry's Parliament, at the time when it repealed so much of the Act as deprived her 'of the name, estate, and dignity of queen',[28] and in lieu of which the king granted her a compensation.

It is possible, if not probable, that Henry disliked his mother-in-law; and in this he was by no means singular, for there never was a woman who contrived to make more personal enemies; but that he ever deprived her of either property or dignity, remains to be proved. Elizabeth Woodville had, in the course of a few years, passed through a series of calamities sufficient to alienate her forever from what must have seemed to her all the fleeting pleasures and mock pageantry of Court life; she had to mourn the deaths of her sons, besides having four daughters wholly dependent on her for their support; it was, therefore, scarcely to be wondered at that, as she grew older, Elizabeth very rarely shared in the gaieties of her daughter's Court. Nevertheless, she appeared there often enough to disperse once and for all the usual assertions that she fell into disgrace with Henry for encouraging the rebellion of the Earl of Lincoln and Lambert Simnel.[29]

What possible advantage could Elizabeth have hoped to gain by countenancing such a rising? Was not her daughter Queen of England? Was it in any way likely that she would plot to dethrone Henry, when, by so doing, she was bound to dethrone her own daughter as well? The Earl of Lincoln[30] had been proclaimed heir to the throne by Richard III,[31] and had become in that capacity the natural supplanter of all her children, whereas Lambert Simnel represented Edward, Earl of Warwick, the son of Clarence, her former bitter enemy, and the grandson of the famous Kingmaker, the ancient and relentless foe of the whole House of Woodville.

Furthermore, had this rebellion proved successful, there can be little doubt but that Lambert Simnel would have quickly disappeared to be replaced by the real Earl of Warwick, the Yorkist claimant. Elizabeth was a clever woman, and she must have been one of the first to realise the great danger by which she and her daughter were threatened, should the rebellion succeed. However, all her fears were allayed when, on 16 June, the rebels were completely defeated at Stoke, Lambert Simnel himself being taken prisoner and Lincoln slain. Henry showed his utter contempt of this impostor by employing him as a scullion in the royal kitchen.[32]

An even greater significance is to be derived from the fact that Elizabeth is reported to have been in confinement about March 1487, whereas on 28 November[33] of that very same year Henry gave further proof of his confidence in her by treating for her marriage with his ally James III, King of Scotland,[34] 'for the greater increase of the love and amity between them'; agreeing, at the same time, that James, the second son of the Scottish king, should marry Princess Catherine, and that the Duke of Rothesay, heir-apparent to the Scottish throne, should marry some other daughter of Edward IV.[35]

This episode is of the greatest importance in that it disproves once and for always the hypothesis of those historians who maintain that Henry was aware that one of the sons of Edward IV was still living, and had confined their mother Elizabeth in a nunnery to prevent her from divulging the secret.[36] If this were true, then it seems absolutely incredible that Henry should have wished to marry her to James III, and her two daughters to two other Scottish princes. Such marriages would have placed her in a situation where she might have published the truth without fear, obtained a sure place of refuge for her son, and seconded her claim with all the armed might of Scotland behind her. All hope of fulfilling these three marriage projects was, however, terminated by the death of James III, who, after losing the Battle of Sauchieburn, was, on 11 June 1488, murdered at Beaton's Mill during his flight.[37]

A little more than a month later Elizabeth was to suffer yet another great loss by the death, on 28 July, of her brother, Sir Edward Woodville, who was slain in the Battle of Saint-Aubin-du-Cormier, in a gallant attempt to aid the Bretons in their struggle for independence from the French.[38] Plunged once more into the depths of woe, the unhappy woman must have longed and even prayed that death would come and spare her all further anguish. She was, however, destined to live for a few years longer, during which time she was to lose her fifth and only surviving brother, Sir Richard Woodville, 3rd Earl Rivers, who died on 6 March 1491.[39] Indeed, of all Elizabeth's many brothers and sisters only Catherine is known to have survived her.[40] This latest bereavement, by which not only the family of Woodville but the peerage became at the same time extinct, must have made Elizabeth realise that she too would soon be called to render an account of her life to her maker.

Proof exists that despite her great sorrow and supposed confinement Elizabeth was occasionally at the Court, and it was in a situation of the highest dignity that she appeared there in public for the last time. Shortly after the queen consort 'had taken to her chamber', previous to her confinement in November 1489, she gave an audience to the French ambassadors, headed by her kinsman, François de Luxembourg, on which important occasion 'ther was with hir Moder Quene Elizabeth, and my Lady the King's Moder'.[41]

One of the last records of Elizabeth Woodville's dealings with Henry VII bears the date of 19 February 1490, when he assigned her an annuity of £400,[42] a sum which would then have been adequate had it been given in lieu of the lands granted to her in the first year of his reign. A receipt[43] signed by Elizabeth on 21 May 1491[44] for the sum of £30, the arrears of her half-year's pension, furnishes yet further proof that less than a year before her death Henry was still paying her a regular annuity. Moreover, the king evidently wished to present his mother-in-law with a Christmas gift, since, on 14 December of this same year, Elizabeth received the sum of 50 marks, which the king ordered to be paid 'unto oure right dere and right welbeloved quene Elizabeth moder unto our most dere wif the quene ayenst the fest of Cristemas next commyng'.[45]

Nevertheless, strange as it may seem, many historians state that she was stripped of everything, since she shortly afterwards retired to the convent of Bermondsey.[46] Here, however, she had every right to be, not as a prisoner, but as a highly favoured inmate; for the prior and monks of Bermondsey were solemnly bound by the deeds of their charter to find hospitality for the representative of their great benefactor, Richard de Clare, Earl of Gloucester, in the state-rooms of the convent.[47] Edward IV was heir to the de Clares,[48] so that Elizabeth had every right, as his widow, to appropriate the apartments specially reserved for the use of the convent's benefactors. Elizabeth had a right of property there; and since it was sometimes the custom in the Middle Ages for persons to seek monastic seclusion when health declined, what better place could Elizabeth single out for her retirement than a convent bound by its charter to receive her?[49] Moreover, hospitality was one of the duties expected of the inmates of religious houses, and to the last it appears to have been the duty they most constantly and willingly fulfilled. In the case of persons of high rank the reception of visitors was an affair of great ceremony and importance. As was probably the case on the arrival of Elizabeth, the monks were summoned from all parts of the monastery by the stroke on one of the great bells, twice repeated. They then hurried into the church, robed themselves, and prepared everything for the reception of the new guest. Upon the queen's near approach, two of the great bells would ring out a peal of welcome, and then the abbot[50] would advance to meet her, saluting her with his blessing, and sprinkling holy water over her. The procession then entered the church, and made a stand before the crucifix, where the visitor prayed. Divine service in honour of the Saviour as the patron saint followed; and at the close of the service, the queen would find the best accommodation the abbey could furnish provided for her use.[51]

It seems, however, highly probable that, with a view to spending the remainder of her days in quiet retirement, the dowager queen effected an amicable arrangement with Henry VII, by virtue of which she surrendered her estates to the king for the consideration of the annuity. At that time, £400 would have been equivalent to about £200,000 today, and one can hardly conceive the miserly king disbursing such considerable sums without a very substantial equivalent. Such an agreement would have suited both parties; Elizabeth would be relieved from all the trouble and expense of administration, and the king would gain what he most certainly desired – a valuable addition to the Crown property.

Thus, it would appear that far from having been despoiled of her estates by Henry VII, the dowager queen had none of which she could be deprived; instead of increasing her unhappiness, he restored her to fame and rank, and granted her a competence; instead of treating her with hatred and contempt, he asked her to be godmother to the Prince of Wales; instead of suspecting her of the absurd intention of plotting against him (and consequently against her own daughter, whom she dearly loved), and imprisoning her for life to avert similar dangers, he agreed to marry her to an independent sovereign, and two of her daughters to that sovereign's sons, with a view to strengthening the alliance between the two countries; and finally, so far from keeping a close prisoner at Bermondsey, where she had the right of property, he allowed her to be present at her daughter's reception of the French ambassadors, some time after the event which, it is said, was the main cause of Henry's rigorous treatment. Such, however, are the effects of historians, repeating the statements of their predecessors without inquiring whether the records do not, as in this case, establish the ignorance or the prejudices of writers in whom implicit confidence has generally been placed.[52]

Early in 1492 her last illness overtook her at Bermondsey, and on her deathbed, on 10 April, Elizabeth dictated the following Will:

In dei nomine, Amen. The Xth daie of Aprill, the yere of our Lord Gode M cccc LXXXXII. I Elizabeth by the grace of God Quene of England, late wif to the most victoriouse Prince of blessed memorie Edward the Fourth, being of hole mynde, seying the worlde so traunsitorie, and no creature certayne, whanne they shall departe from hence, havyng Almyghty Gode fresh in mynde, in whome is all mercy and grace, bequeith my sowle into his hands, beseechyng him, of the same mercy, to accept it graciously, and oure blessed Lady Quene of comforte, and all the holy company of hevyn, to be good meanes for me. I'tm, I bequeith my body to be buried with the bodie of my Lord at Windessore, according to the will of my said Lorde and myne, without pompes entreing or costlie expensis donen thereabought. I'tm, where I have no wordely goodes to do the Quene's Grace, my derest doughter, a pleaser with, neither to reward any of my children, according to my hart and mynde,[53] I besech Almyghty Gode to blisse here Grace, with all her noble issue, and with as good hart and mynde as is to me possible, I geve her Grace my blessing, and all the forsaide my children. I'tm, I will that suche smale stufe and goodes that I have to be disposed trly in the contentac'on of my dettes and for the helth of my sowle, as farre as they will extende. I'tm, yf any of my bloode will of my saide stufe or goodes to me perteyning, I will that they have the prefermente of before any other. And of this my present testament I make and ordeyne myne Executors, that is to say, John Ingilby, Priour of the Charterhouse of Shene, William Sutton and Thomas Brente, Doctors. And I bsesech my said derest doughter, the quene's grace, and my sone Thomas, Marques Dorsett, to putte there good willes and help for the performans of this testamente. In witnesse whereof, to this my present testament I have sett my seale, these witnesses, John Abbot of the Monastry of Sainte Saviour of Bermondesley, and Benedictus Cun, Doctor Fysyk. Yeven the day that yere abovesaid.[54]

Elizabeth lived for about two months after she had made her Will. Finally, on 7 or 8 June 1492[55] – the Thursday or Friday before Whit Sunday – surrounded by her daughters, who throughout her illness had not ceased to pay her the most affectionate attention,[56]

Elizabeth Woodville, the course of whose life had been subjected to so many tragic and terrible vicissitudes, died. Since she had expressed the earnest desire for a speedy and private burial,[57] her funeral took place quietly on Whit Sunday, the twenty-seventh anniversary of her coronation. A most interesting record of Elizabeth's funeral has been handed down to us by an eyewitness.

On Witsonday [10 June] she was accordyng to her desire by water conveied to Wyndesore and ther prevely thorow the littill parke conveied into the castell wtout Ryngyng of any belles or Recyvyng of the dean or chanons in their habits or accompaynyed as whos sayed by wt the prior of the charterhouse of Shen docter brent her chapelain and oon of her executores Edmond Haust maistres grace a bastard dowghter of Kyng Edwarde and upon an other gentilewomen and as it tolde to me oon preest of the college and a clerke Recyved her in the castell. And so prevelty about xi of the clocke in the nyght she was beried wt oute any solempne direge or the morne any solempne masse doon for her owbebytt. On the morne theder came the lord awdeley bysshop of Rochester to doo the Service and the substaunce of the officers of armes of this Realme but that day ther was nothyng doon solemply for her savyng a low hers suche as they use for the comyn peple wt iiij wooden candelstikks abowte hit and a clothe of blacke cloth of gold over hit wt iiij candelstikkes of silver and gilt everyche havyng a taper of noo gret weight and vj sochyns of her armes crowned prynted on that clothe. On the tewsday theder came by water iij of Kynges Edwardes doughters and heirs that is to say the lady anne the lady catherine the lady bregett accompeygned wt the lady marquys of dorset the Duc of buckyngham doughter and nyce of the foresaid qwene. Alsoo the doughter of the Marquiss of Dorsset The lady herbert alsoo nyce to the said qwene the lady Egermont dame katheryne gray dame ... gilford whiche after duryng the derige. And oon the morne that is to say the wensday at the masse of Requyem. And the thre daughters at the hed there gentilwomen behynde the thre ladyes. Alsoo that same tewsday theder came the lordes that folowyn – the lord Thomas marquys of Dorsset soon to the foresaid quene The lord Edmond of Suffolke Therll of Essex The Viscount Welles Sir Charles of Somerset and Roger Coton maister Chaterton. And that nyght began the direge the foresaid bisshop of Rochestre and Vicars of the college were Rectors of the qwer and noo chanons the bishop of Rochestre Red the last lesson at the direges of the chanons the other two but the dean of that college Red noon thowgh he were present at that service nor att direge nor at non at thay was ther never a new torche but old torches nor poince man in blacke gowne nor whod but upon a dozeyn dyvers olde men holdyng old torches and torhes under and on the morne oon of the chanons called maister Vaughan sange our lady masse at the which the lorde marquys offred a piece of gold at that masse offred no man savyng hym selfe and in likewise at the masse of the trenytie whiche was songen by the dean and kneled at the hers hed by cause the Ladyes came not to masse of Requiem and the lordes before Reherced sat above in the qwer. Into thoffryng tyme when that the foresaid lordes and alsoo the officiers of armes ther beyng present went before mylady anne whiche offred the masse peny Instede of the qwene wherefore she had the carpet and the cusshyn hed and the vicount welles toke her thoffryng whiche was a very peney in ded of silver and dame Katherine gray bere the said lady agnes trayne. In tyme she was turned to her place ageyn they everyche of the kings dowghters bere ownes traynes and offred a pece of gold after the ladies had offred in likewise the lord marquys offred a pece of gold than the foresaid lordes offred their pleasirs than offred the dean and the qwer and the poure knyghes then garter kyng of armes wt hym all his company they offred all other esquyres present and yemen and the surnts that wold offre but ther was non affryng to the corps duryng the masse ther was geven certayne money In almes after masse the lord marquys Rewaded ... their costes xl.s. I pray to god to have mercu on her sowle. At this same seasen the qwen her doughter toke her chambre. Wherfore I cawnot tell what dolent howve it she goth in but I suppose she went in blew In likewise as qwen Margaret the wife of Kyng Henry the VI went in whenne her mother the qwene of Ceille deyed.[58]

Thus on the Tuesday following (12 June), Elizabeth was laid to rest in St George's chapel, Windsor, beside the body of her late husband, Edward IV, in the presence of all her daughters with the exception of the queen, who was about to be confined.[59] The actual place of interment of Elizabeth Woodville is supposed to have been discovered on 4 March 1789.

The workmen employed in new paving the choir discovered a decay on the stones which closed up the entrance into the vault where Edward IV had been deposited.[60] Two of the canons and the surveyor, entering the vault, viewed the royal body enclosed in a leaden and wooden coffin, reduced to a skeleton, which measured 6 feet 3 inches ... on the king's coffin lay another of wood, only much decayed, which ontained the skeleton of a woman; who, from the marks of age about the skull, was supposed to be that of his queen, Elizabeth Widville.[61]

No more fitting epitaph could be dedicated to her memory than the delicately beautiful lines of Robert Southey, who thus wrote of her:[62]

Thou, Elizabeth, art here;
Thou to whom all griefs were known;
Who wert placed upon the bier
In happier hour than on the throne
Fatal daughter, fatal mother
Raised to that ill-omen'd station,
Father, uncle, sons, and brother,
Mourn'd in blood her elevation!
Woodville, in the realms of bliss,
To thine offspring thou may'st say,
Early death is happiness;
And favour'd in their lot are they
Who are not left to learn below
Lightly let this ground be prest;
A broken heart is here at rest.

# CONCLUSION

Such is the history of Elizabeth Woodville, to which some highly romantic details have been added, on no apparent authority, by Prévost in a biography of Margaret of Anjou.[1] Her marriage with Edward IV – indeed, her whole life – was a romance in itself, but one can scarcely give credit to the story of her fascinating Warwick, and being used by Margaret at the time of the Second Battle of St Albans as a lure to entrap him.

The spotless purity of Elizabeth's life in a Court of unexampled corruption, the dignified self-restraint with which she endured innumerable wrongs, the constancy which clung to associations of lowlier but happier years, together with her deep maternal devotion, reveal glimpses of a soul which often concealed itself from curious eyes. Grasping and selfish she may have been, but never was a woman raised so high left as friendless as Elizabeth, when, in her awful widowhood, her dowry home became the sanctuary. All her power was then proved to be but the shadow of her husband's royal sun; a power vanished when the orb prematurely set. Yet, from all accounts, she had all gifts of person in her favour, with a beauty set off by glorious golden hair; nevertheless there was something in this ill-fated queen that failed to conciliate friends, and no woman ever contrived to make more personal enemies.

She had, however, a heavy cross to bear. The murder of the two little Princes in the Tower has made a deep impression on the imagination of nearly the whole world, whereas the story of their heartbroken mother has been almost forgotten. That an occasional lack of judgement, and an inability to grasp the wider issues of life, marred the queen's influence and increased her difficulties, merely goes to prove the existence of ordinary human frailty. Limitations and errors were the almost inevitable consequences of sudden exaltation to a throne in a factious and intolerant age, but through the shadows obscuring the *via dolorosa* which Elizabeth trod, can be seen 'that great heart', on which Edward, despite his many infidelities, insensibly relied, and to which he always returned.

This unhappy woman was the victim of the most ghastly circumstances it is possible to imagine. Thwarted in her affections, torn by conflicting interests, deeply outraged and wounded almost to breaking-point in her most sacred feelings, her father, two of her brothers, and three sons having been foully murdered in cold blood, she might well have become insane with sorrow and trouble. Nevertheless, despite her many and great troubles, she remained to the last a brave woman, living for those of her children who were spared to her, and eventually died conscious of the fact that the unprecedented woes of her family appeared to be ended, and that she herself had done her duty to them well and faithfully to the best of her ability.

Although fate had dealt unkindly with Elizabeth in the tragic bereavements which left her a broken-hearted widow and mother, yet that caste but unhappy woman remains the undisputed ancestress of the many noble kings and queens 'fear'd by their breed and famous by their birth', under whose gracious guidance England may still claim to be 'dear for her reputation through the world'.

# MISCELLANEA

Three autographs of Elizabeth Woodville are known to be in existence; two are in the Public Record Office and the other in the British Museum.[1] Of those in the Record Office the first is affixed to a letter to Sir William Stonor,[2] warning him against interfering with the game in her forests, even under cover of a commission from the king, her husband. Elizabeth thus called Sir William to account for his doings:

> Trusty and welbeloved we grete you wel: and where as we understand by report made unto us at this tyme that ye have taken upon you now of late to make maistries withynne our fforest and chace of barnewood and exsille, and that in contempt of us uncourteisly to hunt and slee our deer withynne the same to our grete mervaille and displeasir, we wol ye wite that we entend to sew suche remedy therynne as shall accorde with my lordes laws. And whereas we ferthermore understand that ye purpose under colour of my lordes Commysion in that behalf graunted unto you, as ye sey, hastly to take the view and reule of our game of dere withyn oru said fforest and chace, we wol that ye shew unto us or our counsell your said Commission, if any suche

ye have. And in the mean season that ye spare of huntyng withynne our said fforest or chace, as yewol answere at your perill. Yoven under our signet at our Maner of Grenewiche the first day of August. [1482(?)][3]

Elysabeth.

To our trusty and welbeloved Sir William Stonor, knyght.[4]

The second autograph of Elizabeth Woodville is to be found on a receipt given by her in May 1491 for the arrears of her annuity of £400 allowed her by Henry VII.[5] Another letter, dated 19 August 1481, which, however, is unsigned, from the queen to the forester of Blackmore, is also preserved in the Record Office,[6] and reads thus:

We wol and charge you that ye deliver or do to be delivered unto oure trusty and welbeloved Syr William Stonor, knyght, or unto the bringer herof in his name, one buk this season: to be taken of oure gifte within our Forest of Blackmore, any restrainte or commaundement to you directed to the contrary hereof notwithstanding. And thise oure letters shalbe your sufficient warrant animpst us in that behalve. Yeven under oure signet at my Lordes Castell of Wyndesore the xix day of August the xxj yere of my said lordes Reigne.

To our trusty and welbeloved the maistre fforester our fforest of Blackmore, and to all other fforesters and kepers ther in his absence, and to every of them.

If, therefore, there is any truth in the old saying that a woman's character can be judged by her writing, then the two letters bearing Elizabeth's signature, not to mention the other, certainly convey the impression that a pertinacious clinging to her rights as queen was one of the most salient traits in her character.

Like her husband, Edward IV, and her brother, Anthony, Earl Rivers, Elizabeth appears to have been a lover of books, and one of William Caxton's patrons. It is indeed probable that the royal patronage of Caxton was due in no small degree to the influence of herself and Rivers.[7] One must, however, not overlook the fact that Elizabeth's friendship with the Earl of Worcester almost certainly contributed towards the interest taken by the king and Earl Rivers in this printing-press. Caxton wrote an appreciation of the earl, in which he referred to him as 'noble, vertuous and well disposed'.[8] Not long after Elizabeth had become queen she paid £10 for a book,[9] and a copy of the Romance of the Saint Graal in French prose[10] also belonged to her, and in her widowhood, if not earlier, she owned a copy of the *Recuiel des Histories de Troyes* from Caxton's press.[11] There also exists a small book which belonged to her daughters Elizabeth and Cecily. This is an account, in French, of the death and testamentary disposition of Sultan Amarath.[12]

Edward IV and his queen appear to have shown considerable interest in Caxton's Westminster Press almost as soon as it was installed. In what was probably the very first product of this press,[13] *A Boke of the Hoole Lyf of Jason*, published around 1477, Caxton was able to state that it was 'under the shadowe' of the king's noble protection that he had 'enterprised taccomplish this sayd litil boke'. And while he did not venture to present this book to the king

for asmuch as I doubte not his good Grace hath it in Frensh, which he wel understandeth', he did presume by the king's permission, and 'by the supportacion of our most redoubted liege lady, most excellent princesse the quene, to presente it this sayde boke unto the most fayr. And redoubted young lorde. My lorde the Prynce of Wales, our tocomyng souerayne ... to thentent he may begynne to lerne rede Englissh not for any beaute or good Endyting of our Englissh tonge that is therin, but for the nouelte of the histories.[14]

Thus, whatever posterity may find to say against Edward IV and his queen in other ways, it will ever be to their honour and glory that William Caxton found in them two of his earliest and most faithful patrons.

Of Elizabeth's recorded acts the one which stands most to her credit is the refounding and endowment of Queens' College, Cambridge, 'as the true foundress by right of succession' to her late mistress and rival, Margaret of Anjou.[15]

In the hall of this college is to be seen her portrait, which has been engraved in Agnes Strickland's *Queens of England*.[16]

# APPENDIX 1
# PORTRAITS

The outstanding portrait of Elizabeth Woodville is undoubtedly the small panel portrait measuring 30.4 by 22.2 centimetres which has been ascribed by the owner, Dr William A. Shaw of the Public Record Office, to Edward IV's painter, John Stratford of London.

Dr Shaw describes this portrait as the 'first surviving genuine panel portrait of native English origin'. On 8 July 1461, Edward IV granted Stratford the office of King's Painter.[1] Dr Shaw maintains that two years later, in 1453, the portrait in question was painted representing Elizabeth Woodville as a widow with a widow's veil, prior to her marriage with Edward IV. Dr Shaw further maintains that the three better-known portraits of Elizabeth – namely, those at Queens' College, Cambridge, at the Ashmolean Museum, Oxford,[2] and in the Royal Collection at Windsor Castle – are but poor copies of this panel portrait, in that they preserve traces of the widow's veil, but describe her as queen.[3]

Besides this panel portrait and the three copies at Queens' College, Cambridge, the Ashmolean Museum, and Windsor, there are also three other portraits of Elizabeth Woodville in stained glass. Of these the finest is in the window of the North Cross or Martyrdom chapel in Canterbury Cathedral.[4] In Mr Bernard Rackham's opinion the face of the queen is no conventional portrait, but was intended as a faithful rendering of Edward IV's consort,[5] and is supposed by many to be the work of John Prudde, the king's glazier at Westminster.[6]

The two remaining portraits in stained glass are to be found in the north aisle of St George's chapel, Windsor, and in the north porch of Thaxted church, Essex.[7]

Elizabeth has also been portrayed as a member of the Skinners' Fraternity of Our Lady's Assumption. There is a full-page portrait of her in coronation robes in the *Illuminated Book of the Fraternity of Our Lady's Assumption*, in the possession of the Skinners' Company.[8] Over a dress of scarlet and ermine the queen, holding orb and sceptre, wears a long blue robe, edged and fastened with gold. Beneath the crown her golden hair falls to her shoulders. Rose pink and pale pink, combined with a pale but vivid green, figure largely in the background to the portrait, and in the border of flowers and leaves.

Beneath the portrait of the queen is the following inscription: 'Oure moost goode and graciouse Quene Elizabeth, Soster unto this oure Fraternite of oure blissed Lady and Moder of Mercy Sanct Mary Virgyn the Moder of God.'[9]

No date is given in the book for the enrolment of Elizabeth as a Sister, but the date on the opposite page is that of the eleventh year of Edward IV's reign – namely, 1472.

Elizabeth is also depicted with Edward IV, the Prince of Wales and Earl Rivers in an illuminated manuscript at Lambeth Palace entitled the *Dictes and Sayings of the Philosophers*.[10] This cannot, however, be considered as a true portrait; it is rather an illuminated miniature in the manuscript.

Finally it must not be overlooked that there are actually five portraits of Elizabeth in Queens' College, Cambridge. Besides the old panel portrait on wood in the Combination Room, and the copy of this portrait painted by Hudson in the Hall,[11] there are three others in the President's Lodge, of which two are in the

Gallery, and the third in the Audit Room.[12]

The portrait of Elizabeth which has been most generally reproduced is undoubtedly the one in the Combination Room of Queens' College, Cambridge.[13]

A further engraving of Elizabeth by J. Faber, senior, is to be found in *The Founders of Oxford and Cambridge Colleges.*[14]

# APPENDIX 2
# ORIGINAL DOCUMENTS

*Letter of King Edward IV to the Keeper of his Privy Seal, after his return to the throne in 1471, for letters patent in reward of William Gould, a butcher.*

Right reverend fadre in God, right trusty and welbeloved, we grete you well; lating you wit that for the grete kyndnesse and true hert that oure welbeloved William Gould, citezen of London, bocher, shewed unto us and unto our dearest wife the Quene, in our last absence out of this oure Roialme, every weke, then yeving unto hir for the sustentacion of hir household half a beef and ij motons; and also aftir oure Feld of Tewkysbury, at her being in the Towre, brought C. oxen into a medow beside oure said Towre for the [ki]lling of the same, whereof the Kentishmen, and other at tymes, oure rebels, shipmen, toke of the said bests I. And ledde away ... an to his great hurt and damage, we have yeven and graunted unto the saide William, in recompense of his sad hurts, and for other causes us moveing, our letters of licence, that he by himself, his factours, or attorneys, maye charge a Ship called the Trynyte of London, of the portage of XXX. Ton or within, in any porte or place of this oure Roialme, with oxe hids, ledde, talowe, and alle other merchandises except staple ware, and the saide Ship, so charged and defensibly araied, for the defense of the same, with suche a maistre and nowmbre of mariners as the saide William, his factours or attornes, shall name unto you in oure Chancerye, to goo out of this oure saide Roialme into what parties by yonde the Sea it shall like him or theim; and there to discharge and recharge the same Ship with all maner goods and merchandises leefull; and retourne into this oure saide Roialme, and all other places under oure obeissance: and so to discharge and recharge the saide Ship, with the saide goods, wares, and merchanidses, and goo and com as often as it shall please him or theim, during oon hole yere, without any lett or impediment of us or eny of oure officers and ministres; paing unto us therfor all maner costumes, subsides, and duetees unto us for the same due and apperteynyng, any act, stateute, ordinance, provision, or restraint hadde or made into the contrarye notwithstanding. Wherefore we wol and charge you that undir oure Prive Seale, being in youre ward, ye do make herupon our Letters to be directed unto oure Chancellor of England, commaunding him by the same to make herupon our Letters Patentes undir oure Great Seale in due forme, and thies our Letters shal be your warrant. Yeven undir oure Signet at oure Palois of Westminster the xxiiij day of Feverier ... of our reign.

To the reverend fadre in God our right trusty and welbeloved the Bishop of Rochester, keper of our Prive Seale.[1]

Abbreviations:

L.R. – *Liber Recept. Scaccarii,* The Book of the Receipt of the Exchequer.

P.S. – Privy Seal. Writs.

S.B. – Signed Bills.

1485. *Restitution of Queen Elizabeth Woodville by Henry VII.*

The kinge, our soveraine lorde, for certain considerations him
moveing, by the advise and assent of the lores spirituells and
temporells, and comunes, in thys present Parlement assembled,
and by auctoritee of the same, enaxteth ordeineth, and
stabilisheth that Elizabeth, late wyfe to Edward the iiii, late
king of England, have and enjoye from henceforth all such
estate, dignitee, preeminence and name as she should or might
have had or doune if noe acte of Parlement had been made
ayenst ne touching her in the time of Richard the iii, late, in
dede and not of right, king of England. And that the same
Elizabeth, by the same name the wich she so might have had
if none acte had been made ayenst her, be abled to plede and
impleded in all manner of accions, and to yeve, graunte, take,
and receive all manner of hereditaments, possessions, goodes,
cattells, and other thinges; and allso have and maintaine all
such acciones of debte and account as she should or might have
had or doune, and the same to be of such force and effecte as
if no acte of parliament had been made ayenst ne touchinge
her in the tyme of the reigne of the said late pretended King
Richard. Excepted for such debts and accompts as have been
duly paid and made after the beginning of the said usurped
reigne of the said late pretended King Richard; whereof all
persones which have made any such payments or accompts be
thereof ayenst the said Elizabeth quite and discharged.

Published by W. Campbell, *Materials for a History of Henry VII*, I
(London, 1873), p. 121.

4 March 1486. *Henry VII's grants to Elizabeth.*

Grant for life to Elizabeth, queen of England, widow of King
Edward IV, of the lordship and manors of Waltham, Magna,

Badowe, Masshebury, Dunmow, Lyeghes, and Farneham, in co. Essex, parcel of the duchy of Lancaster, of the office of feodary and bailiff in the said lordships and manors, together with knights' fees, advowsons of churches etc.

L.R. 163b.

W. Campbell, *Materials for a History of Henry VII*, I (London, 1873), p. 338.

*5 March 1486. Henry VII's compensation to Elizabeth for the residue of her dowry.*

Grant to Elizabeth, queen of England, wife of Edward IV, which recites: That by patent, under the seal of the duchy of Lancaster, dated 4 March, I Hen. VII, the lordships and manors of Waltham, Great Badowe, Masshebury, Dunmowe, Leighes and Farnham, co. Essex, parcel of the said duchy, and the offices of feodary and bailiff in the said lordships and manors, and all other appurtenances, had been granted to her, for life, in part compensation for her dowry. The present patent further grants to her, for life, in compensation for the residue of her dowry, the following yearly payments; viz., 102*l* 15*s* 6*d* out of the fee-farm of the town of Bristol and suburbs thereof; 20*l* out of the fee-farm of the borough or town of Bedford; 22*l* 19*s* 3¾*d* out of the fee-farm of the city of Norwich, and of the improved rent of the same; 50 marks a year payable by the convent of St Albans as farm during its voidance, 60*l* out of the farm of the manor and hundred of Barton Bristol, co. Glouc., by the hands of Henry, Duke of Warwick, and his heirs, and the sheriff of Gloucestershire; 40*l* out of the fee-farm of the town of Ipswich, co. Suffolk; 40*l* a year parable by the monastery of St Edmund for the custody of the abbey and the temporalities thereof; 9*l* 16*s* 9*d* a year out of the surplusage of the manor of Lowystoft

and the hundred of Luddynglond, co. Suff., by the hands of
the heirs male of Michael de la Pole, Earl of Suffolk, and
of the other castles and lands specified in the roll of Hen
V (roll 7) assigned to him, to the value of 500*l* a year; 34*l*
12*s* out of the farm of the town of Notyngham, and the
improved rent thereof; 30*l* out of the farm of the town of
Derby; 40*l* of and for the manor of Hedyngton, with the
hundred of Bolyngton without the Northern Gate of Oxford,
by the hands of William Wilcotes and his heirs, or by the
sheriff of Oxfordshire and Berks; 12*l* out of the farm of the
manor of Pourestok, co. Dorset; by the hands of John de
Wroxhalle and his heirs, and the sheriff of Dorset; 15*l* for the
hundred of Calne, and the water-mill in Calne, co. Wilts, by
the hands of William de Zouch de Totneys, knt, and his heirs
and the sheriff of Wilts; 35*l* out of the fee-farm of the town
of Oxford; 46*l* out of the fee-farm and improved rent of the
town of Southampton; 10*l* out of the farm as well of the two
parts as of the third part, of the manor of Godyngton, cos
Oxon. and Bucks., by the hands of Richard Damory and his
heirs, and the sheriff of Oxfordshire and Bucks.; 12*l* out of
the farm or custody of the town of Shaftesbury, by the hands
of the abbess and convent of Shaftesbury, and the sheriff
of Somerset and Dorset; 12*l* out of the farm of Kynton, by
the hands of Nicholas Segrave and his heirs, and the sheriff
of Warwick and Leicester; 100*s* out of the free-farm of the
wapentake of Goscote, by the hands of the same; 116*s* out
of the farm of the moiety of the town of Tamworth, and
of the improved rent thereof; 12*l* 18*s* 5½*d* out of the fee-
farm of the hundred of Framlond, co. Leic., by the hands
of Rogert Bellers, 108*s* 4*d* out of the farm of the honors of
Bonon', Peverell, and Hagnet, cos. Bucks., Northampton,
and Leicester, and of the castle and honor of Huntyngdon
with its appurtenances, in the counties of Hunts., Cambridge,

Beds., Bucks., and Northampton, which belonged to John Hastyngis, Earl of Pemrboke; 70*l* out of the ancient farm and improved rent of the town of Cambridge; 20*l* 17*s* 6*d* out of the farm and improved rent of the town of Shrewsbury; 12*l* out of the fee-farm of the manor of Forde, by the hands as well of Nicholas de Audeley (brother and heir of Thomas, son and heir of James de Audeley) and his heirs, as of the sheriff of Shropshire; 10*l* 6*s* 8*d* out of the hands as well of the abbot and convent of Halesowen, as of the sheriff of Stafford; 9*l* out of the custody of the manors of Kynfare and Storton, and of the forest of Kynfare (which custody Edward Attewode, late a yeoman of the king, held at the like farm, for term of the life of Henry Mortimer, by grant of the same Henry), by the hands as well of Hugh Tyrell, brother and heir of John Tyrell, and his heirs, as of the sheriff of Stafford; 20*l* out of the free-farm of the town of Malmesbury, with the three hundreds thereto pertaining, by the hands as well of the abbot and convent of Malmesbury, as of the sheriff of Wilts.; 15*l* out of the farm of Radwell, by the hands as well of the heirs of Hugh de Veer and Dionisia de Montcenis, his widow, as of the sheriff of Essex and Herts. Further grant, for life, in compensation as aforesaid, of the manors or lordships of Havering atte Boure and Bradwell, co. Essex; the castle, a shelp called Hadlegh Ree, co. Essex, and dredging for muscles in Tilbery Hope, co. Essex; the manors or lordships of Banstede and Walton, alias Wauton, co. Surrey, with the park and warren, and all lands and tenements in Charlewode, co. Surrey; the manors of Langley Marreys and Wirardesbury, co. Bucks.; the manors and lorsdhips of Cokeham and Bray, co. Berks, with all rents pastures and purpresturse in the parish of Bray, in the forest of Windesore, and assarts, wastes, purprestures, and rents of the same, etc. in the said two manors and forest and the seven hundreds of

Cokeham and Bray, co. Berks., with the issues thereof; the castle, manor, lordship and hundred of Odyham, co. Hants.; the manor, town, and barton of Gyllyngham, co. Dorset; the manor and lodship of Cosseham, co. Wilts.; the lordship and manor of Merleburgh, and the borough of Marleburgh, co. Wilts.; the hundred of Selkesey, alias Selkeley, and the perquisites of courts of Berton, near Marleburgh, aforesaid; all assarts of the forest of Savernak, with the agistment and pannage within the forest, and all other appurtenances to the same lordship, manor, burgh and hundred pertaining, held by Humphrey, late duke of Gloucester, and all rents of assarts, etc. in that forest; the castle, manor, park, borough and lordship of Devises; the manor and town of Ronde, and the forest of Milkesham, Pevesham, and Chippenham, and all rents and farms of assarts, etc. in that forest; the manors of Merston Meysey, co. Wilts., Hampsetede Marchall, with the parks, etc., co. Berks, , and Benham, alias Benham Lovell, co. Berks.; two messuages, two plough lands, 40 acres of meadow, 20 acres of wood, with the appurtenances, in Holdenham and Westbroke, co. Berks., parcel of the said manor of Benham Lovell; the manors of Swalowfeld, co. Berks., and the Great Wrattyng, alias Talworth Wrattyng, co. Suff.; and the manor, lordship and forest of Fekhenham, co. Worc., and all rents and farms of assarts, etc. in that forest.

P.S. No. 759, Pat., p. 3, m. 25 (3) and 24 (4).

W. Campbell, *Materials for a History of Henry VII*, I (London, 1873), p. 347–50; *Cal. Pat. Rolls*, I, 75; J. Gairdner, *Letters and Papers illustrative of the Reigns of Richard III and Henry VII*, II (London, 1863) p. 368.

1487. *Writs under the Privy Seal, Easter Term, 2 Henry VII.*

To the lady queen, for payment of all profits, and issues of all

lands, honors and castles lately belonging to Elizabeth, late wife of Edward the Fourth.'
W. Campbell, *Materials for a History of Henry VII*, II (London, 1873), p. 142.

1 May 1487. *Transfer of Elizabeth Woodville's jointure lands to her daughter, the queen consort.*

'Henry, by the grade of God, etc. To the treasourer and chamberlains of our Eschequier that nowe be and that for the tyme hereafter shalbe, greting. Wher as of late by thadvise of the lords and other nobles of our counsaill for diuers consideracions vs and theym moeuyng have seased into our hands all honors, castelles, manoirs, lordships, knights fees, aduousons, and alle othr lands and tenements, with their apportenaunces and all maner fefermes and annuitees by vs late assigned vnto Queene Elizabeth, late wif to the full noble prince of famous memorye Edward the Fourth, and all and every of the saide honoures, castells, manoirs, lordships, knights fees, aduousons, and all other lands, tenements with their appertenaunces, fefermes, and annuities hauve assigned vnto our derrest wif the quene. Wherfor we woll and charge you that all suche sommes of money as is comen to charge you that all suche sommes of money as is comen to your handes of any the p'misses, that ye anon vpon the sight of thies our letters make paiement vnto our said wif, or to suche persone or persounes as she hath and shall appointe and assigne to receyue the same. And from hensfourth yerely in liekwise we woll and charge you that alle the issues, profits and reuvnues that hreafter shall growe of the premises and euery of them ye paie and deliuer to our said wif and to her receyuours.' Given at Couentre.
P.S.

W. Campbell, *Materials for a History of Henry VII*, II (London, 1873), p. 148–9; A. F. Pollard, *Reign of Henry VII from Contemporary Sources*, I (London, 1913), p. 46–7.

1487. *Writs under the Privy Seal, Michaelmas Term, 3. Hen. VII.*

To the Queen Elizabeth, late wife of Ed. IV.--cc marcs.
W. Campbell, *Materials for a History of Henry VII*, II (London, 1873), p. 225.

30 May 1488. *Grant of 400 marks to Elizabeth Woodville.*

The king to the treasurer and the chamberlains of the exchequer: 'Forsomoche as we of our especial grace hauve graunted vnto oure dere moder Quene Elizabeth cccc. Marks yerely towards the mayntenaunce of hir estate, we therfore wol and charge you that at and for the terme of Midsommer next commyng aftre the date herof, ye content and pay vnto oure saide moder hir deputie or assignay in that behalf c. marks sterlinges in partie of paiement of the said cccc. Marks, and so furthe quarterly c. marcs, vnto tyme ye haue othrewise from vs in commaundement, etc. etc. Given at the castel of Wyndesore.'
S.B.
W. Campbell, *Materials for a History of Henry VII*, II (London, 1873), p. 319–20.

5 June 1488. *Grant for £6 to Elizabeth Woodville for a ton of wine.*

Mandate to the treasurer and chamberlains of the exchequer to pay in ready money to the king's 'right dere moder Quene Elisabeth, or to the bringer herof in hir name,' the sum of six pounds, 'graunted vnto her by wey of rewarde for a tonne of wyne towardes hir costes and expenses. Given at the castel of Wyndesore.'

S.B.

W. Campbell, *Materials for a History of Henry VII*, II (London, 1873), p. 322.

19 February 1490. *Elizabeth receives an annuity of £400.*

Grant for life to the king's liege woman, Elizabeth the Queen, late the wife of Edward IV, of an annuity of 400*l* at the receipt of the exchequer. Without fine or fee in the hanaper.

*Pat. Roll* 5 Henry VII, memb. 16 (20); *Cal. Pat. Rolls*, I, 302.

14 December 1490. *Elizabeth Woodville receives a grant of 50 marks for her expenses at Christmas.*

Mandate to the treasurer and chamberlains of the exchequer, to pay in ready money, 'without prest or other charge', sum of 50 marks, 'vnto oure right dere and right welbeloued quene Elizabeth moder vnto oure most dere wif the quene,' to whom the said sum has been granted, by way of reward, 'ayenst the fest of Cristemas next commyng. Given at the paloys of Wesminster.'

S.B.

W. Campbell, *Materials for a History of Henry VII*, II (London, 1873), p. 555.

21 May 1491. *Signed receipt of Elizabeth Woodville for the sum of £30 the arrears of her half-year's pension.*

Be hyt remembyrd that I Quene Elyzabethe lete wyffee to the excelent prynce Kyng Edward the iiijth have reseyvede xxi

day of May the vj yere of King Henry the viith of John Lord
Denham treasorer of Ynglong be the handdes of Thomas
Stolys on [e] of the reseyte, xxxli in party of payment of ccli
due to me at ester last past as hyt aperyth be my annuete
grauntyd be the Kyng. In wytnes wher of I have endosyd thys
byll wythe my hand the day and yere above said.

 Elysabeth.

Public Record Office. Museum. Pedestal 20. (Ancient Deeds A.
15109)

*Archaeologia Cantiana*, I, p. 147; W. G. Harvey, *Handwriting of
the Kings and Queens of England*, p. 38.

# APPENDIX 3
# THE CHILDREN OF EDWARD IV
# & ELIZABETH WOODVILLE

1. Elizabeth, born at Westminster, 11 February 1466.

2. Mary, born at Wesminster, 12 August 1467.

3. Cecily, born at Westminster, 20 March 1469.

4. Edward, born in Westminster Sanctuary, 2 November 1470.

5. Margaret, born at Windsor, 19 April 1472.

6. Richard, born at Shrewsbury, 17 August 1473.

7. Anne, born at Westminster, 2 November 1475.

8. George, born at Windsor before 12 April, 1477.

9. Catherine, born at Eltham early in 1479.

10. Bridget, born at Eltham, 10 November 1480.

*Married Daughters of Elizabeth Woodville*

1. Elizabeth, queen of Henry VII, married 18 January 1486, died 11 February 1503.

2. Cecily, married (1) John, Viscount Welles before December 1487.[1] (2) Thomas Kymbe or Kyme of Boston, Lincs,[2] between 8 February 1499 and January 1503.[3] Died 24 August 1507.[4]

3. Anne, married Thomas Howard, Duke of Norfolk and Earl of Surrey on 4 February 1495.[5] Died shortly after 22 November 1511.[6]

4. Catherine, married William Courtenay, Earl of Devon, before October 1495.[7] Died 15 November 1527.[8]

*Unmarried Daughters*

1. Mary, died on 23 May 1482.[9]
2. Margaret, died on 11 December 1472.[10]
3. Bridget, died about 1517.[11]

*Sisters of Elizabeth Woodville*

1. Margaret, married to Thomas, Lord Maltravers, heir of the Earl of Arundel, in October 1464, died before 6 March 1491.[12]
2. Anne, married (1) before 15 August 1467, William, Lord Bourchier, heir of the Earl of Essex.[13] (2) After 12 February 1483, George Grey, Earl of Kent, and Lord Grey of Ruthin, brother of her sister Joan's husband. Died 30 July 1489.[14]
3. Jacquetta, married John, Lord Strange of Knockyn.[15] Dead in 1481.
4. Joan (or Eleanor), married Anthony, Lord Grey of Ruthin, heir of the Earl of Kent.[16] Dead in 1491.
5. Catherine, married (1) in 1466 Henry, Duke of Buckingham.[17] (2) Between 2 November 1483, and 7 November 1485, Jasper Tudor, Duke of Bedford.[18] (3) Sir Richard Wingfield.[19] Died sometime before 1513.[20]
6. Mary, married in September 1466 to William Herbert, 2nd Earl of Pemrboke, son and heir of Lord Herbert, 1st Earl. He was created Earl of Huntingdon on 4 July 1479. She was dead in 1481.[21]
7. Martha, married to Sir John Bromley of Bartomley and Hextall, Shropshire.[22]

*Brothers of Elizabeth Woodville*

1. Anthony Woodville, Baron Scales[23] and 2nd Earl Rivers. Executed in 1483.
2. Sir John Woodville, married in January 1465 to Catherine

Neville, Dowager Duchess of Norfolk, aunt of Warwick the Kingmaker.[24] Executed in 1469.

3. Lionel, Bishop of Salisbury. Dead before 23 June 1484.

4. Sir Edward Woodville, Admiral. Killed at St Aubin du Cormier on 28 July 1488.

5. Sir Richard Woodville, 3rd and last Earl Rivers. Died in 1491.

Two other brothers, Lewis and John Woodville, are said to have died young.[25]

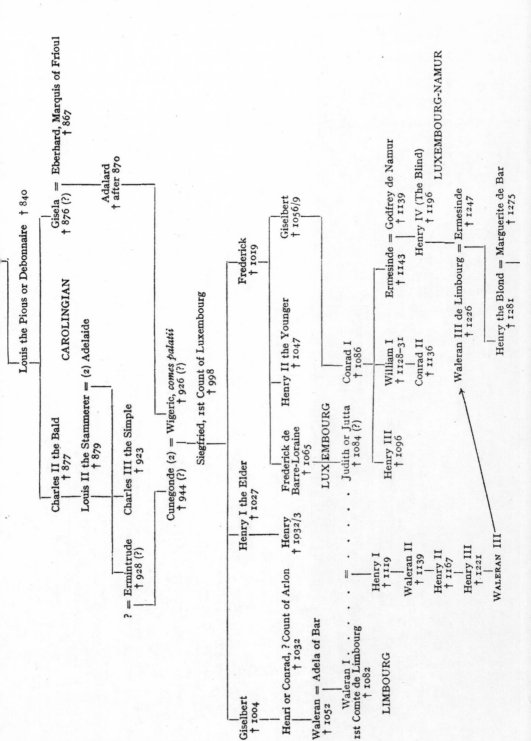

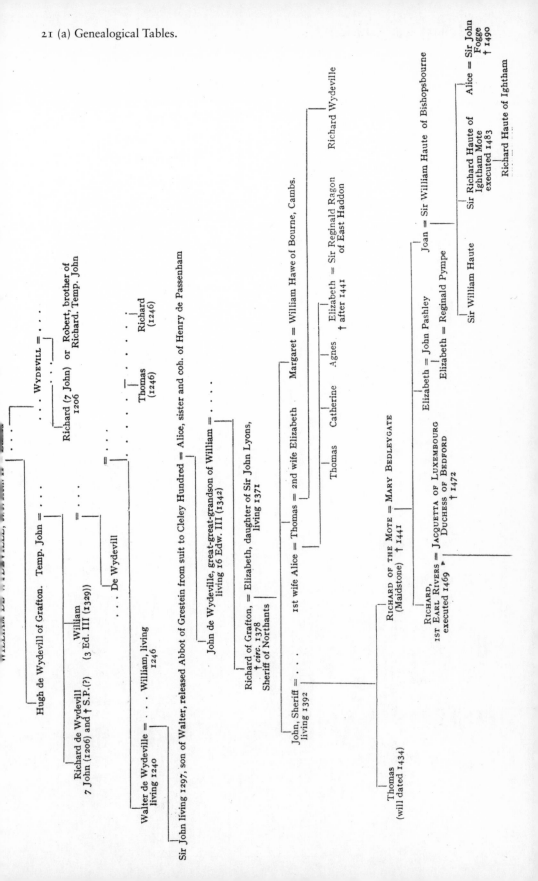

RICHARD, 1ST EARL RIVERS = JACQUETTA OF LUXEMBOURG, DUCHESS OF BEDFORD
executed 1469 † 1472

Thomas Lord Scales † 1460

Elizabeth (1) Lady Scales † 1473 } = { Anthony, 2nd Earl Rivers, married Mary Fitz Lewes (2), executed 1483
Mary Fitz Lewes (2)

John Woodville, executed 1469, married Catherine Dowager Duchess of Norfolk

Lionel, Bishop of Salisbury † 1484(?)

Edward Woodville (Admiral) † 1488 at St. Aubin du Cormier

Richard, 3rd and last Earl Rivers † 1491

Sir John Grey of Groby (1) † 1461 at St. Alban's = Elizabeth Woodville 1437–1492 = (2) Edward IV † 1483

Margaret Countess of Arundel † before 1491

Anne Countess of Kent † 1489

Jacquetta Lady Strange of Knockyn † 1481

Joan Lady Grey of Ruthyn † 1491

Catherine Duchess of Buckingham † 1513

Mary Countess of Huntingdon † 1481

Martha Lady Bromley of Barnsley and Hawkstall (Shrops.)

Thomas Grey, Marquis of Dorset cr. 1475 † 1501 = (1) Anne, daughter of Duke of Exeter † 1467 (2) Cecily, Baroness of Harington and Bonville † 1530

Thomas II, Marquis of Dorset † after 1535 = Margaret Medley

Henry Grey, cr. Duke of Suffolk 1551 † 1554

Thomas Grey, Marquis of Dorset † 1530

Charles Brandon (2) Duke of Suffolk † 1545 = Mary (1) = Louis XII of France † 1515
Mary † 1533

Frances † 1559

Henry Grey † 1554 = Frances

Lady Jane Grey (Queen) executed 1554

William of Orange † 1650 = Mary † 1660

William III † 1702 ... O.S.P. ... Mary II † 1694

Charles II † 1685

James II = Anne Hyde deposed 1688 † 1671

Anne † 1714

Edward VI † 1553

Arthur † 1502

Henry VII Tudor † 1509 = Elizabeth † 1503

Henry VIII Tudor † 1547

Mary I † 1558

Elizabeth † 1603

Henrietta Maria = Charles I ex. 1649

Margaret † 1541 = James IV of Scotland † 1513

Mary † 1482

Cecily † 1507

Edward V † 1483

Margaret † 1472

Richard, Duke of York † 1483

Anne † 1512

George † 1479 (?)

Catherine † 1527

Bridget † circ. 1527

TUDOR

James V = Mary of Lorraine † 1542 † 1560

Darnley = Mary Queen of Scots † 1567 † 1587

James (VI) I = Anne of Denmark of England † 1625 † 1619

STUART

Elizabeth † 1662 = Frederick V, Elector Palatine † 1632

Sophia of Brunswick † 1714 = Ernest Augustus Duke of Hanover † 1698

George I † 1727

George II † 1760

Frederick † 1751

George III † 1820

George IV † 1830

William IV † 1837

Edward Duke of Kent † 1820

HANOVER

Albert of Saxe-Coburg † 1861 = Victoria † 1901

Edward VII † 1910

George V † 1936

Edward VIII abdicated 1936

George VI

WINDSOR

## Elizabeth Woodville's Seal

Elizabeth Woodville's seal contains an escutcheon of King Edward's and her arms and quarterings, impaled under a coronet composed of four crosses pate, and as many *fleurs-de-lis*, and between them eight *fleurs* of a lesser size; and supported by the White Lion of March on the right side, and on the left with a greyhound accolled and chained, which last was the supporter of the Nevilles' earls of Westmoreland as appears in their seals. The queen bears therein, quarterly of six pieces, three in chief and three in base; the first quarter is Argent a Lion Rampant, *queve forche* Gules crowned Proper, and was the paternal coat armour of her mother's father, Pierre, Comte de St Paul. Secondly, quarterly, Gules a Star Argent, and Azure Seme of Fleur de Lys Or, the third as the second, the fourth as the first, by the name of Baux, and were the arms of Elizabeths' grandmother, Margaret, daughter of Francesco (de Baux) del Balzo, Duke of Andria. Thirdly, Barry of ten Argent and Azure, over all a Lion Rampant Gules, being the arms of Henry the Blond, Count of Luxembourg, from whom the younger branch of the House of Luxembourg descended. Fourthly, Gules charged with a Red Rose and Or, being the arms of her great-grandmother, Susanna, daughter of Nicholas Orsini, Count of Nola, and wife of Francesco del Balzo (de Baux), Duke of Andria. The fifth is Gules, three Pallets varry, Argent and Azure on a Chief, Or, a Label of Five Points Azure, borne by the name of St Pol, and was the arms of Mahaut, Countess of St Pol, the wife of Guy (VI) de Luxembourg, the great-great-grandfather of Queen Elizabeth, who in the sixth and last quarter placed her paternal coat of Woodville, namely Argent a Fess and Canton, Gules. Thus were these several coats marshalled for the honour of this queen, to shew the illustrious nobility of her maternal descent. The titles on this seal, and those in her instrument, to which it is annexed, are alike, in which she styles herself, *Elizabetha Dei gracia Regina Anglie et Francie Domina. Hibernie.* It bears the date *Sub magno sigillo Nostro apud Castrum de Wyndesore vicesimo sexto die Maij Anno Regni metuendissimi Domini mei Regis Edwardi quarti post conquestum Anglie sexto.*[26]

# NOTES

## Historical Introduction

1. William de la Pole, 4th Earl and 1st Duke of Suffolk (1396–1450)
2. Richard 'Plantagenet', (I), (1411–60), only son of Richard, Earl of Cambridge, by his first wife Anne Mortimer, sister of Edmund, Earl of March. He was descended from Edward III by both parents; since his father was second son of Edmund of Langley, 1st Duke of York, Edward III's fifth son, and his mother was a daughter of Roger Mortimer (VI), 4th Earl of March, himself grandson of Lionel, Duke of Clarence, Edward III's third son.
3. Edmund Beaufort I, son of John Beaufort I, Earl of Somerset, who was the eldest son of John of Gaunt by Catherine Swynford.
4. John Talbot (I), Earl of Shrewsbury.

## 1 Birth & Early Life

1. Nicolas Vignier, *Histoire de la Maison de Luxembourg*, pp. 245–6; Anselme, *Histoire de la Maison Royale de France*, III, 726. Cf. *Notes and Queries*, 8th series, II, 431; George Smith, *Coronation of Elizabeth Woodville*, p. 41.
2. Cf. T. Fuller, *The Worthies of England*, II, 161, London, 1811. 'Sure I am, if this Grafton saw her not first a child, it beheld her first a queen.'

   T. Philipott (*Villaire Cantianum*, p. 230, Lynn, 1776) and E. Hasted (*History of Kent*, II, 97, Canterbury, 1782), probably failing, like Dugdale (II, 230) to distinguish Richard Woodville the elder from his son (cf. *Dict. Nat. Biog.*, XXI, 885), contend that she was born at the More, Maidstone, and she is sometimes referred to (cf. *Archaeologia Cantiana*, I, 147) as 'one of the two women of Kent who had the honour to become Queen of England'.
3. The date 1431 given by Agnes Strickland (*Lives of the Queens of England*, II, 316) is clearly absurd, being four years before the Duke of Bedford's death (15 September 1435). All remaining doubts regarding the date of Elizabeth's birth can now be said to have been finally dispelled by the inscription on the panel portrait of Elizabeth in the possession of Dr W. A. Shaw of the Record Office. On this portrait, painted in 1463, her age is given as 26. This would make the year of her birth 1437. For a description of this panel portrait see Appendix 1.
4. Baker, *Northamptonshire*, II, 161. See also J. G. Nichols, *The Topographer and Genealogist*, I, 160.
5. Baker, *Northamptonshire*, II, 161; J. Bridges, *Northamptonshire*, I, 299.
6. Woodville was liable to provide 'half a soldier' (*dimidium militem*). See T. Hearne, *Liber Niger Scaccarii*, p. 213 and n. 2.
7. Hearne, *ibid.* p. 1. Cf. *Dict. Nat. Biog.*, XIII, 58; M. A. E. Green, *Lives of the Princesses of England*, I, 224.
8. Baker, II, 161; Bridges, I, 299.

9. *Ibid.*

10. Baker, II, 161; cf. Bridges, I, 299.

11. Baker, *ibid.*

12. Bridges, *ibid.*; Baker, *ibid.* As Baker rightly states (II, 161) there is no little difficulty in adjusting the genealogical position of the parties in these suits; Baker considers Hugh to be the grantee of Cleley Hundred in the time of John, and the head of the six generations mentioned in the *Quo Warranto* of 3 Edward III (1329). Baker, II, 116; cf. Bridges, I, 280. Since, however, the line was continued by his son William, it may be fairly inferred that his son Robert here mentioned, and probably then heir, died without issue.

13. Baker, II, 162. In 1326, during the rebellion of Isabella and Mortimer, a Robert de Wyvill is mentioned as being the Keeper of the Privy Seal of the future Edward III. See *Ord. Privy Council*, VI, clxvi.

14. Richard was Sheriff from 35 to 41 and 44 Edw. III; MP 36, 37, 39, 42, 47 and 50 Edw. III, and I Richard II. Cf. Baker, II, 166; J. Bridges, *Northamptonshire*, I, 6, 10; F. Whellan, *Northamptonshire*, 92, 93; *Cal. Pat. Rolls*, Edward III, vols XII, 457; XIII, 49, 85, 148, 191, 228, 331, 420; XV, 102.

15. John Woodville was Sheriff in 4, 9, 14 Richard II; MP 6, 7, 11, and 14 Richard II. Bridges, I, 6, 10; Whellan, 92, 93; *Cal. Pat. Rolls*, Richard II, vol. III, 168, 389, 545, 549.

16. Baker, II, 162. Cf. *Cal. Pat. Rolls*, Henry VI, III, 426. For Thomas's Will, see Baker, II, 162–3. This Thomas was Sheriff in 8 Henry IV; 3, 8 and 9 Henry V; 1, 7 and 12 Henry VI; MP 2 Henry V and 4 Henry VI. Bridges, I, 6, 10; *Cal. Pat. Rolls*, Henry VI, I, 555. For the manorial history of Grafton, see Baker, II, 160; Bridges, I, 298.

17. G. E. C(okayne), *Complete Peerage* (Old Series), VI, 371; *Genealogist* (New Series), VI, 199. According to many accounts – viz. Baker, II, 166; Bridges, I, 300; *Hist. MSS. Comm.*, 9th report, p. 113, *Dict. Nat. Biog.*, XXI, 885 – Sir Richard's mother was 'Joan Beauchamp, heiress of a Somersetshire family'.

18. Dugdale (II, 230) failed to distinguish him from his son.

19. *Gesta Henrici V* (ed. B. Williams), pp. 9, 277; Dugdale, II, 230.

20. Longnon, *Paris pendant la Domination Anglaise*, p. 106.

21. Longnon, pp. 105–6; Monstrelet, *Chronique* (ed. Douet d'Arcq), IV, 138.

22. *Ord. Privy Council* (ed. Sir H. Nicolas), II, 167; Hall, *Chronicle* 130; Ramsay, I, 36. Cf. Shakespeare, *Henry VI*, pt. I Act I, Sc. iii.

23. *Ord. Privy Council*, III, 245, 329; Dugdale, II, 230; *Dict. Nat. Biog.*, XXI, 885.

24. *Excerpta Historica*, 249–50; cf. p. 234, n. 2.

25. *Cal. Pat. Rolls*, Henry VI, II, 489, 518.

26. *Ord. Privy Council*, IV, 82; Rymer, *Foedera* X, 605; Doyle, III, 141; *Dict. Nat. Biog.*, XXI, 885.

27. Chapter 1, note 16.

28. Baker, II, 166; G. E. C., VI, 371. He was living in July 1441, when he is mentioned as a Justice of the Peace in Kent. *Cal. Pat. Rolls*, Henry VI, III, 584.

29. Leland, *Collectanea*, II, 491; Nicolas, *Chronicle of London*, 114; Doyle, *Official Baronage* III, 141.

30. Rymer, *Foedera*, X, 454.

31. J. Du Clercq, *Memoires*, liv. V, ch. XVIII, p. 373; J. Stevenson, *Wars of the English in France*, II, 436; Doyle, III, 141.

32. Waurin (ed. Hardy), IV, 64.

33. Dugdale, II, 230.

34. *Cal. Pat. Rolls*, Henry VI, II, 516.

35. *Rot. Parl.*, IV, 498.

36. Stow, *Annals*, p. 376 (ed. 1615); Waurin (ed. Hardy), *Chronique*, IV, p. 207; Du Clercq, *Memoires*, liv. V, ch. XVIII, 373.

37. *Rot. Parl.*, IV, 498; F. Devon, *Issues of the Exchequer*, p. 436; Ramsay, *Lancaster and York*, I, 494. Cf. G. E. C., II, 72; *Cal. Pat. Rolls*, Henry VI, III, 53.

38. Sir Richard Woodville's father had won the approval of the King's Council by refusing to allow Humphrey, Duke of Gloucester to enter the Tower of London in 1425.

39. Rymer, *Foedera*, X, 677.

40. *Somerset Record Society*, XXII, 195–6. Cf. G. Smith, *Coronation of Elizabeth Woodville*, p. 45.

41. *Cal. Pat. Rolls*, Henry VI, III, 72; J. E. Doyle, *Official Baronage*, III, 141; cf. G. Smith, *l. c.* p. 45.

42. British Museum, Add. MS. 23,938. *Computus J. Breknoke.*
43. Public Record Office, Accounts of Keepers of Queen Margaret's Jewels.
44. Waurin, *Chronique* (ed. Hardy), IV, 257; Doyle, *Official Baronage*, III, 141; *Chronicle of John Stone*, p. 25.
45. Rymer, *Foedera*, X, 828; *Paston Letters* (ed. J. Gairdner, 1901), I, 41; Chastellain, *Chronique*, III, 455.
46. Stow, *Annals*, p. 379; *Dict. Nat. Biog.*, XXI, 886. Cf. R. Flenley, *Six Town Chronicles*, p. 115.
47. N. Harris Nicolas, *A Chronicle of London*, p. 127; Gregory, *Chronicle*, p. 183; Waurin (ed. Hardy), IV, 326; Stow, *Annals*, p. 278; Ramsay, II, 37.
48. Cf. *Cal. Pat. Rolls*, Henry VI, III, 523; V, 205.
49. Doyle, *Official Baronage*, III, 141; G. E. C., *Complete Peerage* (Old Series), VI, 371.
50. *Cal. Pat. Rolls*, Henry VI, V, 185; Doyle, III, 141; G. E. C. (Old Series), VI, 371. Flenley, *Six Town Chronicles*, p. 123, gives 2 June. For his choice of title see *Dict. Nat. Biog.*, XXI, 886.
51. Cf. *Cal. Pat. Rolls*, Henry VI, V, 385; Doyle, III, 141.
52. R. Flenley, *Six Town Chronicles*, p. 129.
53. *Ibid.*, p. 131.
54. *Paston Letters* (ed. J. Gairdner), I, 128.
55. J. Anstis, *The Register of the Most Noble Order of the Garter*, II, 146; Doyle, *Official Baronage*, III, 141; *Ord. Privy Council*, VI, 101; *Dict. Nat. Biog.*, XXI, 886. Rivers's stall-plate as a Knight of the Garter has been reproduced by H. St John Hope in *Stall Plates of the Knights of the Garter*, Plate LX. Cf. Also *The Ancestor*, III, 176.
56. *Ord. Privy Council*, VI, 105; Ramsay, II, 146; Doyle, III, 141; G. E. C. (Old Series), VI, 371.
57. Cf. *Cal. Pat. Rolls*, Henry VI, V, 444, 478.
58. Stow, *Survey of London* (ed. C. L. Kingsford), I, 91; Ramsay, II, 146; *Dict. Nat. Biog.*, XXI, 886.
59. *Ord. Privy Council*, VI, 276; Beaucort, *Histoire de Charles VII*, VI, 46. Cf. Doyle, III, 141.
60. *Rot. Parl.*, V, 309, 341; *Paston Letters*, I, 334.
61. *Ord. Privy Council*, VI, 276; *Rot. Parl.*, V, 341; Ramsay, *Lancaster and York*, II, 191 and n. 2.
62. *Ord. Privy Council*, VI, 292; *Foedera*, XI, 374, 415.
63. See chapter 1, notes 2 and 3.
64. Further proof of Queen Margaret's friendship to Sir Richard Woodville's wife is to be found in the fact that after the Second Battle of St Albans (1461) the citizens of London requested her to plead with the queen on behalf of the city. See Great Chronicle, fol. 165; C. L. Kingsford, *Chronicles of London*, p. 173; *Cal. Of Milanese State Papers*, I, 50.
65. Hall's *Chronicle* (ed. Ellis), p. 365.
66. *Archaeologia*, XXIX, 132; *Dict. Nat. Biog.*, X, 973. See also T. Bliss and G. Grant Francis, *Some Account of Sir Hugh Johnys*, pp. 5–7.
67. British Museum, *Royal MS.* 17B, XLVII, fol. 165.
68. Mr George Smith, in his excellent book, *The Coronation of Elizabeth Wydeville* (p. 28) states that this letter refers to a Dame Elizabeth Wodehille, a wealthy widow. This may be correct; on the other hand, it must not be overlooked that the name of Woodville is known to have been written in no less than six different ways. See Baker, *Northamptonshire*, II, 161.
69. British Museum, *Royal MS.* 17B, XLVII, fol. 166.
70. This name is rendered almost illegible owing to an inkstain, but it appears to be Wodehill or Wodehull.
71. This, according to Sir Hugh's monument, was in 1451; therefore these two letters, which are dateless, must have been written *after* that year. Cf. R. C. Hoare's edition of the *Itinerary of Giraldus Cambrensis*, I, 266.
72. Edward, Lord Ferrers, died on 18 December 1457. Dugdale, *Baronage*, I, 719.
73. See C. L. Kingsford in *Dict. Nat. Biog.*, VIII, 636. Hall (*Chronicle* (ed. Ellis), pp. 264, 365) states that Sir John Grey was knighted by Henry VI 'at the battle'. Stow (*Annals*, ed. 1615, p. 515) states that he was knighted on the day of the battle (17 February 1461) with twelve others at Colney. However, the inquisitions taken in 1458 after his father's death style him a knight. Moreover, Henry VI was a prisoner in Warwick's hands before the battle, and Colney was on

the line of march of the Yorkists, not of the Lancastrians. Cf. G. E. C., *Complete Peerage*, V, 361, n.c.

74. Dugdale, I, 719.

75. Thomas, her eldest son by Sir John Grey, is described as being aged 37 and more in 1492, in *Inquisitiones post mortem*, ch. II, vol. VII, no. 2; Exch. II, file 461, no. 4. Cf. Baker, II, 166; G. E. C., *Complete Peerage*, V, 362; *Notes and Queries*, 8th Series, II, 431.

76. Public Record Office. Duchy of Lancaster, 285–8. Household Accounts of Queen Margaret. Cf., however, George Smith, *Coronation of Elizabeth Woodville*, p. 27.

77. There was, according to Miss Strickland (*Queens of England*, II, 313), a 'well known paper' called the *Journal of Elizabeth Woodville* dealing with her life when courted by Sir John Grey. See *Church Times* of 11 February 1898. This 'Journal' appears to be pure imagination. Cf. Miss Benger's article, 'Elizabeth Woodville, An Autographic Sketch of the Fifteenth Century', published by Alaric A. Watts in his *Literary Souvenir*, pp. 37–61. Cf. Also T. R. Potter, *The History of Antiquities of Charnwood Forest*, pp. 108–9.

78. See chapter 1 note 75. C. L. Kingsford in the *Dict. Nat. Biog.*, VIII, 644, appears to place Thomas's birth a few years too early, since Elizabeth herself was not born till 1437. Cf. G. E. C., *Complete Peerage*, V, 362, n.c.

79. The actual date of his birth has never yet been discovered. He must, however, have been born not later than 1461, when his father was killed.

80. See Introduction.

81. Gregory, p. 205; Fabyan, pp. 634–5; Whethamstede, I, 368; Du Clerq, *Memoires*, liv. IV, ch. I, p. 3; Ramsay, II, 221; R. Flenley, *Six Town Chronicles of England*, p. 148.

82. See C. L. Scofield's article in *The English Historical Review*, XXXVII, 253–5.

83. Great Chronicle, fol. 158 *verso*; J. S. Davies, *An English Chronicle* (Camden Society, vol. LXIV), p. 85; C. L. Kingsford, *London Chronicle*, p. 170; Worcester, p. 478; Du Clercq, *Memoires*, liv. IV, ch. Iii, p. 12; *Three Fifteenth-Century Chronicles* p. 72; Gregory, p. 206; Scofield, I, 52.

84. *Paston Letters*, III, 204–4. Cf. Waurin (Dupont), II, 205–6; Scofield, I, 51–2.

85. The actual date of their liberation us unknown; Warwick probably brought them over with him when he invaded England in June that same year. They certainly fought on the Lancastrian side at Towtown in March 1461. See *Cal. State Papers, Ven.*, I, 105–6. Waurin (Dupont), II, 236 and 276–80, states that Warwick brought his prisoners back to England some time after the Battle of Northampton (10 July 1460); Rivers and his son were in the vanguard of King Henry's army at Towton, where they were both captured.

86. Ramsay, II, 223.

87. William of Worcester, 480; Ramsay, II, 226.

88. Ramsay, II, 227–8.

89. Ramsay, II, 232.

90. *Rot. Parl.*, V, 375–97; Ramsay, II, 234–5; E. C. Lodge and G. A. Thornton, *English Constitutional Documents*, 1307–1485, pp. 34–6.

91. Ramsay, II, 237.

92. Sir John Grey was one of those commissioned in the county of Leicester, on 21 December 1459, and later, to collect forces to resist the Duke of York and his adherents when they entered the realm. *Pat. Rolls*, 38 Henry VI, p. 1., m.14 d, p. 2, m. 25 d – *Cal. Pat. Rolls*, Henry VI, vol. VI, 560, 603. Cf. G. E. C., *Complete Peerage*, V, 361, n.c.

## 2 The Accession of Edward IV & His Marriage with Elizabeth

1. William of Worcester (p. 488) gives Chipping Norton, while Gregory (p. 217) gives Burford.

2. Stratford, *Edward IV*, 41, n. 2.

3. *Cal. Milanese Papers*, I, 54; Gregory, 215. Cf. *Archaeologia*, XXIX, 347.

4. Ramsay, II, 230.

5. The combined forces of Edward and the Earl of Warwick probably numbered between 6,000 and 7,000 men. Cf. Oman, *Political History*, IV, 404.

6. Great Chronicle, fol. 165; W. Worcester, 489; Ramsay, II, 248; Flenley, *Six Town Chronicles*, pp. 161–2, 167. For a full account of Edward's claim to the Crown see S. B. Chrimes, *English Constitutional Ideas in the the Fifteenth Century*, pp. 31–2.

7. Great Chronicle, fol. 167; Worcester, 489; *Three Fifteenth-Century Chronicles*, p. 173; J.

S. Davies, *An English Chronicle*, p. 110; N. Harris Nicolas, *A Chronicle of London*, p. 141; Ramsay, II, 248–9; Flenley, 162.

8. Great Chronicle, fol. 167 *verso*; *Rot. Parl.*, V, 464. Cf. *Archaeologia*, XXIX, 127–30; Hearne's 'Fragment', p. 286; Flenley, p. 162.

9. Great chronicle, fol. 169; *Chronicle of John Stone*, p. 83; Oman, *Warwick the Kingmaker*, p. 126. For a description and map of the battlefield see Cyril Ransome's article in *The English Historical Review*, IV, 460–6. Cf. Also Ramsay, II, 271; Waurin (Dupont), II, 278–9; William Grainge, *The Battles and Battlefields of Yorkshire*, pp. 57–93; *Archaeologia*, XXIX, 343–7; Richard Brooke, *Visits to Fields of Battle in England*, pp. 81–129.

10. *Cott. MS. Vit.*, A. XVI, fol. 122; *Chronicle of John Stone*, p. 83; Nicolas, *Chronicle of London*, p. 142; Stow, *Annals*, p. 416; *Three Fifteenth-Century Chronicles*, p. 162. Cf Gairdner, Paston Letters, II, 18 and n. 1; Ramsay, II, 275–6; Oman, IV, 409; *Notes and Queries*, and S., X, pp. 106, 153, 196, 237; L. Stratford, *Edward IV*, p. 55; R. B. Mowat, *Wars of the Roses*, p. 158; Scofield, I, 183.

11. Cf. Thomas More, *Life of Richard III* (ed. Lumby), p. 2; Armstrong, *Richard III*, pp. 79–81.

12. Cf. Grafton, *Chronicle* (ed. Ellis), II, 79; Hall's *Chronicle*, p. 341.

13. Oman (*History of the Art of War in the Middle Ages*, II, 412) describes him as 'one of the first of the medieval generals who showed a complete appreciation of the value of time in war'.

14. Laurence Stratford, *Edward IV*, p. 322. Cf. Also R. B. Mowat's admirable account of the work of Edward IV in his *Wars of the Roses*, ch. XXII, pp. 265–73.

15. Straford, *Edward IV*, p. 330. Cf. Hall's *Chronicle*, p. 341; More, *Richard III* (ed. Lumby), p. 3, 'The common people oftentymes more esteme and take for greater kindness a lyttle courtesye, than a great benefyte.'

16. Sir John's mother, the Dowager Baroness Ferrers, was cousin-german to Roger de Hardwycke.

17. G. E. C. (ed. 1915), IV, 207.

18. G. E. C., IX, 606 (1936).

19. Add. MS. 37,447, fol. XLIX. Cf. MS. of Joseph Hardwicke of Knightsbridge, 1753; H. Coore, *Elizabeth Woodville*, p. 10; A. T. Turner, *Hardwycke Annals*, p. 6; J. W. Hardicke-Jones, *Hardwycke of Hardwycke and Burcote*, p. 5.

20. Issue Rolls, Appendix 480; Strickland, II, 324. Cf. Waurin (Dupont), II, 298–9.

21. Scofield, *Edward IV*, I, 178.

22. Privy Seals; Scofield, I, 177.

23. Writs of Privy Seal, file 783, no. 113, 12 June; file 784, no. 252, 20 July. Rivers's pardon passed the Great Seal on 12 July, and Sir Anthony's on 23 July. *Cal. Pat. Rolls*, Edward IV, I, 97. Rivers's younger son, Sir Richard Woodville, appears to have had to wait till 8 February 1462 for his pardon. Pardon Roll 1–6, Edw. IV, m. 39. Cf. The letter written by Count Ludovico Dallugo, the Milanese envoy, to the Duke of Milan on 30 August 1461: 'I held several conversations with this Lord Rivers about King Henry's cause, and he answered me that the cause was lost irremediably.' *Cal. Venetian Papers*, I, 111–12; *Cal. Milanese Papers*, I, 101–2. Cf. also F. Devon, *Issues of the Exchequer*, p. 468.

24. Cf. Henry Coore, *Elizabeth Woodville*, p. 16, who states that Elizabeth first met Edward at a hunting expedition at Grafton in the autumn of 1462.

25. For these discoveries we are indebted to the scholarship of Mr George Smith of Great Bedwyn, Wilts. See his *Coronation of Elizabeth Wydeville*, pp. 29–32.

26. MS Record Office, Feet of Fines, Divers Counties., XXXIV, Henry VI, Case 293, File 72, no. 63.

27. G. E. C., *Complete Peerage*, V, 359–62.

28. Record Office, *Early Chancery Proceedings*, Bungle 27, nos 268, 269, 271.

29. Recorded in the report of the Historical Manuscripts Commission. Report of MSS. Of R. R. Hastings, I, 301. Cf. Armstrong, *Richard III*, p. 139, n. 34.

30. This daughter, Anne, was married *circa* 1486 to George Talbot, 7th Earl of Shrewsbury. G. E. C. (Old Series), VII, 139.

31. The heir to the Asteley lands had been Sir Edward Grey, Sir John's father. G. E. C., V, 359.

32. George Smith, *op. cit.*, pp. 29–32.

33. G. E. C., *Complete Peerage* (New Edition), V, 359–62.

34. See Baker, *Northamptonshire*, II, 179. Cf. *Notes and Queries*, X Series, VII, 27. Cf. also the *Mercury and Herald of Northampton*, 18 December 1936, p. 4.

35. Bradgate was Grey's patrimony by reason his descent from the earliest of our Norman nobility. It had been part of the inheritance of Petronilla, daughter of Hugh de Grandmesnil, later created Baron Hinckley, one of William the Conqueror's tenants *in capite*; the estate descended from her through a co-heiress of Blanchemains, 3rd Earl of Leicester to the line of Ferrers Groby, and by the heiress of the Ferrers to Sir Edward Grey, father to Elizabeth's husband. It was the chance of war that made Elizabeth a suppliant widow. William Burton, *Leicestershier*, pp. 112–4; A. Bloxham, *Bradgate Park*; J. Nichols, *History and Antiquities of the County of Leicester*, II, pt 2, pp. 661–6, and IV, pt 2, 629–33; L. W. Vernon Harcourt, *His Grace the Steward*, pp. 192–9; G. E. C. (New Series), *Complete Peerage*, VII, 532.

36. Elizabeth eldest son Thomas, later Marquis of Dorset, was the great-grandfather of Lady Jane Grey. Dugdale, *Baronage*, I, 719–22; Sir H. Nicolas, *Memoirs of Lady Jane Grey*, pp. ii–vi; G. E. C.; *Complete Peerage*, IV, 418–21.

37. Cf. Philippe Erlanger, *Marguerite d'Anjou*, p. 243: *Edouard IV jette un long regard sur la belle suppliante et ... les destins de l'Angleterre sont changes.*

38. *Chronicle*, p. 264.

39. C. A. J. Armstrong, *The Usurpation of Richard III*, p. 75, quoting Mancini's *De Occupatione Regni Anglie*, states that the king actually went so far as to place a dagger at Elizabeth's throat.

40. T. Fuller, *Worthies of England*, II, 161. 'The lady put herself into a chaste posture, neither forward to accept, nor forward to decline his favour.' Cf. Shakespeare, *Henry VI*, Pt. 3, III, 2; W. Habington, 'History of Edward IV', in *Complete History of England*, I, 437.

41. More, *Richard III*, 60–3.

42. See A. R. Bayley, in *Notes and Queries*, vol. 151, p. 408. Cf. Lingard, IV, 573–5. Cf.

43. Hall, p. 367; More, *Richard III*, 61–2; Stow, *Annals*, p. 433. The child's name was Arthur. He married on 12 November 1511, Elizabeth, daughter of Edward, 1st Viscount Lisle, being created Viscount Lisle on 25 April 1523, and died in 1541. See G. E. C. (New Series), VIII, 63; *Letters and Papers of Henry VIII*, I, 489; A. F. Pollard, *Historical Essays in Honour of James Tait*, 231–2, n. 5.

44. Hall, p. 367.

45. J. Anstis, *The Register of the Most Noble Order of the Garter*, II, 178.

46. *Ibid.*

47. Gairdner, *Three Fifteenth-Century Chronicles*, p. xxv; Ramsay, II, 306; Stratford, p. 78; Scofield, I, 332.

48. Household Accounts; Scofield, I, 332.

49. Fabyan, *Chronicle*, p. 654.

50. Hearne's 'Fragment' (p. 293) mentions the interesting fact that 'the priest' that wedded them 'lyeth buried at the minories by London before the High Altar'. In all probability Thomas Leson, incumbent of Grafton from 1462 to 1471. Bridges, I, 301.

51. Great Chronicle, fol. 174 *verso*; Hearne's 'Fragment', p. 293; Gregory, p. 226; *Three Fifteenth-Century Chronicles*, p. 180; Warkworth, p. 3; *Rot. Parl.*, VI, 241; Du Clercq, *Memoires*, liv. V, ch. XVIII, 373. Du Clercq and some other foreign chroniclers state that Elizabeth's relations with Edward had been too intimate before their marriage; Loui XI told the Milanese ambassador Edward had married a widow by whom he had already two children. Mandrot, *Depeches*, II, 304. None of the English chroniclers, however, make any such accusations against Elizabeth.

52. Gairdner, *Three Fifteenth-Century Chronicles*, p. xxv; Ramsay, II, 306; Lingard, IV, 154; Stratford, *Edward IV*, p. 78.

53. Fabyan, p. 654.

54. *Ibid.*

55. Gairdner, *Three Fifteenth-Century Chronicles*, p. xxv; Ramsay, II, 306. Prior to leaving London, Edward had written to the mayor of Salisbury to send men to meet him at Leicester on 10 May. Cf. Hatcher, *Old and New Sarum*, p. 159. Miss Scofield (I, 333, n. 2) refers to Fabyan's account of the king's stay at Grafton as 'erroneous'. Since, however, the Court was at Northampton, only about 10 miles from Grafton, from 1 May to 7 May, the king would have had no difficulty in spending four days with his bride at Grafton Hall during this time.

Such a visit would have aroused little or no suspicion, since, as Miss Scofield herself states, Edward, who had just ordered troops to join him at Leicester on 10 May, had already reached the town by 8 May.

56. Gregory, p. 224; *Three Fifteenth-Century Chronicles*, p. 156.

57. Household Accounts.

58. See chapter 3.

59. For the movements of Warwick in the summer of 1464 see C. L. Scofield's article in *The English Historical Review*, XXI, 732–5.

60. On Warwick's policy see J. Kirk, *Charles the Bold*, I, p. 415; II, p. 15. See also Rymer, XI, 518, 520, 521.

61. Chastellain, V, 22.

62. See C. W. Oman, *Warwick the Kingmaker*, p. 162; Gregory, *Historical Collections of a London Citizen* (ed. Gairdner), p. 226. See also Waurin, *Chronique* (ed. Hardy), V, 456–7; William of Worcester, *Annals*, 500–1; footnotes in J. Kirk, *Charles the Bold*, I, 415; II, 15.

63. Gregory, p. 226.

64. See Appendix 3, Genealogical Tables.

65. Waurin (Dupont), II, 326–8. Cf. Oman, *Warwick the Kingmaker*, p. 162; R. Francis, *Warwick the Kingmaker*, p. 118.

66. It would appear that various agents were employed in England to ascertain whether the people approved of the king's marriage. The result was communicated by Sir John Howard in a letter supposed to have been addressed to lord Rivers, the new queen's father. 'Also my lord, I have bene in dyverse plasese wethein Norfolke, Suffolke and Hessex, and ad komenkasion of thes marygge to fel hwoe the pepel of the konteryes wer depossed and, in good feythe, they ar despossed in the beste voysse and glade ther of. Also I have ben wethe many dyverse astates, to fel theyer hertes, and, [in good feythe] I fowende them al ryte wele despossed, safe on, the wesche I schal henforme yower good lordesche at my next komhenge to yowe be the grase of God, ho have yowe, my ryte spesyal god lord, in his blesed safegard. At Wemsche, the 22 day of September.' See B. Botfield, *Manners and Household Expenses of England in the Thirteenth and Fourteenth Centuries*, pp. 196–7. For a foreigner's opinion of Edward's marriage see Caspar Weinreich's *Danziger Chronik*, printed in Theodore Hirsch's *Scriptores Rerum Prussicarum*, IV, 728–9. Edward's marriage was 'publicly announced' in France by 10 October. See *Cal. Of Milanese State Papers*, I, 114.

67. Fabyan's remark (p. 684) that Edward immediately repented of his hot passion and would have repudiated his wife if he could, appears to be without the least foundation. Cf. J. Calmette, *Louis XI et l'Angleterre*, p. 61, n. 3.

68. See Warkworth, *Chronicle*, p. 3. Cf. Waurin (Dupont), *Chronique*, II, p. 326, note, where is printed Wenlock's view of the marriage. Cf. *Cal. Milanese State Papers*, I, 113; *Cal. Venetian State Papers*, I, 114, in which latter authority it is stated that the peers summoned to the Council at Reading held consultations among themselves in an attempt at finding means to annul the marriage.

69. Rymer, XI, 533; *Cal. Pat. Rolls*, I, 327, 329. The papal bull confirming Neville's election did not reach England until the following summer. It was published in York Cathedral on 4 June 1465. Drake, *Eboracum*, p. 444; Scofield, I, 354.

### 3 *The Coronation of Elizabeth*

1. William of Worcester, 500. Cf. *History of Croy. Cont.*, 551. See also Landsdown MS. 285; fol. 2; *Archaeologia*, XXIX, 133.

2. There is no evidence to prove that Warwick was actually in France demanding the hand of Bona of Savoy at the time Edward's marriage was announced. Cf. Lingard, IV, 161–2, n. 3. Shakespeare (*Henry VI*, Part 3, Act III, Sc. 3) seems chiefly responsible for the general belief in this story.

3. As no other embassy from Castile seems to have come to England before Edward's marriage, this must have been the one that offered him Isabella's hand. Cf. Scofield, I, 320, n. 2; A. F. Pollard, *Historical Essays*, 232–3, n. 1.

4. *Harl. MS.* 433, fol. 235b. See also H. Ellis, Original Letters, series II, I, 152; Gairdner, *Letters and Papers Illustrative of the Reigns of Richard III and Henry VII*, I, xxii, 32.

5. Cf. Philippe Erlanger, *Marguerite d'Anjou*, p. 242: 'A cela pres, l'harmonie regnait. Un femme destruisit tout.'

6. Cf. L. Stratford, *Edward IV*, p. 96.

7. For a list of Edward IV's children by Elizabeth Woodville, see Appendix 3. See also *Notes and Queries*, vol. 153, p. 382.

8. *Edward IV*, p. 96.

9. See chapter 7.

10. Cf. *Cal. Milanese State Papers*, I, 131.

11. J. T. Gilbert, *History of the Viceroys of Ireland*, pp. 386–7.

12. Ramsay, II, 334, n. 3; R. J. Mitchell, *John Tiptoft*, p. 117.

13. *Cal. Pat. Rolls*, I, 294, 437; *Warrants for Issues*, 5 Edward IV, 18 May; R. J. Mitchell, *op. cit.*, pp. 118–21.

14. See the account by Desmond's grandson in the introduction to the 'Carew MSS. 1575–88', pp. cv–cviii, published in the *Cal. Of State Papers*; also the version in the *Book of Howth*, published in the *Calendar of the Carew MS.*, pp. 186–7. Cf. *Letters and Papers Illustrative of the Reigns of Richard III and Henry VII*, I, 68, 73. Cf. also S. Hayman and J. Graves, *Unpublished Geraldine Documents*, I, 12; M. F. Cusack, *History of the Irish Nation*, p. 608; Walter Bensemann, *Warwick, der Konigmacher*, p. 120; Vespasiano da Bistici, *Lives of Illustrious Men of the Fifteenth Century*, p. 337; H. F. Berry, *Statute Rolls of the Parliament of Ireland, 1–12 Edw. IV*, p. vi; Agnes Conway, *Henry VII's Relations with Scotland and Ireland*, p. 44, n. 1; Eleanor Hull, *History of Ireland*, pp. 270–1. G. H. Orpen disputes the authenticity of this episode in *The English Historical Review*, XXX, 242–3. For an account of Desmond's life see *Dict. Nat. Biog.*, VII, 147–8; E. Hull, *History of Ireland*, pp. 269–71.

15. G. E. C., (New Series), IV, 248, n.b.

16. Cf. Worcester, p. 513; *Annals of the Four Masters*, IV, 1051–3; Ramsay, II, 334.

17. This child received the name of Edward, and later became Earl of Worcester. Dugdale, II, 41. Cf. G. E. C., (Old Series), VII, 402–3; Scofield, I, 438; R. J. Mitchell, *John Tiptoft*, p. 125.

18. *Issue Rolls, Easter 9 Edw. IV*, 8 May.

19. Oman, *Political History*, IV, 424. For a list of the queen's brothers and sisters, see Appendix 3.

20. Warkworth, *Chronicle*, pp. 3–4: '[The Earl of Warwick] took to him in fee as many knights … as he may be strong; and King Edward did that he might to feeble the earl's power.' Cf. Nat. Library, Paris, F. ital. 1649, fol. 168. See also J. Kirk, *Charles the Bold*, I, 418.

21. William of Worcester, p. 500; Ramsay, II, 320; Oman, *Political History*, IV, 424; Stratford, p. 97; Scofield, I, 397. G. E. C. (New Series), I, 250; Doyle, *Official Baronage*, I, 79. The marriage was celebrated in October 1464. See G. E. C., *Complete Peerage*, I, 250 and n.b.; *Paston Letters* (ed. J. Gairdner), II, 257. Their daughter Margaret married John de la Pole, Earl of Lincoln. See G. E. C. (New Series), VII, 689.

22. Cf. P. Erlanger, *Marguerite d'Anjou*, p. 244: 'Alors se dechaina une "ruee vers l'or" dont l'histoire offre peu d'equivalents.' Cf. also the attempt made by Elizabeth's brother, Anthony, Lord Scales, in July 1465 to obtain possession of Caister and the lordship of Cotton from Sir John Paston. *Paston Letters* (ed. J. Gairdner), II, 214, and introduction, III, cclvii.

23. Privy Seals.

24. Warrants for Issues, 4 Edw. IV, 8 December; Will. of Worcester, 503; *Cal. Pat. Rolls*, I, 430, 433, 445, 480, 525.

25. Warrant for Issues, 4 Edw. IV, 28 December.

26. L. P. Gachard, *Itinéraire de Phillipe le Bon*, p. 96; Scofield, I, 372.

27. On her mother's side Elizabeth could trace her descent as far back as Charlemagne. See Pedigree in Appendix 3.

28. J. Du Clercq, *Memoires*, liv. V, ch. XVIII, p. 374. French Roll 4 Edw. IV, m. 7, 8 October. Jacques de Luxembourg was the youngest of Jacquetta's three brothers. That Edward was especially keen at all times to lay stress on Elizabeth's ancestry is further illustrated by the fact that in 1474 in a pageant arranged at Coventry for the reception of the Prince of Wales one of the three kings of Cologne was made to proclaim that Elizabeth was descended from the Magi. *Coventry Leet Book*, Part II, p. 393. Cf. *Notes and Queries*, XI, Series II, 449; Armstrong, *Richard III*, p. 132, n. 8. The House of St Pol was also connected with that of Plantagenet in that Beatrice, the second daughter of Henry III, King of England, had, in 1529, married John (II) of Britanny, Earl of Richmond. Their daughter Mary married in 1292 Guy (IV), Comite de St Pol, of whom Elizabeth's mother, Jacquetta, was a direct descendant. See G. E. C. (Old Series), VI, 208, 352–3; Anselme, *Histoire Genealogique et Chronologique de la Maison Royale de France*, I, 448–9. See also pedigree in Appendix 3. Cf. also H. M. Lane, *Royal Daughters of*

*England*, I, 121. Jacquetta's great-uncle, Waleran (III) de Luxembourg, had married, in 1380, Maud, daughter of Joan (later the wife of Edward, 'the Black Prince') and her first husband, Sir Thomas de Holand, Earl of Kent. See G. E. C. (New Series), IV, 325; Lane, *op. cit.*, I, 218.

29. Teller, Rolls, Easter and Mich. 5 Edw. IV; Customs Accounts, Sandwich, 128/8; Warrants for Issues, 5 Edw. IV, 6 May and 6 Edw. IV, 30 September; Treasurer's Account, 5 Edw. IV, 1 March; Accounts and Memoranda of Sir John Howard, *Manners and Household Expenses of England*, p. 467.

30. J. Anstis, *The Order of the Garter*, I, 444 and note.

31. *Cal. Of Letter Books of the City of London: Letter Book in Temp. Edw. IV*, pp. 58–9. Cf. Scofield, I, 375.

32. Privy Seals; Scofield, I, 375.

33. Her three former husbands were: (i) John I (de Mowbray), Duke of Norfolk; (ii) Thomas Strangways; (iii) John, Viscount Beaumont. G. E. C., *Complete Peerage*, IX, 607. Cf. Ramsay, II, 321, n. 1; *Notes and Queries*, 2nd series, VIII, 329; Worcester, 501: 'Maritagium Diabolicum'.

34. Ralph Joslyn. See Great Chronicle, fol. 175; Nicolas, *Chronicle of London*, p. 143.

35. *The London Bridge Masters' Accounts*, 1460–84, fols 94–5, at the City of London Record Office, the Guildhall.

36. See Mary A. S. Hickmore, 'A Royal Pageant', published in the *Tenth Annual Report of the Friends of Canterbury Cathedral*, pp. 51–4.

37. Whit Sunday was in 1465 on 2 June. Cf. J. E. W. Wallis, *English Regnal Years and Titles*, p. 34.

38. Worcester, pp. 501–3; *Three Fifteenth-Century Chronicles*, p. 80; *Chronicle of John Stone*, p. 92; Stow, *Annals*, p. 419; R. Sharpe, *London and the Kingdom*, I, 307; London Journal, 7, ff. 97B and 99b; Nicolas, *Chronicle of London*, p. 143; Great Chronicle, fol. 175.

39. This manuscript was, in 1874, in the possession of Lord Mostyn of Mostyn Hall. (See *Historical Manuscripts Commission, Appendix to 4th Report*, p. 359, No. 226.) It is now in the possession of George Smith, Esq., of Great Bedwyn, Wilts, who has published this invaluable discovery in *The Coronation of Elizabeth Woodville*.

40. Possibly a form of *cropiers*, Anglo-Norman word signifying the housings on a horse's back.

41. There is a magnificent portrait of Elizabeth in her coronation robes in the Illuminated Book of the Fraternity of Our Lady's Assumption in the possession of the Worshipful Company of Skinners. This portrait has been reproduced in colour by John James Lambert, *Records of the Skinners of London, Edward I to James I*, p. 82. See Appendix 1.

42. George Norwych. See *Dict. Nat. Biog.*, XIV, 675; Browne Willis, *History of the Mitred Parliamentary Abbies*, I, 206.

43. Wine used at dessert. The 'void' was the dessert or parting-cup served at the end of a banquet. See Kingsford, *English Historical Literature*, 384, n. 5. Cf. 'The coronation of Anne Boleyn' in Arber's *English Garner*, II, 50. Cf. Philip W. Sergeant, *Anne Boleyn*, p. 167, note.

44. G. Smith, *Coronation*, p. 19.

45. Plancher, *Histoire de Bourgogne*, IV, p. 323. There seems no evidence to support the declaration that these Flemish knights constituted an armed band of mercenaries, ready to aid in enforcing obedience, should the citizens refuse to recognise Elizabeth as queen. The safe conduct issued to Jacques du Luxembourg as early as 8 October (1464) granted him permission to bring with him 100 persons of any degree and any nationality except French. Cf. Scofield, *Edward IV*, I, 372, n. 2

46. Warrants for Issues, 5 Edw. IV, 16 and 20 June.

47. Worcester, pp. 501–3; Du Clercq, liv. V, ch. XVIII, pp. 374–5. As early as March the king had been buying horses, saddles and other tournament necessities. John Wode spent £33 10s for 'stuff' for the jousts to be held on the Monday following the queen's coronation. Wode's purchases included 200 spears, and fifty tilting lances. See Writs of Privy Seal, file 802, no. 1630; Warrants for Issues, 5 Edw. IV, 24 May. Cf. Wardrobe Accounts, 2–5 Edw. IV (Exchequer L.T.R.) roll 6, m. 55–6; Scofield, I, 377.

48. George Smith, *The Coronation of Elizabeth Woodville*, p. 8.

49. The house stood in Knightrider Street, near St Paul's. Stow, *Survey of London*, I, 247–8. Cf H. A. Harben, *Dictionary of London*, p. 452; C. L. Kingsford, *The English Historical Review*, XXXIX, p. 277.

50. *Cal. Pat. Rolls*, I, 463.

51. Account Books of the Receiver-General of Queen Elizabeth, 6–7 Edw. IV; Miscellaneous Books, Exchequer T.R. no. 207. Cf. Scofield, I, 377–8.

## 4 *The Birth of Princess Elizabeth & the Disaffection of Warwick*

1. Waurin (Dupont), II, 330; Ramsay, II, 314.
2. Worcester, p. 505; Ramsay, II, 320.
3. Stow, *Annals*, p. 419; *Chronicle of John Stone*, p. 93.
4. *Chronicle of John Stone*, p. 93.
5. *Chronicle of John Stone*, pp. 93–4; *Three Fifteenth-Century Chronicles*, p. 80; Warkworth, p. 5 and notes pp. 40–3; Devon, *Issues*, p. 490. Cf. Du Clercq, liv. V, ch. XLIX, pp. 55–6.
6. Great Chronicle, fol. 175 *verso*; *Add. MS.* 6113, FOL. 48B; *Three Fifteenth-Century Chronicles*, p. 80; Nicolas, *Chronicle of London*, p. 143; J. Anstis, *Order of the Garter*, II, 79 and note; Stow, *Annals*, p. 419; *Gentleman's Magazine*, January 1831, CI, pt I, p. 24; *Ibid.*, September 1832, p. 200; *Archaeologia*, XXVI, 277, n. 3. N. H. Nicolas, *Privy Purse Expenses*, p. xxxi, n. 1, and Gilbert West in *Notes and Queries*, vol. 153, p. 382, give the date as 1465. However, Gabriel Tetzel, who has handed down to us a detailed description of the churching of the queen, had, in February 1466, just arrived in England. See *Des Bohmischen Herrn Leo's Von Rozmital Ritter-, Hof- und Pilger-Reise durch die Abenlande: Beschreiben durch Gabriel Tetzel von Nurnberg*, printed in vol. VII of the *Bibliothek des Literarischen Vereins in Stuttgart*. Cf. also Mrs Henry Cust, *Gentlemen Errant*, p. 35; *The Athenaeum* for 16 November 1844. Furthermore, the Letters of Safe Conduct for Leo von Rozmital and his companion were issued by Edward IV were issued by Edward IV on 26 February 'Anno Regni nostri quinto' (1466). These letters are printed in *Des Bohmischen Hern Leo, etc.*, pp. 42–3. All further doubt on this point would appear to be removed on consulting *Hist. Cont. Croyland*, p. 551, which reads: 'Elizabetha nata 1465, secundum Ecclesia Anglicanae, 1466 Ecclesia vero Romanae, Mense Februarii.'
7. Fabyan, p. 655.
8. Exchequer T.R., Council and Privy Seal, file 89, m. 49 (19 January).
9. Fabyan 655; Hearne's 'Fragment', p. 295; Kingsford's *London Chronicle*, p. 179; Worcester, p. 505; *Three Fifteenth-Century chronicles*, p. 181; *Hist. Croy. Cont.*, p. 551; *Harl. Ms.* 543, f. 130; *Add. MS.* 6113, f. 84b.
10. This ceremony must have taken place sometime after 20 March, as on that date Edward IV issued letters summoning Tetzel and his companions to Westminster Palace. See *Des Bohmischen Hern Leo, etc.*, p. 44. Cf. Mrs H Cust, *loc. cit.*, p. 35. Cf. also *The Athenaeum* for 16 November 1844.
11. Many uncomplimentary remarks have been made with regard to Elizabeth's attitude at this banquet (cf. Scofield, I, 398). The reader must, however, bear in mind that the silence at English banquets was proverbial (see Mrs Henry Cust, Gentlemen *Errant*, p. 494, n. 6). Furthermore, it would seem to have been the custom for noble ladies to sit at the queen's feet during a banquet, since at the coronation banquet of Elizabeth's daughter, Elizabeth of York, the Countesses of Oxford and Rivers knelt on each side of her (*Lelandi Coll.*, IV, 226). It seems highly probable that the attitude of Elizabeth was quite correct, but that on this occasion Tetzel was purposely given a wrong impression by Warwick and others who were jealous of Elizabeth, and of her sudden rise to fame.
12. *Des Bohmischen Herrn Leo's von Rozmital Reise*, etc., pp. 155–7. Cf. Mrs Henry Cust, *Gentlemen Errant*, pp. 36–9; Scofield, I, 395–6.
13. William of Worcester, pp. 505–6; G. E. C. (New Series), II, 390; Doyle, *Official Baronage*, I, 256. See also Appendix 3.
14. *Cal. Pat. Rolls*, II, 25; G. E. C. (New Series), V, 138; Doyle, II, 282. Cf. Ramsay, II, 321, n. 4.
15. Williams of Worcester, p. 506. His father had deserted from the Lancastrian ranks at Northampton and was created Earl of Kent on 30 May 1465. See G. E. C., *Complete Peerage* (Old Series), VII, 274. Cf. Baker, II, 166; Oman, *Political History*, IV, 424; Stratford, *Edward IV*, 97.
16. Worcester, p. 506; G. E. C. (Old Series), VI, 214; Doyle, III, 17. Lord Herbert's daughter was betrothed to Viscount Lisle at the same time that Mary Woodville was betrothed to Lord Dunster. Household Accounts, 6–7 Edw. IV, Accounts, etc. (Exchequer K.R.), bundle 412, no. 2. Warwick had a claim to the title of Lord Mohun of Dunster, as heir of Salisbury. Cf. Ramsay, II, 321, n. 6.

17. *Harlian Society, Visitation of Shropshire in 1623*, p. 75. Cf. Dugdale, II, 231; G. Smith, *Coronation of Elizabeth Wydeville*, p. 52.

18. Great Chronicle, fol. 175; Ramsay, II, 321 and note 5; Doyle, III, 142.

19. Treasurer's Account. Warrants for Issues, 5 Edw. IV, 1 March; *Cal. Pat. Rolls*, I, 516. See also Household Accounts, etc. (Exchequer K.R.), bundle 411, no. 15. Cf. Doyle, III, 142; Scofield, I, 398 and n. 1.

20. *Foedera*, XI, 581; Waurin (Dupont), II, 331; Ramsay, II, 333; L. W. Vernon Harcourt, *His Grace the Steward*, pp. 392, 407–11.

21. Cf. William of Worcester, p. 506; *Ad Secretam displiceniam comitis Warwici et Magnatum Angliae*.

22. William of Worcester, p. 507; G. E. C., *Complete Peerage*, IV, 418; Stratford, *Edward IV*, p. 105.

23. William of Worcester, p. 507; Ramsay, II, 322, and n. 1; Scofield, I, 397.

24. Hall, p. 265.

25. See Stow, *Annals*, p. 421. Six oxen were served at a single breakfast in his house, and anyone who had an acquaintance among his servants was at liberty to take away as much as he could carry on his dagger. Cf. C. L. Scofield, *Edward IV*, I, 399.

26. Cf. Great Chronicle, fol. 174 *verso*; *Cont. Croyland*, p. 551.

27. See Scofield, I, 400.

28. Waurin (Dupont), II, 333–4. Cf. Oman's *Warwick the Kingmaker*, p. 169.

29. Waurin (Dupont), II, 333–4. Cf. Bensemann, *Warwick*, p. 112; Armstrong, *Usurpation of Richard III*, p. 134, n. 14.

30. Cf. Lord Lytton's version in his *Last of the Barons*, Book IV, ch. 2.

31. For a description of Warwick's embassy in France see J. Calmette, *Louis XI et l'Angleterre*, pp. 83–7.

32. Cf. *Excerpta Historica*, pp. 173 and 214.

33. For a description of this tournament see *Excerpta Historica*, pp. 171–212; C. L. Scofield, *Edward IV*, I, 414–20; W. H. Black, *Historical Illustrations of the Reign of Edward IV*, pp. 2–44. Cf. Great Chronicle, fols 176–176 *verso*.

34. The queen's uncle, Jacques de Luxembourg, was actually one of the Burgundian envoys, and had already visited the English Court in that capacity in March 1465. Rymer, *Foedera*, XI, 540; *Cal. Pat. Rolls*, I, 439; Du Clercq, *Memoires*, liv. V, ch. XXIII, 400; Scofield, I, 373. Cf. J. Kirk, *Charles the Bold*, I, 414.

35. Chastellain, *Chronique*, V, 311–12. Cf. J. Calmette, *Louis XI et l'Angleterre*, p. 75. As early as January 1467, Earl Rivers, Elizabeth's father, had headed an English embassy to the Burgundian Court. See Rymer, XI, 576. Cf. *Excerpta Historica*, p. 223, n. 6.

36. See Scofield, I, 419, n. 3.

37. *Excerpta Historica*, p. 213; Olivier de la Marche, *Memoires*, pp. 493–4.

38. *Excerpta Historica*, p. 214; Olivier de la Marche, *Memoires*, pp. 493–4; R. Putnam, *Charles the Bold*, p. 160.

39. Haynin, II, 193; Chastellain, V, 227; Ramsay, II, 323.

40. *Chronicle of John Stone*, pp. 99–100; Waurin (Dupont), II, 344, n. 3; Scofield, I, 425.

41. *Rot. Parl.*, V, 571; Waurin (Dupont), II, 344; Stow, *Annals*, p. 419.

42. Cf. Great Chronicle, fol. 174 *verso*: 'And much hert brenning was evyr aftyr atwene the sayd Erle and the Quenys blood soo long as he lyvid.'

## 5 Elizabeth & the Burgundian Alliance

1. Waurin (Dupont), II, 348.

2. Privy Seals, Edw. IV. Worcester, p. 510; Waurin (Dupont), II, 344–8; Haynin, I, 200. Edward was at Windsor from 6 July to 14 August. Cf. Ramsay, II, 326, n. 5.

3. Waurin (Dupont), II, 347. Cf. Brugière de Barante, II, 285.

4. Household Accounts, 6 and 7 Edw. IV.

5. Worcester, p. 510; *Paston Letters*, VI, 107. Cf. *Gentleman's Magazine* for September 1832, p. 200; J. Tighe and J. E. Davis, *Annals of Windsor*, I, 385; H. M. Lane, *Royal Daughters of England*, I, 311.

6. Household Accounts 6 and 7 Edw. IV. Mention is made in the Household Accounts of the payment of £22 18s to one Robert Chamberlain for conducting the French ambassadors to Windsor.

7. Rymer, *Foedera*, XI, 631; Green, *Lives of the Princesses of England*, II, 396, 403, n.; Scofield, I, 428–9.

8. Worcester, p. 510; Lingard, IV, 160; Oman, *Warwick the Kingmaker*, p. 173.

9. French Rolls, 7 Edw. IV, m. 5; Signed Bills, file 1499, no. 4207; Rymer, *Foedera*, XI, 590, 598. Cf. *Excerpta Historica*, p. 223 and n. 6; *Archaeologia*, XXVI, p. 272, n.d.; Scofield, I, 430 and n. 3.

10. Worcester, p. 511; Rymer, XI, 590; Chastellain, V, 312.

11. Clarence's mother was Isabel's great-aunt.

12. Worcester, p. 511; Waurin (Dupont), III, 192.

13. Worcester, p. 511; Waurin (Dupont), III, 193 (*Piece justificative*, VII); Oman, *Warwick*, p. 174; Scofield, I, 443.

14. This reconciliation took place about the middle of January 1468. Worcester, 512–3. Cf. Ramsay, II, 328, n. 3.

15. Hearne's 'Fragment', p. 296; *Cot. MS. Nero* c. IX; *Excerpta Historica*, p. 227.

16. Great Chronicle, fol. 177.

17. *Chronicle of John Stone*, p. 103.

18. Scofield, I, 456.

19. Haynin, II, 59; O. Cartellieri, *The Court of Burgundy*, 133.

20. For full details of the marriage see *Archaeologia*, XXXI, 327–38; *Excerpta Historica*, pp. 227–9; La Marche, III, 101–20; IV, 95–144; Haynin, II, 17–62; Waurin (Dupont), II, 368þ72; *Bulletins de la Com. Royale d'Histoire, Belgique*, Series I, V, 168–74; Gilliodts-van-Severen, *Inventaire des Archives de Bruges*, V, 565, *et seq.*, E. Munch, *Die Furstinnen des Hauses Burgund-Osterreich*, I, 10–36; Brugière de Barante, *Histoire des Ducs de Bourgogne*, II, 308–10.

21. Cornelius was a servant of Sir Robert Whitingham, one of Margaret of Anjou's companions in exile. Cf. Scofield, I, 454.

22. Worcester, p. 514.

23. Gregory, p. 237.

24. Sir Thomas Cooke had been Lord Mayor of London in 1462–3, and was created a Knight of the Bath at Queen Elizabeth's coronation. See Great Chronicle, fols 171 and 172 *verso*; Stow, *Survey of London* (ed. Strype), II, Book V, p. 122. Cf. *Biographia Britannica*, IV, 194.

25. Great Chronicle, fol. 177; *MS. Cott. Vitellius* A., XVI, fol. 179' Gregory, p. 236; Fabyan, p. 656; Holinshed, p. 287; Worcester, pp. 515–16.

26. Great Chronicle, fol. 177. Cooke had united with sixty-two other wealthy Londoners in giving a bond for £10,000 to the Duke of Burgundy's officials, thus helping to make possible the marriage of this princess and Charles the Bold. Cf. Scofield, I, 453.

27. Great Chronicle, fol. 178 *verso*; *Cal. Pat. Rolls*, II, 103. Cf. Worcester, p. 515.

28. E. Foss, *Judges of England*, IV, 443.

29. Worcester, p. 516.

30. Following the failure of this small rising, Harlech Castle, which had till then held out against the Yorkists, surrendered to Lord Herbert on 14 August.

31. B. B. Orridge, *Citizens of London*, p. 27. Cooke's wife was the adughter and heiress of Philip Malpas. See also B. B. Orridge, Illustrations *of Jack Cade's Rebellion*, pp. 1–23. Cf. Scofield, I, 459, n. 4.

32. Sir John Fogge was connected with the Woodvilles by marriage, in that he had married a first cousins of Elizabeth's, Alice Haute, daughter of Sir William Haute and Joan Woodville, Elizabeth's aunt. See pedigree in Appendix 3. Cf. *Archaeologia Cantiana*, XXXVII, 120.

33. See Great Chronicle, fol. 177 *verso*; Worcester, p. 515, B. B. Orridge, *Citizens of London*, p. 27; Orridge, *Illustrations of Jack Cade's Rebellion*, pp. 11–13.

34. Fabyan, p. 656; C. L. Kingsford, *London Chronicle*, p. 179; Gairdner, *Collections of a Citizen of London* (Gregory), pp. xxxii–v and 236–7; Warkworth, p. 5; Scofield, I, 460.

35. Great Chronicle, fol. 180 *verso*; Worcester, p. 515; Fuller, *Worthies*, II, 207–8.

36. *Cal. Pat. Rolls*, II, 98.

37. London Journal 7, fol. 182.

38. William Prynne, *Aurum Reginae*, pp. 68–104; Great Chronicle, fol. 181; Stow, *Annals*, p. 420; Stratford, p. 124; Scofield, I, 461.

39. Fabyan (ed. Ellis), pp. 656–7; Kingsford, *London Chronicle*, p. 179. Among Exchequer Miscellanea 8/27 are some enrolled writs for levying the 'Queen-Gold', ranging from 5 to

20 Edw. IV. It would appear, therefore, that Cooke was not the only victim of Elizabeth's pertinacious clinging to her rights as queen. Cf. B. B. Orridge, *The Citizens of London and their Rulers*, pp. 26–7, and *Biographia Britannica*, iv, p. 94. For a full account of the many tributes to Queen-Gold paid to Elizabeth, see William Prynne, *Aurum Reginae*, pp. 68–104.

40. Great Chronicle, fol. 180 *verso*; Stow, *Annals*, p. 420; Gairdner, *Collections of a Citizen of London* (Gregory), pp. xxxiii–xxxv; Hall's *Chronicle*, p. 369; Gairdner, *Richard III*, pp. 98–9. Cf. Holinshed (ed. Hooker), III, 670. Evidence that this case was notorious is clearly shown from the reference made to it by the Duke of Buckingham prior to the accession of Richard III. See More (ed. Lumby), *Richard III*, P. 68.

41. Already in January (1468), evidence of the great unpopularity of the Woodvilles was forthcoming when a band of men had raided the Kentish estate (the Mote, Maidstone) of Earl Rivers, killing his deer and breaking down his fences, the Mote itself being saved from pilalge only by the flight of the servants with the valuables. Waurin (Dupont), III, 193; Ramsay, II, 328; Oman, *Political History*, IV, 429; Stratford, p. 119; Scofield, I, 435.

42. Baker, MS., XLII, 160; C. H. Cooper, *Annals of Cambridge*, I, 216; W. J. Searle, *Queens' College*, p. 72; J. H. Grey, *Queens' College*, p. 29.

43. The first evidence of her interest in the college is provided by a licence in mortmain dated 25 March 1465, in which the college is said 'to exist by virtue of the patronage of Elizabeth, Queen of England, our most dear consort'. R. Willis, *The Architectural History of the University of Cambridge*, I, LXV. The first Statutes 'for the founding and establishing of the college' were given by letters patent to Queen Elizabeth on 10 March 1475. *Cal. Pat. Rolls*, I, 495; C. H. Cooper, *Annals of Cambridge*, p. 216; W. J. Searle, *Queens' College*, p. 72; J. H. Grey, *Queens' College*, p. 12, 31; Scofield, II, 439.

## 6 The Rebellion of 1469

1. Waurin (Dupont), II, 348.

2. *Paston Letters*, V, 28.

3. *Ibid.*, V, 30; Francis Blomefield, *Norfolk*, III, 167. Edward, as can be seen from the dates of his Privy Seals, was at Windsor on 29 May and at Norwich on 19 June, at Walsingham on the 21st and 22nd, and at Lynn on the 26th/

4. See *Dict. Nat. Biog.*, XVI, 1319.

5. Oman, *Warwick*, p. 183; Ramsay, II, 339, n. 2.

6. *Harl. Ms.*, 543. Cf. Lingard, IV, 164. See also J. O. Halliwell's *Notes to Warkworth*, pp. 46–51; Cf. *Cal. Milanese State Papers*, I, 131; E. C. Lodge and G. A. Thornton, *English Constitutional Documents*, p. 87.

7. *Three Fifteenth-Century Chronicles*, p. 183. Montagu had been created Earl of Northumberland on 27 May 1464. *Cal. Pat. Rolls*, I, 332; G. E. C. (New Series), IX, 91.

8. Oman, *Warwick*, p. 184.

9. Sir John Conyers's son had married Warwicks' first cousin, Alice, daughter of William (Neville), Lord Fauconberg and Earl of Kent. G. E. C. (New Series), V, 282, 286; (Old Series), VIII, 114. Ramsay (II, 338) is mistaken in stating that Sir John Conyers himself was married to Warwick's cousin. This is clearly impossible, as Sir John married Margery, daughter of Sir Philip Darcy. She died in April 1469. See G. E. C. (New Series), IV, 67. Their son John, who was slain at Edgecote (Warkworth, p. 7) was certainly married to Alice before 1463. See G. E. C. (New Series), V, 286.

10. London Journal 7, fol. 195.

11. *Cont. Croyland*, 553; Lingard, IV, 165.

12. Warrants for Issues, 9 Edw. IV, 30 June; *Cal. Pat. Rolls*, II, 163.

13. *Paston Letters*, V, 28–33, 35; *Hist. Croy. Cont.*, p. 542; Warkworth, p. 25.

14. *Chronicle of John Stone*, pp. 109–11; Scofield, I, 494.

15. *Paston Letters*, V, 35–6; Oman, *Warwick*, p. 184; Scofield, I, 493.

16. Warkworth, p. 6; Waurin (Dupont), II, 403; Dugdale, I, 307; Ramsay, II, 337; Oman, *Warwick*, p. 185; Scofield, I, 494.

17. Scofield, I, 495 and n. 1.

18. Vatican Library, *Archives Brevi*, arm. XXXI, no. 12, fols 09 and 110 *verso*. Cf. Rymer, *Foedera*, XI, 638. James Goldwell was, in 1469, the king's proctor at the Court of Rome. He was appointed Bishop of Norwich on 4 October 1472. *Cal. Pat. Rolls*, II, 125–6. Cf. *Chronicle of John Stone*, p. 118.

19. This manifesto has been published by J. O. Halliwell in his *Notes to Warkworth*, pp. 46–51, from Ashmole MS. 1160. See also E. C. Lodge and G. A. Thornton, *English Constitutional Documents*, p. 87.

20. Warwick's great popularity in Kent was the result of his exploits as Captain of the Sea in 1458. Cf. *Dict. Nat. Biog.*, XIV, 284.

21. Chastellain, V, 485, 486, 499; Commynes (Mandrot), I, 217; London Journal 7, fol. 198; Sharpe, *London and the Kingdom*, I, 310; Oman, *Warwick*, p. 185; Scofield, I, 496.

22. Waurin (Dupont), II, 405; Oman, *Warwick*, p. 186.

23. Waurin (Dupont), II, 405.

24. See Chapter 6 note 27.

25. See Chapter 6 note 31.

26. For an account of this battle see Ramsay, II, 341–2; Oman, *Warwick*, p. 187.

27. Historians do not agree as to the exact scene of this remarkable incident. Ramsay (II, 343) thinks that it was 'at Honiley or Olney, 3 miles west of Kenilworth'. Professor Oman (*Political History*, IV, 434) says 'Olney, Bucks, on the edge of Northamptonshire'. Laurence Stratford (*Edward IV*, pp. 145–7), who has made a special study of this question, considers that 'Olney, by Coventry, has the best claim'. Cf. *Cont. Croyland*, p. 551; *Gentleman's Magazine*, XII, 616, December 1839.

28. The king was probably captured during the night of 30 July. He had written a letter to the town of Coventry from Nottingham on 20 July. Coventry Leet Book, II, 345. The Privy Seals show that Edward was at Coventry on 2 August and, at Warwick Castle from 8 August to 13 August, and at Middleham on the 25th and 28th. Ramsay, II, 343; Stratford, *Edward IV*, PP. 145–7; Scofield, I, 497. Cf. Waurin (Dupont), III, 3.

29. Holinshed, Chronicles, III, 673. There appear to be no grounds for the ancient and seemingly erroneous supposition that the queen's father and brother were captured at Chepstow, and executed at Coventry. Holinshed is far more likely to be correct in giving Grafton, the principal manor of the Woodvilles, as the scene of their capture. Cf. also Brugière de Barante, II, 342; G. Baker, *Northamptonshire*, II, 164; *Gentleman's Magazine*, XII, 615, December 1839. J. O. Halliwell in *Archaeologia* (XXIX, 138) gives 20 September as the date of their execution: this would appear to be incorrect, since at that time Warwick was fully occupied in dealing with Humphrey Neville's insurrection. Cf. Scofield, I, 503.

30. *Paston Letters*, V, 29–30. Cf. R. H. Mason, *History of Norfolk*, pp. 95–96.

31. Roger Ree. See R. H. Mason, *History of Norfolk*, p. 534; cf. *Paston Letters*, V, 34, n. 3.

32. 18 July.

33. *Paston Letters*, v, 34.

34. Chamberlain's Accounts from Michaelmas 9th Edw. IV to the following Michaelmas. Cf. Henry Harrod in *Norfolk Archaeology*, V, 32–7.

35. *Hist. Croy. Cont.*, p. 542; Scofield, I, 493.

36. *Cal. Milanese State Papers*, I, 131–2; London Journal 7, fol. 198B; Scofield, I, 498.

37. See Chapter 6 note 26.

38. *Rot. Parl.*, VI, 232. Cf. Ramsay, II, 347 and n. 2; Oman, *Political History*, IV, 435. She was charged with having bewitched the king into marrying her daughter. The charge, which was preferred by one Thomas Wake, while the king was in captivity at Warwick, was quashed at a great council held on 19 January 1470. Cf. *Cal. Pat. Rolls*, 9 Edw. IV, pt. II, p. 190; Scofield, I, 498–9.

39. *Cal. Milanese State Papers*, I, 131–2l Scofield, I, 498.

40. London Journal 7, fol. 198B; Scofield, I, 498, n. 2.

41. On 2 August Edward signed at Coventry, on the 9th, 12th and 13th at Warwick, and on the 25th and 28th at Middleham. Ramsay, II, 343, n. 7. There is not the slightest doubt that Edward was Warwick's prisoner during this time. In the bill of attainder against Clarence in 1477 the duke is accused of 'jupartyng the Kyngs royall estate, persone and life in straite warde putting him thereby from all his libertie, after procryng grete commicions. *Rot. Parl.*, VI, 193. Cf. Waurin (Dupont), III, 4, note; Lingard, IV, 168, n. 1; Plancher, IV, cclxxv.

42. Waurin (Dupont), III, 5 & 6, n. 1, and 8, note. R Putnam, *Charles the Bold*, p. 266; Brudgiere de Barante, II, 343.

43. Ramsay II, 344. Sur Humphrey Neville was captured and executed at York on 29 September. Cf. Scofield, I, 503; *Dict. Nat. Biog.*, XIV, 262.

44. *Cont. Croyland*, pp. 551–2; Warkworth, p. 7. Cf. Waurin (Dupont), III, 5–6 and 9, n. 2. The

authorities on this period disagree as to whether Edward was liberated, or whether he escaped. L. Stratford (*Edward IV*, p. 137) refuses to commit himself; C. L. Scofield (I, 503) states quite definitely that Edward was liberated by Warwick and brought to London by the Archbishop of York. Reinhold Pauli, *Geschichte von England*, V, 386; Lingard, IV, 170, n.; Oman, *Warwick*, pp. 190–2; R. Francis, *Warwick*, pp. 139; Walter Bensemann, *Warwick der Konigmacher*, p. 129; J. F. Kirk, *Charles the Bold*, II, 19: share Miss Scofield's opinion. Contemporary writers are inclined to disagree with Miss Scofield. In France (*Cal. Milanese State Papers*, I, 133) it was reported that Edward had escaped from Warwick's hands while out hunting. Polydore Vergil (p. 124) also holds this view, which has been immortalised by Shakespeare in *Henry VI*, pt III, Act IV, sc. 5.

45. *Paston Letters*, V, 63–3. Cf. Scofield, I, 503, n. 5.

46. Writs of Privy Seal, file 830, no. 3025; Fabyan, p. 657; Hearne's 'Fragment', p. 301; Warkworth, p. 8; Ramsay, II, 347; Scofield, I, 506. Cf. Flenley, *Six Town Chronicles*, p. 163.

47. Eldest son of Warwick's brother John, Lord Montagu, Earl of Northumberland.

48. *Cal. Milanese State Papers*, I, 129; *Lords' Report, Appendix*, V, 377. The title was granted on 5 Janaury 1470. G. E. C. (New Series), *Complete Peerage*, II, 72; *ibid.*, IX, 93.

49. Cf. Oman, *Warwick*, p. 131; R. Francis, *Warwick*, p. 141l Stratford, pp. 140–1.

50. Letters of Luchino Dallaghiexia of Milan in *Cal. Milanese State Papers*, I, 129; Warrants for Issues, 9 Edw. IV. In anticipation of her delivery the yeomen of beds spent £53 18s for a feather bed with a bolster, cushions, and many ells of fustian, holland, cloth, crimson, damask, etc. Scofield, I, 482. Cf. *Gentleman's Magazine* for September 1832, p. 200.

## 7 Warwick's Fleeting Triumph

1. Waurin (Dupont), III, 12.

2. *Chronicle of Rebellion in Lincolnshire*, pp. 6–10; Hearne's 'Fragment', pp. 301–2; Waurin (Dupont), III, 14–15; Ramsay, II, 349; Oman, *Warwick*, p. 195; cf. Flenley, *Six Town Chronicles*, p. 164.

3. *Cal. Pat. Rolls*, II, 205; Rymer, XI, 654; Vernon Harcourt, *op. cit.*, 412; R. J. Mitchell, *John Tiptoft*, 129.

4. *Cal. Pat. Rolls*, II, 211; Scofield, I, 534.

5. Scofield, I, 522.

6. Apart from his cruelty, Worcester is famous for his scholarship and interest in learning, besides being a traveller of cultivated taste. *Dict. Nat. Biog.*, XIX, 893. Cf. C. H. Williams, *Cambridge Medieval History*, VIII, 439–40; R. J. Mitchell, *John Tiptoft*, 135 *et seq.*

7. *Rot. Parl.*, VI, 144; Rymer, XI, 652; Waurin (Dupont), III, 17. The confession of Sir Robert Welles is printed in *Excerpta Historica*, pp. 282, *et seq.* Professor Oman (*Warwick*, p. 198, and *Political History*, IV, 437) and also R. Francis (*Warwick*, pp. 144–5) suggest the possibility that Edward was tempted by his victory at Empingham to revenge himself on Warwick and Clarence, and therefore invented Welles's 'confession', by which act he made them appear responsible for an insurrection with which they really had nothing to do. It should, however, be noted that Warkworth (p. 8 and notes, pp. 51–9), who was never a friend of Edward's, believed the revolt to have been the work of Warwick and Clarence. Cf. *Cont. Croyland*, p. 553; Hearne's 'Fragment', p. 301; L. Stratford, *Edward IV*, p. 150; Scofield, I, 515–5.

8. J. Anstis, *Order of the Garter*, I, 353, n.a.

9. Plancher, *Histoire generale et particuliere de Bourgogne*, IV, 387, and cclxi *et seq.* Cf. Brugière de Barante, II, 348.

10. Waurin (Dupont), III, 28–9, n. 2. Cf. Haynin, II, 92.

11. Commynes (Mandrot), I, 200, and n. 2. Cf. Waurin (Dupont), III, 31; Brugière de Barante, II, 343.

12. Commynes (Mandrot), I, 200, n. 3. Plancher, *Histoire generale*, etc., IV, 388 and cclxi *et seq.*; Scofield, I, 520, n. 1. Cf. R. Putnam, *Charles the Bold*, p. 273.

13. *Chronicle of John Stone*, pp. 113–4.

14. *Ibid.*, p. 113.

15. Chastellain, V, 422. Cf. Scofield, I, 522.

16. For full details see 'The Manner and Guiding of the Earl of Warwick at Angers', in *Chronicles of the White Rose*, p. 229. Cf. Chastellain, V, 467–8; *Cal. Milanese State Papers*, I, 138–42. It would appear almost certain that this marriage actually took place some time in December 1470. See National library, Paris, F. fr. 20,865, fol. 500 *verso*, printed in Waurin

(Dupont), III, 45, note. Cf. also Monstrelet, *Nouvelles Chroniques*, III, 35; Lingard, IV, 177; J. Calmette, *Louis XI et l'Angleterre*, 125, n. 4. A dispensation for this marriage would appear to have been granted by Louis II d'Harcourt, the Patriarch of Jerusalem, on 28 November 1470. On about 13 December, the vicar-general of Bayeux blessed this union at Amboise. This is made perfectly clear in the document dealing with that priest's expenses which has been published by J. Calmette, *Louis XI, etc.*, pp. 319–20. The original is in the National Library, Paris; F. fr. 6759, fol. 144 *verso*. Cf. also Waurin (Dupont), III, 41; Commynes (Mandrot), I, 202, note; Plancher, IV, 389. Further proof is furnished by Fortescue's *The Governance of England* (ed. Charlse Plummer), Appendix B, 348–9, in which mention is made of 'Articles sentre fro the Prince, to therle of Warrewic his fadir in law, for to be shewed and consumed by hym to king Henry his fader ... an° M.cccc. LXX°'.

17. Oman, *Warwick*, p. 204; Putnam, p. 285; Francis, p. 148.
18. Commynes (Mandrot), I, 203; Waurin (Dupont), III, 113–4; Oman, *Warwick*, p. 204; Stratford, 161; Scofield, I, 560.
19. *Arrival*, p. 10; *Hist. Croy. Cont.*, p. 554; Scofield, I, 560.
20. Oman, *Warwick*, p. 204.
21. Commynes (Mandrot), I, 204, n. 2; Chastellain, *Oeuvres* (ed. Kervyn de Lettenhove), V, 469.
22. Lord Fitzhugh was married to Warwicks' sister, Alice. See G. E. C. (New Series), V, 429. Cf. *Dict. Nat. Biog.*, XIV, 282.
23. Warkworth, p. 9.
24. Warkworth, p. 10; Waurin (Dupont), III, 49, n. 2. Scofield, I, 536.
25. Charter Rolls, 8–10 Edw. IV, m. 1; Signed Bills, file 1501, no. 4330; *Cal. Pat. Rolls*, II, 206; Dugdale, I, 308; *Paston Letters*, V, 71.
26. Commynes (Mandrot), I, 205; Waurin (Dupont), III, 47, note; Chastellain, V, 501–2.
27. Hearne's 'Fragment', published in his edition of Sprott's *Chronica*, p. 306.
28. Chastellain, V, 502–4.
29. King's Lynn Corp. MSS., Hall Book II, fol. 284. Cf. Winifred I. Haward, 'Economic Aspects of the Wars of the Roses in East Anglia', *English Historical Review*, XLI, 179.
30. Warkworth, p. 12; Commynes (Mandrot), I, 206–8; Basin, *Histoire des regnes de Charles VII et de Louis XI*, II, 246; Plancher, *Histoire generale, etc.*, IV, 390; J. Lappenberg, *Urkundliche Geschichte des Hanischen Stahlhofes zu London*, pp. 51–2; Rugiere de Barante, II, 355.
31. Stratford, p. 166.
32. For a detailed account of Edward's reception by Louis de Gruthuyse see Armand de Behault de Dornon, *Bruges: sejour d'exil des rois d'Angleterre, Edward IV et Charles II*. Cf. also J. B. Van Praet, *Recherches sur Louis de Bruges*, p. 10. Gruthuyse was among those Burgundians who came over for the famous tournament in 1467, remaining behind for over a motnh after the departuer of the Bastard of Burgundy. Waurin (Dupont), II, 342, n. 1; Scofield, I, 420 and 427, n. 5.
33. Warkworth, 13. Cf. London Journal 7, fol. 223B; R. R. Sharpe, *London and the Kingdom*, III, 385.
34. London Journal 7, fols 223b–24; Stow, *Annals*, p. 422; R. R. Sharpe, *London and the Kingdom*, III, 385–6.
35. Great Chronicle, fol. 184 *verso*; *Cotton MS. Vitell*. XVI, fol. 129 *verso*; Chastellain, V, 487; Fabyan, pp. 658–9; *Paston Letters*, V, 85; C. L. Kingsford, *Chronicles of London*, p. 182.
36. R. R. Sharpe, *London and the Kingdom*, III, 386.
37. *Ibid*.
38. Great Chronicle, fol. 184 *verso*; Stow, *Annals*, p. 422.
39. R. R. Sharpe, *London and the Kingdom*, III, 386.
40. *Harl. MS.*, 543, fol. 172; London Journal 7, fols 223b–4; Stow, *Annals*, p. 422. See C. L. Scofield's article in *The English Historical Review*, XXIV, 90.
41. Writs of Privy Seal, file 838, n. 3417 (Ellis, *Original Letters*, Series II, vol. I, 140); Warrants for Issues, 49 Hen. VI, 30 October; Scofield, I, 546.
42. The ancient chroniclers disagree with regard to the date of Prince Edward's birth, but all doubt is now removed, not only by the document (*Cal. Pat. Rolls*, II, 365), which, quoted by Miss Scofield (I, 546, n. 3) mentions a grant made to the pricne of the issues of the duchy of Cornwall from Michaelmas to 10 Edw. IV till 2 November following 'on which day he was born', but also by two further documents quoted in *The Gentleman's Magazine* (a) for January 1831, p. 24, and (b) for September 1832, p. 200. (a) *Addit. MS.*, 6113, Fol. 59B. 'The second daye of Novembre was borne at Westminster in the seyntwary, my lorde the prince, the king

that tyme beinge out of the lande in the parties of Flaundres, Hollande and Zelande.' (b) 'D'n's Edwardus primogenitus filius Regis Edwardi iiij. Princeps Wallie, q$^i$ nat 9 fuit de aiarum d'ni 1470.' Cf. G. J. Nichols, *Grants of Edward V*, p. vi, note b. All doubt would now seem to have been finally removed.

43. R. Widmore, *History of Westminster Abbey*, p. 116.

44. Marjory Cobb had already attended the queen in this capacity, since on 15 April 1469 she had received a grant of £10 yearly from the issues of the County of Stafford. See *Cal. Pat. Rolls*, II, 154. She was still assisting the queen over six years later, for on 8 November 1475, six days after the birth of the Princess Anne, she was granted £10 yearly from the issues of the County of Devon. *Cal. Pat. Rolls*, II, 457.

45. *Add. MS.*, 4611, fol. 222. See also Ellis, *Original Letters*, 2nd Series, I, 140; *The Genealogist*, IV, 126–7.

46. See Browne Willis, *History of the Mitred Parliamentary Abbies*, I, 206–7; *Dict. Nat. Biog.*, XIII, 447.

47. Great Chronicle, fol. 186.

48. *MS. Vitell.* A. XVI, fol. 130 *verso*; Fabyan, pp. 659–60.

## 8 The Death of Warwick

1. *MS. Vitell.* A. XVI, fol. 130 *verso*; London Journal 7, fol. 224; Waurin (Dupont), III, 43; *Cont. Croyland*, p. 554; Warkworth, p. 11; Fabyan, p. 658; Stow, p. 423; Ramsay, II, 359.

2. Commynes (Mandrot), I, 220; Oman, *Warwick*, p. 208.

3. Great Chronicle, fol. 184 *verso*; Warkworth, p. 11; Sharpe, *London and the Kingdom*, III, 385.

4. On 2 January 1471. *Cal. Pat. Rolls*, II, 233; Scofield, I, 543.

5. Ellis, *Original Letters*, Series II, I, 139; Chastellain, *Oeuvres*, V, 494; Stratford, p. 176; Scofield, I, 543.

6. Commynes (Mandrot), I, 210; Oman, *Warwick*, p. 213; R. Francis, *Warwick*, p. 154.

7. *Arrivall*, p. 10; *Cont. Croyland*, p. 554; Waurin (Dupont), III, 114; Oman, *Warwick*, p. 213; Stratford, p. 176; Scofield, I, 560.

8. For the instructions given to this embassy see Waurin (Dupont), III, *Pieces justificatives*, VIII, 196–204.

9. A Treaty of Alliance between Louis XI and Prince Edward of Lancaster against Charles the Bold had been signed at Amboise on 28 November (1470). For the contents of this treaty see Plancher, *Histoire*, IV, *Preuves*, CCXCIII.

10. Waurin (Dupont), III, 55–6; Commynes (Lenglet), II, 197; Haynin, II, 97; Brugière de Barante, II, 373.

11. Van Praet, p. 10; Commynes (Mandrot), I, 215; Commynes (Lenglet), II, 197; Waurin (Dupont), III, 55; Scofield, I, 562.

12. Great Chronicle, fol. 187 *verso*; Commynes (Mandrot, I, 215; Planchet, IV, 391; Brugière de Barante, II, 373. Cf. *The Genealogist*, III, 65–8.

13. 14 March is given as the date of Edward's landing.

14. Henry Percy, the newly restored Earl of Nothumberland, although he did not actually join Edward, was held to have rendered 'notable good service' to the Yorkist cause by preventing Montagu from raising Yorkshire against the small invading force. Warkworth, p. 14; *Arrivall*, p. 6; *Dict. Nat. Biog.*, XV, 583; Stratford, pp. 178–80; Scofield, I, 570–2.

15. *Arrivall*, p. 3–5; Warkworth, pp. 13–4; *Hist. Croy. Cont.*, p. 554; Kingsford's *London Chronicle*, p. 183; Fabyan, p. 660; Waurin, III, 101–5; Oman, *Political History*, IV, 442. Cf. also *Cal. Milanese State Papers*, I, 153. The Lancastrian chroniclers (Fabyan, p. 660; Polydore Vergil, p. 516; Holinshed, p. 303) go so far as to say that Edward was compelled to swear on the Sacrament that he had no desire to be king again. Whereas Lingard (IV, 571–2), Professor Oman (*Warwick*, p. 218), and R. Francis (*Warwick*, p. 162) are inclined to believe this, neither Ramsay (II, 366) nor Scofield (I, 570) mentions this event, while both Pauli (*Geschichte*, V, 401, n. 1) and L. Stratford (*Edward IV*, p. 178) are of the opinion that this episode was a slander invented in later times.

16. Stow, *Annals*, 423. This would appear to be the only suitable explanation of Montagu's extraordinary inaction at this critical juncture. Cf. Lord Lytton, *The Last of the Barons*, Book XI, ch. 5; H. J. Swallow, *House of Neville*, 224.

17. Great Chronicle, fol. 188.

18. Waurin (Dupont), III, 111; *Archaeologia*, XXI, 115–7.

19. *Rot. Parl.*, VI, 477; *Foedera*, VIII, 165; *Paston Letters*, II, 243; Ramsay, II, 367. Cf. *Gentleman's Magazine*, XXII, 599, December 1844. As late as 30 March Clarence had written to Vernon in Warwick's favour. *Hist. MSS. Comm. 12th Report*, App. IV. Cf. Bensemann, *Warwick*, p. 153, n. 8.

20. *Arrivall*, p. 11. According to the Great Chronicle (fol. 189 *verso*) Clarence joined Edward on the night before the Battle of Barnet.

21. *Arrivall*, p. 11; Waurin, III, 114–5; Commynes (Mandrot), I, 217; Haynin, II, 126.

22. Warkworth, p. 15; Waurin (Dupont), III, 120.

23. See Foss, *Judges of England*, IV, 459; *Dict. Nat. Biog.*, XX, 57.

24. *Arrivall*, p. 17; Warkworth, p. 15; Waurin (Dupont), II, 96; Commynes (Mandrot), I, 216–7. Cf. Waurin, III, 120–4.

25. Great Chronicle, fol. 188 *verso*. Edward is said to have promised the archbishop a pardon provided he kept King Henry out of sanctuary. Warkworth, p. 26; Leland, *Collctanea*, II, 508. Cf. Lingard, IV, 185 note; Stratford, 184.

26. *Arrivall*, p. 17.

27. *Ibid.* Cf. Waurin (Dupont), III, 123; and *Political Poems and Songs*, II, 274: 'The kyng comfortid the quene and ladyes eke; his swete babis full tendurly did kys; the yong prynce he behelde and in his armys did bere. Thus his bale turynd hym to blis; aftur sorrow joy, the course of the world is. The sighte of his babies relesid parte of his woo; thus the wille of God in every thyng is doo.' See also C. L. Kingsford, *English History in Contemporary Poetry, Lancaster and York*, p. 43.

28. Holinshed, *Chronicle*, III, 311.

29. *Arrivall*, pp. 18–20; Fabyan, p. 661; Warkworth, p. 16; Waurin, III, 124–8. For plans and full accounts of this battle see Oman, *History of the Art of War in the Middle Ages*, II, 416–8, and plate xxxiii, p. 422; Ramsay, II, 370; A. J. K[empe] in *The Gentleman's Magazine*, XXII, 243–55, September 1844. Cf. also Richard Brooke, *Visits to Fields of Battle*, pp. 205–11. Cf. also the account of the battle in the letter written by Margaret, Duchess of Burgundy, to her mother-in-law, Isabella of Portugal, printed in Waurin (Dupont), III, *Pieces Justificatives*, X, 210–5. An old miniature representing this battle has been reproduced in *Archaeologia*, XXI, 14, pl. 1.

30. Great Chronicle, fol. 190.

31. Great Chronicle, fol. 190 *verso*. Warkworth, p. 17. Cf. Waurin (Dupont), III, 128 and 213; Haynin, II, 128.

32. *Constitutional History of England*, III, 228.

33. Cf. also H. J. Swallow, *De Nova Villa, or, The house of Nevill*; Oman, *Warwick the Kingmaker*, pp. 236–43; Walther Bensemann, *Richard Nevil, der Konigmacher*; R. Francis, *Warwick the Kingmaker.*

## 9 The Death of Henry VI & the Reception of Louis de Gruthuyse

1. Warkworth, p. 18; Waurin (Dupont), III, 129.

2. For a detailed account of this battle see the article by Canon William Bazeley in *Trans. Of Bristol and Gloucestershire Archaeological Society*, XXVI, 173–93. Cf. Richard Brooke, *Visits to Fields of Battle in England*, pp. 131–55; Oman, *History of the Art of War in the Middle Ages*, II, 419–22 and plate xxxiii.

3. There are many versions as to the exact way in which this unfortunate prince met his end. To judge, however, from the evidence of contemporary writers, it seems clear that he was 'taken, fleinge to the towne wards and slayne in the field'. *Arrivall*, p. 30. Cf. Commynes (Mandrot), I, 220: 'Et fur le prince de Galles tue sur le champ.' Cf. also *Croyland Cont.*, 555–6; *Three Fifteenth-Century Chronicles*, p. 184; *Chronicle of Tewkesbury* (Harl. MS. 545), fol. 132, dors.; *Chronicle of London*, p. 144; Commynes (Lenglet), I, 166; Waurin (Dupont), III, 139. Warkworth, never a friend to the Yorkists, merely states (p. 18) that 'ther was slayne in the felde, Prynce Edward whiche cryede for socoure to his brother-in-lawe the Duke of Clarence'. This is probably the most exact account. The Yorkist centre were pursuing their enemies townwards with Clarence in command; possibly the prince saw and appealed to him as he was cut down. This is well within the bounds of possibility, since Edward had placed Clarence beside him in the centre, as he was uncertain to what extent his brother could be trusted. Furthermore, in the letter written by the citizens of London to the Bastard of Fauconberg on 8 May 1471, the prince is reported as 'slain', and lower down as 'taken and slayn'. See London

# Notes

Journal 8, fols 5 *et seq*. Cf. *Archaeologia Cantiana*, XI, 359–64. The story that the prince was led before Edward IV, who hit him in the face with his gauntlet, and then had him murdered in his presence, first occurs in the chronicles of the next century (Great Chronicle, fol. 191 *verso*; Fabyan, p. 462; Holinshed, III, 688; Stow, p. 424; Polydore Vergil, p. 152), all strongly tinged with Lancastrian prejudice. Too much importance should not, therefore, be attached to them. Most of the greatest authorities on this period, with the important exception of Lingard (IV, 189, n. 1) are of the opinion that the prince was slain in the course of the battle. See Stubbs, III, 228; R. Pauli, V, 409, n. 2; Ramsay, II, 381 and n. 3; Oman, *Political History*, IV, 447; clements Markham, *Richard III*, p. 75 and 188–92; L. Stratford, p. 198, n. 1; Scofield, I, 587. Their opinion would appear to be confirmed by the fact that two days after the Battle of Tewkesbury, Clarence wrote to Henry Vernon, one of the squires of Edward IV's body, that 'Edward, late called prince ... with other estates, knights, squires and gentilmen, were slayn in playn bataill' (see *Hist. MSS. Comm. Report* 12, App. 4, p. 4). In *Archaeologia*, XXI, 11–23, and plate II (p. 14) there is a description of the battle, and a miniature from a manuscript in the Library at Ghent, depicting Prince Edward's death.

4. See Edward IV's letter to Henry Vernon, written from Worcester on 8 May, where he states that 'Margarete late called quene is in our handes'. See *Hist. MSS. Comm. Report* 12, App. 4, p. 5. Margaret remained in captivity for five years, being confined first in the Tower, then at Windsor, and finally at Wallingford Castle. According to Miss Strickland (*Lives of the Queens of England*, II, 308), the rigour of Margaret's imprisonment 'was ameliorated through the compassionate influence of Elizabeth Woodville'.

5. *Arrivall*, p. 34. Cf. Waurin (Dupont), III, 142. Wakworth (19–20) seems to have antedated the whole episode by one week.

6. *Arrivall*, p. 34.

7. Great Chronicle, fols 192–3; *Cont. Croyland*; 556; Waurin (Dupont), III, 143; Kingsford, *English Historical Literature*, p. 375; from Arundel MS. 28, fol. 25 *verso*.

8. *Arrivall*, p. 38; Waurin (Dupont), III, 144; Lingard, IV, 191; Stratford, p. 201; Scofield, I, 593.

9. For an account of Fauconberg's rising, see R. R. Sharpe, *London and the Kingdom*, I, 314–6; J. R. Scott in *Archaeologia Cantiana*, XI, 359–64. Cf. *Archaeologia*, XXI, 20–2, and plate IV, p. 14; *Dict. Nat. Biog.*, VI, 1104.

10. On 13 October 1472.

11. *Add. Ms.*, 6113, fol. 100b. Cf. *Archaeologia*, XXVI, 280; Kingsford, *English Historical Literature*, 382.

12. Edward IV pensioned Majory Cobb, midwife with £12 per annim, and Dr Serigo with £40. *Add. MS.* 4614, fols 340–1. Cf. *Cal. Pat. Rolls*, II, 154, 247; p. 124, n. 2. He also rewarded butcher Gould by granting him leave to load a royal ship, called the *Trinity of London*, with 'oxehides, ledde, talowe and all other merchandises except staple ware'. *Add. MS.* 4614, fols 222–3. Cf. also Ellis, *Original Letters*, Series II, vol. I, 140–2; *Genealogist*, IV, 126–7. Abbot Thomas Millyng, the queen's benefactor in sanctuary, was summoned to the King's Privy Council, nominated chancellor to the Prince of Wales, and, in 1474, elected to the bishopric of Hereford. See R. Widmore, *History of Westminster Abbey*, pp. 116–7; *Dict. Nat. Biog.*, XIII, 447; Browne Willis, *History of the Mitred Parliamentary Abbies*, I, 206.

13. *Cal. Pat. Rolls*, III, 133.

14. See *Archaeologia*, XLVII, 366, note a.

15. According to the official Yorkist account, Henry 'toke it to so great dispite, ire, and indignation, that of pure displeasure, and melancoly he dyed': *Arrival*, p. 38. (Cf. Waurin (Dupont), III, 144.) However, the general verdict of the time was that Henry had been quietly put out of the way. Most authorities agree that he was slain either by, or, as is more probable, in the presence of, Richard, Duke of Gloucester. See *MS. Cott. Vitell.* A XVI, fol. 133; Fabyan, p. 662; *Chronicles of London* (C. L. Kingsford), 185; Kingsford, *English Historical Literature*, p. 370 and n. 2, 374; Flenley, *Six Town Chronicles*, p. 168; Warkworth, p. 21; R. Pauli, *Geschichte*, V, 412–3; J. Gairdner, *Richard III*, p. 17; Clements Markham, *Richard III*, p. 290–4; M. E. Christie, *Henry VI*, p. 369; J. O. Halliwell, Introduction to *Warkworth*, pp. xi–xix; Philip Lindsay, *Richard III*, P. 158–60. For a discussion of authorities see Ramsay, III, 386, n. 3. See also Rawdon Brown, *Calendar of State Papers in the Archives and Collections of Venice*, I, 128; W. H. St John Hope, 'The Discovery of the Remains of Henry VI in St George's Chapel, Windsor', *Archaeologia*, LXII, pt. II, 533–542.

16. *Chronicle* (ed. Halliwell), p. 21.

17. Gloucester probably brought the death warrant from the king, and remained at the Tower to see that its contents were carried out. Shakespeare (*Henry VI*, pt 3, Act V, sc. vi) must once again be held responsible for the general belief that Gloucester himself was the murderer. Cf. Great Chronicle, fol. 193 *verso*; Clements Markham, *Richard III*, 290.

18. Cf. chapter 9 note 43.

19. *Rot. Parl.*, VI, 9; *Cal. Pat. Rolls*, II, 283; Signed Bills, file 1502, no. 4385; J. G. Nichols, *Grants of Edward V*, P. VII, and n.

20. *Paston Letters*, III, 17.

21. *Ibid.*

22. *Add. MS.* 6113, fol. 103B; Stow, *Annals*, p. 425.

23. Stow, *ibid.*; Kingsford, *English Historical Literature*, p. 379.

24. This quarrel had arisen from the fact that Clarence claimed the earldoms and the whole remaining estates of the Earl of Warwick through is wife Isabel Neville, and was determined to give up nothing to his brother with Anne, Warwick's second daughter, whom Richard intended to marry. Cf. Ramsay, II, 399; *Archaeologia*, XLVII, 409–27.

25. *Paston Letters*, V, 135–6.

26. *Paston Letters*, V, 137; Green, *Princesses of England*, III, 437; F. Madden in *Gentleman's Magazine*, (25 January) 1831; E. W. Brayley, *History and Antiquities of Westminster*, II, 104 and plate XIII; Nicolas, *Privy Purse Expenses*, p. xxii; Sandford, *Genealogical History*, p. 419; Ramsay, II, 469; Gilbert West in *Notes and Queries*, vol. 151, p. 382; Lane, *Royal Daughters of England*, I, 314.

27. G. E. C., *Complete Peerage*, II, 72.

28. Cf. Armand de Behault de Dornon, *op. cit.*, pp. 145–9.

29. C. L. Kingsford, *English Historical Literature in the Fifteenth Century: The Record of Bluemantle Pursuivant*, pp. 379–88.

30. See J. B. B. Roquefort, *Glossaire de la langue romane*, II, 148; *Marteaux: Jeu des petits palets*. This seems to imply that it was a game with balls,closely resembling marbles.

31. Nine-pins, made of ivory.

32. According to the belief of this and earlier periods, this was supposed to guard against the existence of poison in the cup. See Sir F. Madden in *Archaeologia*, XXVI, n. 4, p. 277.

33. A small or middle-sized horse.

34. *Archaeologia*, XXVI, 276–8.

35. Catherine, sister of Queen Elizabeth.

36. Cf. W. E. Mead's edition of the *Squyr of Love Degre*, p. 37, l. 841: 'Your blankettes shall be of fustyane, your shetes shall be of cloth of Rayne.'

37. 'A other of astate.'

38. It seems probably that one should read *congy* (leave) here instead of *cuppe*. See Sir Frederic Madden's note in *Archaeologia*, XXVI, 280.

39. 13 October. Cf. Van Praet, p. 14.

40. *Add. MS.* 6113, fol. 103b. See also *Archaeologia*, XXVI, 278–80; R. R. Tighe and J. E. Davis, *Annals of Windsor*, I, 367–71.

41. *Add. MS.* 6113, fol. 100b. Cf. *Archaeologia*, XXVI, 282–4.

42. *Rot. Parl.*, VI, 160; Scofield, II, 54.

43. *Sloane MS.* 3479. A full list of the Prince's Household is given by J. R. Scott in *Memorials of Scott of Scotts Hall*, 175. See also J. G. Nichols, *Grants of Edward V*, p. VII.

44. Rivers's appointment was sealed on 10 November. Signed Bills 1506, no. 4578; *Cal. Pat. Rolls*, II, 417. Cf. *Cal. Milanese State Papers*, I, 176; J. G. Nichols, *Grants of Edward V*, p. VII, n.

45. Lingard, IV, 221.

46. It is certain that Edward was resident at Shrewsbury sometime during 1473. This is to be seen in the account of the sequestrators of Alberbury in the archives of All Souls' College, and entitled: 'He sunt expense quas Will. Ap David (and three others) procuratores adminsitrationis sequestri fructuum et proventuum ecclesie de A. expenderunt circa ipsam adminsitraco'em A.D. M.ccc. LXX. III. "Item Will'us ap David, pro essendo apud Salop. Quum dominus Rex erat ibi"'. Cf. H. Owen and J. B. Blakeway, *History of Shrewsbury*, I, 230, n. 5.

47. Cf. L. W. Tanner in *Archaeologia*, LXXXIV, 5, n. 3, who points out that on this day the prince received the king a 'purple velvet gown and the Garter'.

48. According to the notes in *Add. MS.* 6113 already cited, Richard was born on 17 August 1472. This is, however, impossible, as Princess Margaret was born as late as 19 April 1472. In an old chronicle at Shrewsbury (Taylor's MS.) in the library of the Royal Free Grammar School for the year September 1472–September 1473 stands the following entry: 'This yeare the Duke of Yorke was borne in the Blacke frears within the towne of Shrewsbury, the which frears standethe under Saint Mary's churche in the sayde town estward.' This entry, coupled with the fact that the queen was certainly at Shrewsbury in August 1473, suggests that the prince was born on 17 August of *that* year. It would appear that the compiler of *Add. MS.* 6113, though correct as to the actual day, made a slight mistake in copying the year, when recording this prince's birth. See Gilbert West in *Notes and Queries*, vol. 153; pp. 381–2, and vol. 166, p. 69. See also the articles published in The Times of 1 December and 12 December 1933, the latter of which Mr W. Westley Manning published evidence of Chester Herald's receipt for money given to him by the Duke of Burgundy on his bringing news of Richard's birth. This receipt has been photographed and reproduced in *Archaeologia* LXXXIV, p. 5, plate 1, fig. 1. Since his receipt is dated 3 September 1473, this important piece of evidence, coupled with Mr Lawrence E. Tanner's recent discoveries, published in *Archaeologia*, LXXXV, 5 *et seq.*, would seem to offer conclusive proof that Miss Scofield, (II, 60) was perfectly justified in fixing 17 August 1473 as the date of this unfortunate prince's birth. Cf. Owen and Blakeway, *History of Shrewsbury*, I, 230; *Shropshier Archaeological Society Transactions*, 1st series, vol. 3, p. 247; T. Auden, *Shrewsbury*, III; cf. also Mancini, who states that at the time of Elizabeth his mother's flight to sanctuary, Richard was 'a boy of eight years'. Mancini (ed. Armstrong, *Usurpations of Richard III*, p. 97) made a slight miscalculation, sicne in June 1483, the prince was nearly ten years old.

49. See chapter 4.

50. Anne died soon after 26 August 1467. Cf. William of Worcester, p. 507; *Rot. Parl.*, VI, 216, 242; G. E. C., *Complete Peerage*, IV, 418.

51. This session lasted from 6 June to 18 July.

52. *Rot. Parl.*, VI, 104–9. Cecile Bonville was the daughter and heir of William Bonville (III) and Catherine, daughter of Richard Neville, Earl of Salisbury. Cf. G. E. C., IV, 418; Ramsay, II, 403.

53. *Rot. Parl.*, VI, 108. Cf. *Cal. Pat. Rolls*, II, 456.

54. *Rot. Parl.*, VI, 108. In the *Cal. Pat. Rolls* 17 Edw. IV 9 May, there is an entry stating that Elizabeth was lately indebted to William, Lord Hastings in 2,500 marks 'for the custody and marriage of the king's kinswoman Cecily, Marchioness of Dorset, Lady Haryngton and Bonville'. Cf. *Cal. Pat. Rolls*, III, 36. Cecily was Lord Hastings's step-daughter. G. E. C. (New Series), VI, 373.

55. On 14 August 1472. Charter Roll 11–14 Edw. IV, m. 5. He appears to have resigned this title to the king on being created Marquis of Dorset. Cf. G. E. C., IV, 418, n.b.

56. Charter Roll 15–22 Edw. IV, m. 13. Cf. G. E. C., IV, 418. This was the sixth Marquessate ever bestowed. See G. E. C., V, App. H., 798–9. Cf. Stow, *Annals*, pp. 428–9.

## 10 The Death of Clarence

1. Scofield, II, 128.

2. *Excerpta Historica*, 366–79; Scofield, II, 128–9.

3. *Cotton MS. Vespasian*, C. XIV, fol. 244; Scofield, II, 125.

4. Great Chronicle, fol. 197; Stratford, p. 234.

5. Great Chronicle, fol. 197 *verso*. It is unnecessary here to enter into the details of the ignominious failure of Edward's 'invasion' of France. For an account of this episode of his reign see L. Stratford, pp. 226–49; Scofield, II, 113–51; J. Calmette, *Louis XI et l'Angleterre*, pp. 186–216; J. Kirk, *Charles the Bold*, III, 133–72.

6. Michelet, *Histoire de France*, IX, 309. Cf. Commynes (Mandrot), I, 454, and II, 6; Stow, *Annals*, p. 434; Brugière de Barante, II, 687.

7. F. Madden in *Gentleman's Magazine*, pp. 24–5, (January 1831); Stow, *Annals*, p. 429; Green, *Princesses of England*, IV, 1 *et seq.*; Gilbert West in *Notes and Queries*, vol. 151, p. 381. G. E. C. (New Series), IX, 619; Lane, *Royal Daughters of England*, I, 315.

8. *Cotton Vespasian MS.*, C. XIV, fol. 572; Scofield, II, 163.

9. J. Anstis, *Order of the Garter*, II, 197. Cf. Stow, *Annals*, 429; Tighe and Davis, *Annals of Windsor*, I, 373.

10. J. Anstis, *Order of the Garter*, II, 197; Cf. Ashmole, *Order of the Garter*, p. 172; Stow, *Annals*, p. 429. This ceremony appears to have been an annual occurrence, in that, five years later, Piers Curteys, Keeper of the King's Wardrobe, was ordered to provide 'of the lyveries of the noble Ordre and right worchiful fraternitee and brotherhood of St George, and of the Garter ... for our beloved wyf the Quene, oru derest son the prince, oure right dere and welbeloved children oure son the Duke of Yorke, and the Ladies Elezeabeth, Cecile, and Mary oure Daughters ... yerely ayenst the fest of Saint Geroge for the tyme aforesaid'. Privy Seal, 6 June, 21 Edw. IV. Cf. J. Anstis, *Order of the Garter*, II, 210, note I.

11. *Harl. MS.* 48, fols 78–91. Cf. Sandford, *Genealogical History*, pp. 391–2, who has made the mistake of dating the ceremony 1466. Cf. Scofield, II, 167–8; Lane, *Royal Daughters of England*, I, 311, n. 1.

12. Ramsay, II, 419.

13. Cf. C. A. J. Armstrong, *The Usurpation of Richard III*, translated from Mancini's *De Occupation Regni Anglie*, p. 77. 'The queen then (following on Edward's restoration) remembered the insults to her family and the calumnies with which she was reproached.'

14. *Cont. Croyland*, p. 561. Cf. Lingard, IV, 217. According to Mancini (Armstrong, *Usurpation of Richard III*, pp. 75–6 and p. 138, n. 34), Clarence is reported not only to have 'vented his wrath by his bitter and public denunciation of Elizabeth's obscure family', but further to have proclaimed that the king had married a widow in violation of established custon, and that she was, therefore, not the legitimate wife of the king.

15. Ramsay, II, 419.

16. Cf. National Library, Paris, F. fr. 10,187², fols 123–4; Scofield, II, 478–9.

17. Cf. Commynes (Mandrot), II, 8, Haynin, II, 233; La Marche, III, 243; Plancher, IV, 481; E. Munch, *Die Furstinnen des Hauses Burgund-Osterreich*, I, 47; Brugière de Barante, II, 565; Stratford, p. 282; Scofield, II, 185.

18. According to the old legend, Melusina, the serpent-witch, a water nymph of Lusignon, was the supposed ancestress of the House of Luxembourg, from which Elizabeth's mother was descended. See J. P. Bullet, *Dessertation sur la Mythologie Francaise*, p. 9; S. Baring Gould, *Curious Myths of the Middle Ages*, pp. 482–3. Cf. C. Roy, *Melusine*; Jules Baudot, *Les Princesses Yolande et les ducs de Bar*, 1st Part.

19. *Rot. Parl.*, VI, 173; *Third Report of the Deputy Keeper of Public Records*, vol. III, Appendix II, pp. 213–4.

20. Oman, *Political History*, IV, 461.

21. Clarence probably referred to the old legend that Elizabeth's ancestors were descended from Melusina, the water-witch. Since the family of Luxembourg had actually altered their pedigree in order to claim this descent, this is by no means so unlikely as it may now appear. Cf. chapter 10 note 18.

22. *Rot. Parl.*, VI, 193–5. The reader must bear in mind that the reality of witchcraft and sorcery was not questioned in the fifteenth century.

23. *Cont. Croyland*, 561.

24. *Ibid.*, pp. 561–2.

25. Anne Mowbray was born on 10 December 1472. G. E. C., *Complete Peerage* (New Series), IX, 610.

26. *Narrative of the Marriage of Richard, Duke of York, with Anne of Norfolk, the Matrimonial Feast, and the Grand Justing*, a contemporary account of the ceremony printed in W. H. Black's *Illustrations of Ancient State and Chivalry* (Roghburgh Club), pp. 27–40. Cf. F. Sandford, *Genealogical History*, pp. 416–7; Scofield, II, 203–6.

27. *Rot. Parl.*, VI, 193. Cf. W. Cobbett's State Trials, I, 275–6; *Archaeologia*, XLVII, 418–9.

28. For further charges against Clarence, see J. Gairdner, *Richard III*, pp. 31–2; Stratford, pp. 286–7. Mancini (*Usurpation of Richard III*, ed. Armstrong, p. 77) actually states that the queen concluded that her offspring would not come to the throne unless Clarence were removed; and of this she easily persuaded the king. Cf. Molinet, *Chroniques*, II, 377.

29. Gairdner (*Richard III*, pp. 90–1) is inclined to believe that Clarence had got to know of Edward's supposed pre-contract with Lady Eleanor Butler, and that he had attempted to make use of it to the queen's prejudice. Ramsay (II, 488), Lingard (IV, 573–5) and Scofield (II, 213) are, however, of the opinion that the whole idea of a pre-contract was a mere political invention.

30. *Cal. Pat. Rolls*, III, 63. Cf. *Rot. Parl.*, VI, 195; L. W. Vernon Harcourt, *op. cit.*, pp. 412–3; *Archaeologia*, XLVII, 418–9.

31. The actual manner in which Clarence met his death is shrouded in mystery. Commynes (Lenglet, II, 147) says that he was drowned in a butt of malmsey wine and then beheaded. Cf. Great Chronicle, fol. 200 *verso*; C. L. Kingsford, *London Chronicle*, 188 (*MS. Cott. Vitell. A* XVI, fol. 136); Fabyan, p. 666; Olivier de la Marche, III, 70; Mancini (Armstrong), p. 77 and 134, n. 18; Notar Giacomo, *Cronica di Napoli*, p. 141.

32. *Cal. Pat. Rolls*, III, 212. Cf. also *ibid.*, III, 139, 263.

33. Rymer, *Foedera*, XIII, 95; *Cal. Pat. Rolls*, III, 115, 132, 135; Ramsay, II, 425.

34. Shakespeare (*Henry VI*, pt III, Act V, sc. vi; *Richard III*, Act I, sc. I) appears yet again to be responsible for the widely spread theory that Richard alone had planned Clarence's death. It would seem, however, far more probably that Clarence had for some considerable time been hostile to the queen and her relations, and was, therefore, executed at her request. Cf. Mancini (Armstrong, *Usurpation of Richard III*, p. 83): 'They [the Woodvilles] had to endure the imputation brought against them by all, of causing the death of the Duke of Clarence.' Cf. also Plancher (*Histoire*, IV, 481): 'Le roi Edward, et surtout la Reine, qui voyait ses tentatives pour le Comte de Riviere contrarriees par les projets de Clarence, employerent les moyens les plus violens pour les rompre.' Cf. also Hall, *Chronicle*, p. 326; Armstrong, *Usurpation of Richard III*, 134, n. 15.

### 11 The Last Years of Edward IV

1. It is impossible to determine the exact date of this prince's birth. L. Stratford (*Edward IV*, p. 270) gives August 1478 as the correct date: the year is clearly an error, since on 6 July 1478, that prince was created Lord Lieutenant in Ireland. *Cal. Pat. Rolls*, III, 67, 118. Scofield (II, 210, n. 3) points out that Prince George was born at Windsor 'sometime before 15 November 1477', as the king did not go to Windsor at any time between that date and 16 July 1478. Cf. *Household Account Books*, 17–18 Edw. IV, Exchequer K.R. He would appear to have been born at Windsor, since he is mentioned in an official document as 'our son George of Windsor'. *Cal. Pat. Rolls*, 19 Edw. IV, 7 May. Cf. Green, *Princesses of England*, IV, 3, n. 4. Gilbert West in *Notes and Queries* (vol. 153, p. 381) states that 'other authorities record George's birth as having been at Shrewsbury or Windsor in March 1476/77 or 1477/78', but he seems inclined to favour 17 August 1476 or 1477. Owing to the fact that the child was named George, it seems, however, more probably that he was born prior to Clarence's attack on Ankarette Twynho (12 April 1477).

2. *Cal. Pat. Rolls*, III, 67, 118.

3. Rymer, *Foedera*, XII, 171; *Acts of the Parliament of Scotland*, II, 117; *Genealogist* (New Series), V, 103.

4. *Acts of Parliament of Scotland*, II, 120; Rymer, *Foedera*, XXI, 97, 162; Ramsay, II, 437.

5. For Edward's intrigues in Scotland see Ramsay, II, 436; Stratford, pp. 303–4.

6. Scofield, II, 253.

7. The exact date of Catherine's birth is unknown. She was certainly born before 28 August 1479, when Dr John Coke and Bernard de la Forsse went to Spain to offer her as a bride to the son of Ferdinand and Isabella. On the other hand, it is evident, as Nicolas has pointed out (*Wardrobe Accounts of Edward IV*, xxiv, 122) that she had not been born very long at that time, as the wardrobe accounts of April–September 1480 refer to nails used 'about covering of the font' at her christening. Gilbert West (*Notes and Queries*, vol. 153, p. 382) gives the date of her birth as 14 August 1479. Since, however, the Court was at Eltham from the middle of November 1478 to February 1479, it seems more probably that Elizabeth was confined in the winter. Cf. Kingsford, *English Historical Literature*, p. 125; Scofield, II, 253.

8. Stratford, p. 270. Cf. *Gentleman's Magazine*, (January) 1831, p. 25; *Paston Letters*, V, 137; Green, *Princesses of England*, III, 437; Kingsford, *English Historical Literature*, p. 125. He was buried at Windsor, where his sister Mary (ob. 1482) lies beside him. He most probably died of the plague which was raging in England at this time (cf. Ramsay, II, 469; Scofield, II, 249); one Continental chronicler actually says this was the case: see *Chron. D'Adrien de But, Collection de Chroniques Belges Inedites*, p. 538.

9. *Add. MS.* 6113, fol. 59B; *Cely Papers*, p. 46. Cf. Weever, *Ancient Monuments*, p. 128; Stow, *Annals*, p. 432; Nicolas, *Privy Purse Expenses*, etc., p. xxix; Ramsay, II, 470; Green, *Princesses of England*, IV, 44; Gilbert West in *Notes and Queries*, Vol. 153, p. 382; Stratford, p. 270; Scofield, II, 299; Lane, *Royal Daughters of England*, I, 318.

10. Elizabeth's sister Margaret.

11. Madden, *Gentleman's Magazine*, January 1831, p. 25. Cf. More (ed. Lumby), *History of Richard III*, 1. Bridget, who seems to have been a sickly child, became a nun between 1486 and 1492, and died at Dartford Priory apparently before 1513. Green, *Princesses of England*, IV, 46–8; Scofield, II, 299–300.

12. A. Wood, *History of the University of Oxford* (ed. J. Gutch), 1, 637.

13. Wood, *History of the Colleges and Halls of Oxford* (ed. J. Gutch), App. 63. Lionel Woodville succeeded Dr Thomas Chaundler as chancellor of the university in 1479. Cf. *Dict. Nat. Biog.*, XXI, 885; Scofield, II, 440. The royal visit to Oxford cannot, therefore, have taken place as early as 1472, as stated by Strickland (*Queens of England*, II, 349 and n. 2) and Stratford (*Edward IV*, P. 269).

14. Wood (*History of the University of Oxford*, ed. J. Gutch, I, 637) states: 'With them also came the queen's mother Countess of Suffolk.' This is clearly an error in the compilation of the *Annals*, as the queen's mother, who incidentally had never borne the title of Countess of Suffolk, had died in 1472. The compiler of the *Annals* was probably referring to the queen's sister-in-law, Elizabeth, Duchess of Suffolk. Cf. G. E. C., VII, 306 (Old Series). Miss Strickland (*Queens of England*, II, 349 and n. 2), as also Stratford (*Edward IV*, 269), on account of the reference to the queen's *mother*, placed the royal visit to Oxford in 1472. They forget, however, that the Duchess of Bedford died in May 1472, whereas the king's visit to Oxford is plainly stated to have taken place in September. Moreover, it is almost certain that the Duchess of Suffolk would have been one of the royal party, in that her son Edmund de la Pole was at that time at the university. See Wood, *History of the University, etc.*, I, 638; Cf. *Dict. Nat. Biog.*, XVI, 21.

15. *Epistola Academica Oxon.*, II, 447–8, 453–7, 478–9.

16. Wood, *History of the University, etc.*, I, 637–8. Cf. also Maxwell Lyte, *History of the University of Oxford*, 328–9; Scofield, II, 440.

17. *Dict. Nat. Biog.*, VI, 499. Cf. Commynes (Mandrot), II, 91; More, *Richard II* (ed. Lumby), 2.

18. Nat. Library, Paris, F. fr. 4054, fol. 229; Scofield, II, 227–9, and 480–1; Stratford, 291–2.

19. See chapter 10.

20. Plancher, *Histoire de Bourgogne*, IV, 482; Brugière de Barante, II, 565.

21. Plancher, *Histoire*, IV, 482 remarks that the queen was beside herself with anger on account of the scorn with which the Burgundian Courttreated her proposals.

22. She died before 26 November 1481. Cf. *Cely Papers*, p. 79; Scofield, II, 323; G. E. C. (New Series), IX, 610.

23. Cf. Mancini (Armstrong, *Usurpation of Richard III*, 79): 'After the execution of the Duke of Clarence, the queen ennobled many of her family. Besides, she attracted to her party many strangers and introduced them to court, so that they alone should manage the public and private business of the crown ... and finally rule the very king himself.' This account was doubtless due to a certain extent to rumours and slander propagated by the enemies of the Woodvilles.

24. Parliament met on 20 January and rose on 18 February 1483. Ramsay, II, 451–2.

25. G. E. C., *Complete Peerage*, II, 133; *Rot. Parl.*, VI, 205–7. Viscount Berkeley claimed the Mowbray estates through his mother Isabel, eldest daughter of Thomas (de Mowbray), Duke of Norfolk. See G. E. C., *Complete Peerage*, II, 132.

26. This Anne was the daughter of the duchess by Sir Thomas St Leger, and must not be confused with the other Anne, the duchess' daughter by the Duke of Exeter, who, in 1466, was married to Thomas Grey, Marquis of Dorset. See G. E. C., IV, 419, note f; and V, 215, note b. The marriage never took place owing to the fall of the Woodvilles and Greys. Cf. Ramsay, II, 452, n. 2; Lane, *Royal Daughters of England*, I, 293.

27. G. E. C., IV, 419, note f.

28. *Rot. Parl.*, VI, 215–8. Cf. Ramsay, II, 451–2.

29. Commynes (Lenglet), IV, 82; Brugière de Barante, II, 668.

30. Stow, *Annalsm* 434; cf. Stratford, *Edward IV*, p. 312. Scofield (II, 356), however, states that Edward IV spent his last Christmas at Westminster Palace.

31. *Cont. Croyland*, 563; cf. Stratford, p. 312.

32. *Cont. Croyland*, 563; cf. Scofield, II, 356.

33. *Harl. MS.* 4780; Nicolas, *Wardrobe Accounts of Edward IV* P. 159, London, 1830.

34. Stow, *Annals*, p. 434.

35. Great Chronicle, fol. 205; Flenley, *Six Town Chronicles*, 169, 185. For the probable causes of Edward's death see Scofield, II, 365; Mancini (Armstrong), *Richard III*, pp. 73 and 131, n. 5. For an account of his funeral, see J. Gairdner, *Letters and Papers Illustrative of the Reigns of Richard II and Henry VII*, I, vii, App. 1–10; *Archaeologia*, I, 348–55; Scofield, II, 366–8.

36. *Not*, states Scofield (II, 364), apparently, the Will which he had made before his expedition to France, but one of more recent date. Cf. J. Nichols, *Wills of the Kings of England*, p. 345; *Excerpta Historica*, pp. 366–78. See also J. Gairdner's remarks in *Richard III*, p. 44, and C. A. J. Armstrong, *Usurpation of Richard III*, 131–2, n. 7. In the Will of 1475 Queen Elizabeth's name heads the list of executors, while in the later one her name does not figure in the list at all.

37. *Excerpta Historica*, p. 366.

38. There is no proof of Shakespeare's version (*Richard III*, Act I, sc. 1 and 3; II, sc. 1) that Richard shared the general dislike of the queen and her relations. Cf. Mancini (Armstrong, *Usurpation*, p. 79): 'Richard … avoided the jealousy of the queen, from whom he lived far separated.'

39. Strong indications of this fact appear in contemporary records. Cf. J. Gairdner, *Richard III*, 338–9. Jealousy of the Woodvilles is further illustrated by an official communication of app. Oxford University addressed in 1478 to Lionel Woodville, the future chancellor. See *Epistolae Academicae*, ed. H. Anstey (*Oxford Historical Society*, XXXVI, 1898), II, 448. Cf. Armstrong, *Usurpation*, p. 83) also refers to their great unpopularity. Cf. also p. 74, n. 1.

40. For a description of his life see *Dict. Nat. Biog.*, XXI, 881–4.

41. For his life see Dict. Nat. biog., XXI 885. There does not appear to be an atom of truth in the story that Bishop Stephen Gardiner was his natural son. For a full discussion of this question see J. A. Muller, *Stephen Gardiner and the Tudor Reaction*, App. 306–8. Cf. also *Dict. Nat. Biog.*, VII, 859. He was consecrated Bishop of Salisbury in April 1482.

42. Dugdale (*Baronage*, II, 231) has attributed part of the history of Sir Edward Woodville to an imaginary uncle of the same name. Baker (*Northamptonshire*, II, 166) has committed the same error. Most of the great authorities on the period, as also a contemporary chronicler, Mancini (Armstrng, *Richard III*, 79 and 99) agree in stating that Sir Edward was a brother of Elizabeth Woodville. See Oman, *Political History*, IV, 474; J. G. Nicols, *Grants to Edward V*, p. X; W. Busch, *England under the Tudors*, I, 43; J. Gairdner, *Richard III*, 150; H. A. L. Fisher, *Political History*, V, 28; *Dict. Nat. Biog.*, XXI, 887; Scofield, II, 251. See also R. B. Merriman, 'Edward Woodville: Knight-Errant', *Proceedings of the American Antiquarian Society*, XVI, 127–44.

43. This is clearly shown in the case of the Duke of Buckingham, the husband of Elizabeth's sister, Catherine, who sided with Richard against the Woodvilles. Cf. Mancini (Armstrong, *Usurpation*), p. 91.

44. More, *Richard III*, p. 9.

45. On one occasion relations between Rivers and Hastings had become so bad that, probably at the queen's instigation, Edward sent Hastings to the Tower for a time. This may have occurred about the end of June 1477. More, *Richard III*, p. 50. Cf. Mancini (Armstrong, *Usurpation*), p. 85; Stratford, *Edward IV*, P. 300; *Paston Letters*, iii, 195; Scofield, II, 192–3; Shakespeare, *Richard III*, Act I, sc. I.

46. More, *Richard III*, p. 9. See also Mancini (Armstrong), p. 85: 'Hastings was also the accomplice and partner of his (Edward's) privy pleasures.' Cf. Commynes (ed. Calmette), I, 78–9; Lingard, IV, 220; Scofield, II, 4.

47. See Mancini (Armstrong), who states that Hastings and Dorset had been reconciled two days prior to Edward's death. Cf. *Cont. Croyland*, p. 564; Scofield, II, 365.

48. Stubbs, *Constitutional History*, III, 238.

49. Cf. More, *Richard III*, p. 12: 'In effect everyone, as he was nearest of kin unto the queen, so was planted about the prince.'

50. Hastings may even have feared that the Woodvilles might make an attempt to seize Calais, since shortly before Edward IV's death a reinforcement of 500 archers had been ordered. See Ramsay, II, 476, n. 5.

51. *Cont. Croyland*, pp. 564–5. Cf. J. Gairdner, *Richard III*, P. 47. K. H. Vickers, *England in the Later Middles Ages*, 488, suggests that Hastings was acting on a preconceived plan which he, Gloucester and Buckingham had arranged before Edward's death.

## 12 The Usurpation of Richard III

1. J. Gairdner, *Richard III*, p. 47.

2. In the commissions for taxes, issued on 27 April, the names of the Dukes of Gloucester and

Buckingham were not inserted, the leading persons being the Marquis of Dorset, *frater regis uterinus*, Earl Rivers, *avunculus regis uterinus*, Lord Hastings, and others. *Pat. Roll. Edward V.* memb. 7 and 6 in dorso. Cf. *The Ninth report of the Deputy Keeper of the Public Records*, App. II, 7–8; *Cal. Pat. Rolls, Edward V*, 353–5; J. G. Nichols, *Grants of Edward V*, Introd., xiv; Gairdner, *Richard III*, 47 and n. 2. According to Mancini (Armstrong, *Usurpation*, p. 91), Dorset is actually reported to have said, 'We are so important that even without the king's uncle we can make and enforce our decision.'

3. Richard is usually said to have been on his way north when Edward IV died. On receiving the news he is stated by Polydore Vergil (p. 539) to have proceeded to York, where he attended a funeral service for the late king in the Minster. Davies (*York Records*, p. 143, note) and Gairdner (*Richard III*, p. 48) are, however, of the opinion that had any such important events taken place at York, they would hardly have passed unnoticed in the records. Edward IV was already reported to be dead on 6 April, a dirge being sung for him in the Minster on the following day. The mayor and aldermen attended both this and also a requiem mass on 8 April (Davies, *Records*, p. 142). No mention is made of Richard as having been present, and false reports may have muddled up the dates of the services, thus giving rise to the belief that he was present. J. G. Nichols (*Grants of Edward V*, p. xxiv) considers that in the absence of positive evidence it seems more probably that on the day of Edward's death, Richard was at Middleham, his usual private residence.

4. *Cont. Croyland*, p. 565; Polydore Vergil, *Anglica Historia*, p. 685; Lingard, IV, 222; Armstrong, *Usurpation*, p. 139, n. 39.

5. Great Chronicle, fol. 205 *verso*.

6. Cf. Mancini (Armstrong, *Usurpation*, p. 91): 'Buckingham had his own reasons for detesting the queen's kin: for, when he was younger, he had been forced to marry the queen's sister, whom he scorned to wed on account of her humble origin.' Cf. also Mancini, p. 95; More, p. 14: 'These two (Hastings and Buckingham) not bearing each to other much love, as hatred both unto the queen's part, in this point recorded together with the Duke of Gloucester, that they would utterly remove from the king's company all his mother's friends, under the name of their enemies.'

7. Mancini (Armstrong, *Usurpation*, p. 99) actually states that the late king's treasure was divided between the queen, Dorset, and Sir Edward Woodville.

8. On 10 May Sir Thomas Fulford and Halwell were 'ordered to rig them to the sea, in all haste they could, go to the Downs among Sir Edward and his company'. Again on 14 May Edward Brampton, John Wellis and Thomas Grey were directed 'to go with other ships to sea to capture Sir Edward Wydeville', having further instructions to receive as friends all that came 'except the Marquis of Dorset, Sir Edward Wydeville, and Robert Radclyffe'. J. G. Nichols, *Grants of Edward V*, p. ix; Cf. Ramsay, II, 476; Gairdner, *Richard III*, P. 59. Mancini (Armstrong, p. 105) gives a most interesting description of the surrender of this fleet.

9. Great Chronicle, fol. 205 *verso*. Rivers was confined at Sheriff Hutton and Grey at Middleham. *Harl. MS.*, 433, fol. 118 *verso*. Cf. J. Nichols, *Grants of Edward V*, preface, xviii; *Gentleman's Magazine*, 1844, II, pt. 377–9; *Excerpta Historica*, p. 244; Ramsay, II, 492; Flenley, *ibid.*, p. 159; Armstrong, *Usurpation*, p. 152, n. 82.

10. Mancini (Armstrong, p. 103) states, however, that 'since many knew these charges to be false, because the arms in question had been placed there long before the late king's death for an altogether different purpose when war was being waged against the Scots, mistrust both of his (Richard's) accusation and designs upon the throne were exceedingly augmented'. Cf. Armstrong in *Usurpation*, p. 146, n. 61.

11. *Cont. Croyland*, p. 565; More, *Richard III*, p. 409.

12. Thomas Scott or Scotte, Cardinal Archbishop of York. See James Renat Scott, *Memorials of Scott of Scotts Hall*, pp. 154–8; *Notes and Queries*, vth series, vol. VII (1877) *passim*; VIII (1877) *England*, pp. 431–2. Cf. John Lord Campbell, *Lives of the Lord Chancellors of England*, I, 390–400.

13. Hall, *Chronicle*, p. 350. Cf. Great Chronicle, fol. 205 *verso*; *Cont. Croyland*, p. 565; Ross, *Historia Regum Anglie*, p. 213; Fabyan, p. 668.

14. More, *History of Richard III*, p. 20. Cf. Foss, *Judges of England*, IV, 476.

15. Hall, *Chronicle*, p. 350.

16. Cf. More, *Richard III*, p. 21. For this action Rotherham was deprived of office prior to the entry of Edward V and Gloucester to London (4 May). See the letter, written on 2 May

from Northampton, in which the king, then in Gloucester's power, bids Thomas Bourchier, Archbishop of Canterbury, 'see for the saufegarde and sure keping of the gret seale of this oure realme unto our comyng to our cite of London'. Public Record Office. S.C.I./XL, no. 236. Cf. Armstrong, *Usurpation*, pp. 145–6, n. 58.

17. More, *Richard III*, P. 20. Cf. Mancini (Armstrong, *Usurpation*), p. 97.

18. *Cont. Croyland*, pp. 565–6; More, p. 21; K. H. Vickers, *England in the Later Middle Ages*, p. 488.

19. Great Chronicle, fol. 205 *verso*; MS. *Cott. Vitell*. A XVI, fol. 138; Fabyan, p. 668; Ramsay, II, 479; C. L. Kingsford, *Chronicles of London*, p. 190; Gairdner, *Richard III*, p. 54.

20. Great Chronicle, fol. 206. J. Gairdner (*Richard III*, p. 55) is of the opinion that this title was bestowed on Richard in accordance with Edward IV's Will. This would seem to be correct, since in two documents on the Patent Roll, dated 21 April and 2 May, Richard is styled Protector of England. ON 14 May his name was inserted in the new commissions of peace as *carissimo avunculo nostri Ricardo Gloucestriae protectori Angliae. Pat. Roll*, 1 Edw. V, memb. 11d. 8d. In dorso. Cf. also *Ninth Report of the Deputy Keeper of the Public Records*, App. II, 3–6; J. Gairdner, *Richard III*, 55; J. G. Nichols, *Grants of Edward V*, xiii; Armstrong, *Usurpation*, p. 131, n. 7 and 147, n. 62.

21. *Cont. Croyland*, p. 566.

22. J. Nichols, *Grants of Edward V*, pp. 69–70; Rymer, *Foedera*, XII, 185; *Excerpta Historica*, p. 16.

23. *Seventh Report of Deputy Keeper of Public Records*, App II, p. 212. Cf. J. Nichols, *Royal Wills*, p. 347; Gairdner, *Richard III*, p. 55.

24. Cf. chapter 12 note 16.

25. See Simon Stallworth's letter to Sir William Stonor, dated 8 June 1843. 'The quene kepys still Westm, my lord of Salysbury with othyr mo wyche wyll nott departe as yett. Wher so evyr kanne be founde any godyse of my lord Markues [of Dorset] it is tayne.' Public Record Office, S.C.I./XLVI, 207. Printed in *Excerpta Historica*, 16; and in *Royal Hist. Society*, Camden Series III, vol. XXX, 159–60.

26. Gairdner, *Richard III*, 58. Cf. Armstrong, *Usurpation*, p. 146, n. 58.

27. See Simon Stallworth's letter to Sir William Stonor. 'My lord Protector, my lord of Bukynham with all othyr lords ... were at Westm. In the councel chambre from X to ij, butt ther wass none that spake with the qwene.' Public Record Office, S.C.I./XLVI, 208; *Excerpta Historica*, p. 16; *Roy. Hist. Soc.*, Camden Series III, vol. XXX, p. 160.

28. Sir Richard Ratcliffe.

29. Davies, *York Records*, pp. 149. See also J. Gairdner, *Richard III*, pp. 59–60.

30. See chapter 12 note 27.

31. London Guildhall, MS. Journal 9, fol. 23 *verso*. Minutes of the London County Council held on 23 May. Cf. Armstrong, *Richard III*, p. 150, n. 72.

32. P. Vergil, p. 686.

33. Cf. J. Gairdner, *Richard III*, p. 62.

34. *Cont. Croyland*, p. 566.

35. This view has been immortalised by Shakespeare in his *Henry VI* (Part III), Act III, sc. 2, 'I'll make my heaven to dream upon the crown'; Act IV, sc. 1, 'I stay not for love of Edward but the crown'.

36. Shakespeare is again chiefly responsible for the general belief in this story. Cf. *Henry VI* (Part III) Act V, sc. 6, 'Clarence beware; thou keep'st me from the light ... Clarence thy turn is next'. Cf. also the magnificent soliloquies in *Richard III*, Act I, sc. 1, 'Polots have I laid, inductions dangerous .../ to set my brother Clarence and the king/ in deadly hate the one against the other ... and if I fail not in my deep intent, Clarence hath not another day to live.' See George B. Churchill, 'Richard III up to Shakespeare', *Palaestra*, X, 239–45. According to Mancini (Armstrong, *Usurpation*, 77), Richard 'was so overcome with grief for his brother that he could not dissimulate so well, but that he was overheard to say that he would one day avenge his brother's death'.

37. Oman, *Political History*, IV, 475; Pollard, *Historical Essays*, 235.

38. *Richard III*, p. 43.

39. Gairdner, *Richard III*, p. 63.

40. More, p. 44. Cf. Shakespeare, *Richard III*, Act III, sc. 3.

41. Catesby had been much advanced by the patronage of Hastings, and enjoyed great

authority in Leicestershire and Northamptonshire as a result of that nobleman's influence. Cf. Gairdner, *Richard III*, p. 64.

42. More, 45. Cf. Shakespeare, *Richard III*, Act III, sc. 2.

43. Catesby derived considerable profit from Hastings's death. Immediately after Richard's accession he obtained the office of one of the chamberlains of the receipt of the exchequer, a post formerly held by Hastings. On the same day (30 June) he was appointed Chancellor of the Exchequer and Chancellor of the Earldom of March for life. *Harl. MS.* 433, fol. 6. Cf. J. H. Nichols, *Grants of Edward VI*, p. 3. On 6 January 1484, he was chosen as Speaker. *Rot. Parl.*, VI, 238; cf. Ramsay, II, 516.

44. Philip Lindsay ('Errata for Richard III', in *Some Bones in Westminster Abbey*, p. 54) agrees with Miss Mary A. Berkeley 'that Richard's apparently irrelevant comment on Morton's strawberries might have had a covert allusion to an attempt of Morton's to poison him with strawberries, given perhaps by Jane Shore, as a part of the Woodville conspiracy'. This explanation appears to be somewhat far-fetched.

45. More, *Richard III*, p. 47.

46. More, pp. 45–8. Cf. Simon Stallworth's letter of 21 June 1483 to Sir William Stonor: 'As on Fryday last was the Lord chamberleyn hedded some apone noon'. Public Record Office. S.C.I./XLVI, 207. Printed in *Excerpta Historica*, 16, 17; *Royal Hist. Soc.*, Camden Series III, Vol. XXX, 161. Cf. also Shakespeare, *Richard III*, Act III, sc. 4.

47. Cf. More, p. 53: 'Every child might well perceive that it was prepared before.'

48. Cf. Simon Stallworth's letter: 'Mastres Chore is in pisone'. Public Record Office, S.C.I/XLVI, 207. Cf. *Excerpta Historica*, p. 17; *Royal Hist. Soc.*, etc., p. 161.

49. *Richard III*, pp. 69–70.

50. It is hardly likely that Jane Shore had been the mistress of both Hastings and Dorset in the space of two months (April–June 1483). It seems far more probable that as mentioned in Richard's proclamation (*Cal. Pat. Rolls*, 1476–85, p. 371), she was Dorset's mistress. The story of her illicit relations with Hastings appears to have arisen from the fact that the latter, probably at the request of the late king, had taken her 'under his protection'. She cannot have been connected with Dorset at a later date, as firstly she was imprisoned in June 1483, and secondly Dorset, following on Richard's seizure of the crown, had fled first to sanctuary, where he remained till Buckingham's rebellion in October, when, this rebellion having failed, he escaped abroad. If Richard's proclamation was justified, then Jane Shore can only have been Dorset's mistress sometime bewteen 9 April and 13 June 1483, at the tiem she is usually described as having been the *paramour* of Hastings.

51. See Richard's proclamation of 23 October 1483; *Cal. Pat. Rolls*, 1476–85, p. 371; Rymer, *Foedera*, XII, 204; Gairdner, *Richard III* p. 100, and in *The English Historical Magazine*, VI, 262; Ramsay, II, 506. For an account of Jane Shore's life see *Dict. Nat. Biog.*, XVIII, 147–8. Cf. also C. J. S. Thompson, *The Witchery of Jane Shore*; Guy Paget, *The Rose of London*.

52. Cf. Simon Stallworth's letter: 'On Monday last [16 June 1483] was at Westm. Gret plenty of harnest men.' Public Record Office, S.C.I./XLVI, 207. Cf. *Excerpta Historica*, pp. 16, 17; *Royal Hist. Soc., ut sup.*, 161.

53. See Simon Stallworth's letter: 'Yet it is thought ther shalbe XX thousand of my lord protectour and my lord of Bukyngham in London, this weeke.' Public Record Office, S.C.I/XLVI, 207. Cf. *Excerpta Historica*, pp. 16, 17.

54. Some of the great chroniclers (Great Chronicle, fol. 206 *verso*; Fabyan, p. 668; Polydore Vergil, pp. 688–9; More, pp. 41, 45–7) place the delivery of the Duek of York before the execution of Hastings. There is, however, very little doubt that the young duke was taken from sanctuary on Monday 16 June, whereas Hastings was certainly executed on 13 June. See *Cont. Croyland*, p. 566; *Stonor Letters and Papers*, II, 161. Cf. Armstrong, *Usurpation of Richard III*, pp. 149–50, n. 72; Pollard, *Historical Essays*, 233.

55. More, *Richard III*, pp. 25–31.

56. More, p. 32. A previous attempt to persuade the queen to leave sanctuary had been made on 23 May. See London, Guildhall, MS. Journal 9, fol. 23 *verso*. Cf. Armstrong, *Usurpation*, p. 150, n. 72.

57. More, p. 32. Cf. Great Chronicle, fol. 206.

58. More, *History of the Reigns of Edward V and Richard III*, printed in *The Historical Magazine*, III, 18–24.

59. Cf. Simon Stallworth's letter: 'On Monday last … ther was the dylyveraunce of the Dewke

of Yorke to my lord Cardenale ...: and with hym mette my lord of Bukynham in the myddes of the hall of Westm.: my lord protectouir recevynge hyme at the Starre Chamber Dore with many lovynge wordys: and so departed with my lord cardenale to the toure, where he is, blessid be Jhesus mary'. Public Record Office, S.C.I/XLVI, 207. Cf. *Excertpa Historica*, pp. 16, 17; *Royal Hist. Soc.*, Camden Series III, vol. XXX, p. 161. Cf. also Great Chronicle, fol. 206; *MS. Cott. Vitell.*, A XVI, fol. 138 *verso* C. L. Kingsford, *Chronicles of London*, p. 190.

60. Sir Edward Grey, younger brother of Sir John Grey. Cf. G. E. C. (New Series), VIII, 59; *Excerpta Historica*, p. 15, n. 9.

61. Public Record Office, S.C.I./XLVI 207: 'The lord Liele is come to my lord protectour and awaits upon hyme.' Cf. *Excerpta Historica*, pp. 16–17. *Royal. Hist. Soc.*, Camden Series III, vol. XXX, 161.

62. Grafton, *Chronicles*, II, 102.

63. Great Chronicle, fol. 207; Fabyan, p. 669; Armstrong, *Usurpation*, p. 117; Gairdner, *Richard III*, p. 79.

64. Alluding to a silly story that the Duchess of York had been seduced by an archer named Blackburn. *Archeologia*, XIII, 11. Cf. Oman, *Political History*, IV, 462, n.

65. More, *Richard III*, p. 65.

66. *Ibid.*, p. 66.

67. Great chronicle, fol. 207 *verso*.

68. Great Chronicle, fol. 208 *verso*; British Museum MS. *Cott. Faustina B. VIII*, fol. 4 *verso*; J. Nichols, *Grants of Edward V*, p. xviii; Gairdner, *Richard III*, p. 73. Cf. Flenley, *l.c.*, 169.

69. Rows Rolls, 213. Rivers appears to have had some form of trial, but would seem to have been denied his undoubted legal right to trial by his peers. Cf. Oman, *Political History*, IV, 480; Ramsay, II, 492; Lingard, IV, 227; Gairdner, *Richard III*, p. 72. Clements Markham (*Richard III*, pp. 216–7) is, however, of the opinion that this trial was legalyl correct. Mancini (Armstrong, *Usurpation*, 113) states that Richard first attempted to have Rivers and Grey found guilty of treason by a decision of the council, but 'when by means of the council the duke could not compass their execution, of his own authority as protector he ordered dependable officers to put them to death'.

70. MS. *Cott. Faustina B. VIII*, FOL. 4B. More (*Richard III*, p. 55) asserts that tehse executions took place on the same day as that of Hastings (13 June). This may be true of Grey, Vaughan and Haute, but Rivers was certainly alive on 23 June, when he made his Will, at the end of which, immediately after the names of the witnesses, is written: 'My Will is now to be buried before an image of our blessed lady Mary with my Lord Richard, in Pomfrete.' This woulds eem to indicate that Grey was, on 23 June, already dead, and had been interred at Pontefract. Cf. *Excerpta Historica*, p. 248; Rows, p. 214; Ramsay, II, 492; Lingard, IV, 227–8; Oman, *Political History*, IV, 482; *Gentleman's Magazine*, XXII, 377–9 (October) 1844; J. Nichols, *Grants of Edward V*, pp. xvi, note, and xviii; Gairdner, p. 75; Armstrong, *Usurpation*, p. 152, n. 82. Earl Rivers was the noblest and msot accomplished of all Richard's victims. Mancini (Armstrong, *Usurpation*, p. 83) says of him: 'Lord Rivers was always considered a king, serious and just man, and one tested by every vicissitude of life. Whatever his prosperity he had injured nobody, though benefiting many.' For an account of the earl's life and a copy of his Will, see *Excerpta Historica*, pp. 240–8. Cf. also George G. Cunningham, *Lives of Eminent and Illustrious Englishmen*, I, 400–3. Sir Richard Haute or Hawte, Treasurer of Edward V's Household, was Elizabeth's cousin, being the son of William Haute and Joan Woodville, Elizabeth's aunt. *Harl. MS.*, 1431, fol. 5; cf. *Excerpta Historica*, p. 249; Nichols, *Grants of Edward V*, xvi, note; Scofield, II, 158, n. 2. George Smith, *Coronation of Elizabeth Woodville*, p. 63. Cf. also *Archaeologia Cantiana*, XXXVII, 120; and Pedigree in the Appendix.

71. R. Davies, *Extracts from the Records of the City of York*, p. 154.

72. See J. Gairdner, *Richard III*, pp. 84–7.

73. *Rot. Parl.*, VI, 241. Gairdner (*Richard III*, pp. 90–2) is inclined to believe this story, his view being shared by Sir Clements Markham (*Richard III*, pp. 95–6 and 218–9). Both Gairdner and Markham consider that Clarence would appear to have been aware of the pre-contract, and that he was put to death in 1478 for that reason. However, Lingard (IV, 573–5), Ramsay (II, 488), and Scofield (II, 213) are of the opinion that the whole story was merely an invention in order to justify Richard's usurpation. This would seem to be correct, if only for the reason that all the chroniclers agree in stating that at the time of Edward IV's secret marriage with Elizabeth, Warwick had already succeeded in obtaining Louis XI's consent to the marriage of

his sister-in-law, Lady Bona of Savoy, with Edward. Furthermore, Commynes (ed. Mandrot, I, 455; II, 64–5) makes it quite clear that the story of the pre-contract was not told to Richard until Edward IV's death, when Bishop Stillington told him of it – he in all probability invented it – in order to furnish the usurper with sufficient grounds for declaring Edward's children illegitimate. For this question see Lingard, IV, 235, n. 1 and 573–5. Cf. also Gairdner, *Letters and Papers Illustrative of the Reigns of Richard III and Henry VII*, Preface, pp. xvii–xviii. A. R. Bayley in *Notes and Queries*, vol. 151, pp. 408–9; Ramsay, II, 487, n. 6 and 488; W. F. Hook, *Lives of the Archbishops of Canterbury*, V, 375–6; Scofield, II, 213. The Croyland Chronicler (p. 567), although he omits the name, states that the authorship was notorious. Stillington has indeed been imprisoned by Edward IV in 1478, a short time after Clarence's execution (*Stonor Letters and Papers*, II, 42) for 'uttering words prejudicial to the king and his state' (Rymer, *Foedera*, XII, 66). He received a pardon on 20 Juen by paying the king a large sum of money (Commynes (Mandrot), II, 64). Gairdner and Markham consider that the imprisonment of Stillington goes to prove that the bishop and Clarence were alone aware of the pre-contract at this time. It would appear, however, that the true cause of Stillington's imprisonment was that of having violated his oath of allegiance by having associated with Clarence (Rymer, *Foedera*, XII, 66; cf. Lingard, IV, 575). It must not be forgotten that the bishop had been one of the principal workers for the reconciliation of Edward and Clarence prior to the Battle of Barnet in 1471 (Scofield, I, 560), and that Edward may have distrusted him as a friend of Clarence. Furthermore, if the story of the pre-contract was true, it seems an amazing thing that no use was made of it either by the Lancastrians or by the Earl of Warwick in their struggle with Edward IV (Habington, *Edward IV*, p. 438). Further proof that Warwick had no intention of contesting the validity of Elizabeth's marriage is indicated by the fact that he refused to have anything to do with the attempted indictment of her mother Jacquetta on a charge of sorcery, the charge being quashed in council on 19 January 1470 (*Cal. Pat. Rolls*, Edward IV, Pt II, 190; cf. Oman, *Political History*, IV, 435). That no such use was made of any pre-cotnract would seem to offer sufficient proof that it was a pure invention. Finally following the accession of Henry VII in 1485, some of the lords wished to summon Stillington to answer the charge, but the kign did not wish to proceed against him. S. B. Chrimes, *English Constitutional Ideas in the Fifteenth Century*, p. 266, n. 5. See also A. F. Pollard, *Historical Essays*, 231–2, n. 5.

74. *Rot. Parl.*, VI, 240; Gairdner, *Richard III*, p. 93.

75. Great Chronicle, fol. 208; *Cont. Croyland*, p. 566; Fabyan, p. 669; Polydore Vergil, p. 692; Lingard, IV, 237; Gairdner, p. 94 and n. 1; Armstrong, *Usurpation*, p. 156, n. 100.

## 13 The Murder of the Princes in the Tower & the Rebellion of the Duke of Buckingham

1. Great Chronicle, fol. 208 *verso*. For a full account of Richard III's coronation see *Excerpta Historica*, pp. 379–84. Cf. G. E. C., *Complete Peerage* (New Series), IV, 19, n. f; Gairdner, *Richard III*, pp. 100–3; Clements Markham, *Richard III*, pp. 126–7.

2. Fabyan, p. 670.

3. Ramsay, II, 498.

4. *Ibid.*, 511.

5. *Cont. Croyland*, p. 567.

6. Ramsay, II, 502 and n. 2.

7. *Great Chronicle of London*, fol. 208 *verso*: 'But afftr Estyrn (1484) much whysperyng was among the people yt the king hadd put the childyr of King Edward to deth.' Cf. L. W. Tanner in *Archaeologia*, LXXXIV, 2, n. 2. Cf. also C. A. J. Armstrong's edition of Mancini's *De Occupatione Regni Anglie*, p. 113: 'A Strasbourg doctor, the last of his attendants whose services the king [Edward V] enjoyed, reported that the young king, like a victim prepared for sacrifice, sought remission of his sins by daily confession and penance, because he believed that death was facing him' Cf. also Great Chronicle, fols 212 *verso*–213. Indeed, so widespread was the opinion that the princes had been murdered that the French chancellor, Guillaume de Rochefort, actually referred to the fact in his speech to the States General at Tours in the following January (15 January 1484). 'Aspicite, quaeso, quidnam post mortem regis Eduardi in ea terra contigerit, ejus scilicet jam adultos, et egrgios liberos impune trucidari, et regni diadema in horum extinctorem, populis faventibus, delatum.' See the *Collections de Documents inedits sur l'Histoire de France, Series I: Journal des Etats Generaux tenus a Tours en 1484 redige en Latin par Jehan a Masselin* ed. A. Bernier, p. 38. Cf. Georges Picot, *Histoires des Etats*

# Notes

*Generaux*, I, 361–2; Gairdner, *Letters and Papers*, p. xxv, n. 2; Kingsford, *English Historical Literature*, 184, n.; Flenley, *Six Town Chronicles*, pp. 169, 185.

8. J. Gairdner, one of the greatest authorities on this period, has not the slightest doubt that Richard III caused the princes to be murdered. His opinion is also shared by many other authorities, including Ramsay, II, 510–4; Lingard, IV, 576–81; Oman, *Political History*, IV, 481–2, and n. 1; Pauli, *Geschichte*, V, 487 and n. 1; *Archaeologia*, I, 361–83. Sir Clements Markham in his *Richard III* (pp. 246–301) and Philip Lindsay (*Richard III*, pp. 317–30) attribute the crime to Henry VII. In the light of recent discoveries it would seem that Gairdner's version is the correct one. This whole question would appear to have been settled once and for always by the recent research work undertaken Mr Lawrence E. Tanner and Professor William Wright. These two eminent scholars have succeeded in carrying out the most thorough examination of this great historical 'mystery' that has ever yet been attempted. The results of their untiring research work, which, despite Philip Lindsay's adverse criticism in his pamphlet *On Some Bones in Westminster Abbey*, cannot be too highly praised, have been published, together with many interesting illustrations, in *Archaeologia*, LXXXIV, 1–25, under the title of 'Recent Investigations Regarding the Fate of the Princes in the Tower'. Another very important contribution towards the solution of this problem has been made by C. A. J. Armstrong's important discovery of Dominic Mancini's *De Occupatione Regni Anglie*. Mr Armstrong, who first drew the attention of the public to the existence of this manuscript by his article in *The Times* of 26 May 1934, has since published and edited this manuscript under the title of *The Usurpation of Richard III*.

9. Hall's *Chronicle*, pp. 379–80.

10. Gairdner, *Richard III*, P. 105.

11. *Cal. Pat. Rolls*, I Richard III, Part I, p. 361.

12. For these offices see Gairdner, *Richard III*, P. 105.

13. See *Cont. Croyland*, pp. 567–8, who states quite clearly that the princes were alive when Richard started on his progress in July, and the princes were alive when Richard started on his progress, and that they were dead before Buckingham's rebellion broke out in October. Cf. Great Chronicle, fol. 210; Ramsay, II, 511.

14. Ramsay II, 503. Cf. Oman, *Political History*, IV, 484; A. E. Conway, 'The Maidstone Sector of Buckingham's Rebellion', *Archaeologia Cantiana*, XXXVII, 97–120. The outstanding rebels in the Maidstone sector were relations or connections by marriage of the Woodvilles, Hautes, Guildfords.

15. Cf. Great Chronicle, fol. 210. 'It was not long after, were it for the foresaid causes or other, but that the Duke of Buckingham estarnged him from the king.'

16. Ramsay, II, 499.

17. Gairdner, *Richard III*, p. 116.

18. Morton had been arrested by Richard's orders on 13 June 1483 at the time of Hastings's execution. The University of Oxford having petitioned for his release (Wood, *History of the University of Oxford*, I, 640), he was placed in the custody of the Duke of Buckingham at Brecon Castle. Cf. Gairdner, *Richard III*, 68–9.

19. Both Henry and Buckinham could claim descent from Edward III through the Beauforts in the female line. Buckingham's mother was the daughter of John Beaufort's younger son, Edmund, whereas the daughter of the elder son, John, was Margaret, mother of Henry, Earl of Richmond. Henry therefore had the better claim. Cf. Lingard, IV, 244, n. 1. Cf. Great Chronicle, fol. 212 *verso*. 'Henry made speedy provision for to come to England to clayme the crowne as his ryght.'

20. R. J. Woodhouse, *The Lief of John Morton*, p. 74. Cf. *Dict. Nat. Biog.*, XIII, 1049.

21. See *Cont. Croyland*, pp. 567–8. See also Polydore Vergil (pp. 697–8) who states quite clearly that Buckingham joined a conspiracy already on foot. Cf. Ramsay, II, 504, n. 4; *Archaeologia Cantiana*, XXXVII, 103; Great Chronicle, fol. 213: 'But how soo evyr they [the Princes] were put to deth certayn it was that before that daye [in all probability the day of Buckingham's proclamation (15 October 1483)] they were departed this world.'

22. Hall, 'Richard III', *The Historical Magazine*, III, 53 (1791).

23. Margaret Beaufort, Countess of Richmond and Derby, daughter and heiress of John Beaufort, 1st Duke of Somerset, and mother by Edmund Tudor, Earl of Richmond, of Henry VII.

24. Hall in *The Historical Magazine*, III, 53, 1791.

25. *Ibid.*, 54.

26. For an account of Dorset's escape see Mancini (Armstrong, *Usurpation*), p. 113. Cf. also Great Chronicle, fol. 208 *verso*; Fabyan, 670.

27. Three of Elizabeth's brothers – Lionel, Bishop of Salisbury, Sir Edward and Sir Richard Woodville – were among the leaders of this rebellion. Cf. Ramsay, II, 503; Gairdner, *Henry VII*, p. 15. On the failure of the insurrection all fled to join Richmond in Brittany. It is noteworthy that in July 1483, immediately after his accession, Richard III had sent Dr Hutton to the Duke of Brittany to 'fele and understand the mynde and disposicion of the duke anempst Sir Edward Wodevile and his reteignue, practizing by all meanes to him possible to enserche and knowe if ther be extended any enterprise out of land upon any part of this realm.' *Harl. MS.*, 433, fol. 241; Gairdner, *Letters and Papers*, I, 23. Cf. Gairdner, *Richard III*, p. 150; *Henry VII*, P. 15; B. A. Ppcquet du Haut-Jusse, *Francois II, duc de Bretagne, et l'Angleterre*, p. 416.

28. John and Reginald Pympe were brothers, and their stepmother, Philippa St Leger, was the second wife of Sir John Guildford. Their sister Anne had married Sir Richard Guildford prior to Buckingham's rebellion; Reginald's wife, Elizabeth Pashley, was a cousin of Elizabeth Woodville, while John's wife was a niece of Sir John Cheyney. Sir William Haute was a first-cousin of Elizabeth Woodville, being the son of Sir William Haute of Bishopsbourne, and Joan Woodville, Queen Elizabeth's aunt. Sir John Fogge was the husband of this Sir William Haute's sister, Alice. See A. E. Conway, 'The Maidstone Sector of Buckingham's Rebellion', *Archaeologia Cantiana*, XXXVII, 97–120. Cf. also pedigree in Appendix.

29. Great Chronicle, fol. 210 *verso*; Owen and Blakeway, *History of Shrewsbury*, I, 236.

30. Owen and Blakeway, *ibid.*, p. 238, n. 1.

31. Great Chronicle, fol. 210 *verso*; *Cont. Croyland*, p. 567; Fabyan, p. 671; Hall, pp. 394–5; Ramsay, II, 507; *Dict. Nat. Biog.* XVIII, 588. G. E. C., *Complete Peerage*, II, 389–90.

## 14 *The Desperate Plight of Elizabeth & the Death of Richard III*

1. *Richard III*, Act IV, sc. 4.

2. On this day Henry gave the Duke of Brittany a receipt for a loan of 10,000 crowns of gold, dated at Paimpol, near Brehat (*Add. MS.* 19398, fol. 33; cf. *Dict. Nat. Biog.*, IX, 521).

3. Great Chronicle, fol. 209; *Rot. Parl.*, VI, 242. Cf. Gairdner, *Richard III*, p. 157.

4. Hall in *Historical Magazine*, III, 61.

5. *Ibid.*

6. Ellis's *Original Letters*, Second Series, I, 149 from *Harl. MS.* 433; Cf. Hall, p. 406; Gairdner, *Richard III*, pp. 156–6.

7. *Cont. Hardyng's Chronicle*, p. 536. Cf. *Cont. Croyland*, p. 570.

8. Polydore Vergil, p. 210.

9. *Rot. Parl.*, VI, 263; Rymer, *Foedera*, XII, 259.

10. Cf. chapter 13.

11. Nevertheless, Philip Lindsay (*Kings of Merry England*, p. 584) would have us believe that during Richard's reign, 'he and Elizabeth remained the best of friends'. It is, however, hardly likely that any woman would ever 'respect or perhaps love' the man whom she knew to be responsible for the deaths of her brother (Anthony Lord Rivers), her yougn sons, and Sir Richard Grey. The very fact that Elizabeth remained for ten months in sanctuary would seem to disprove that statement.

12. *Patent Rolls*, 1 May, I Richard III, pt. 2; *Cal. Pat. Rolls*, I Richard III, 397–401.

13. E. J. M. Routh, in her *Lady Margaret*, pp. 52–3, also holds this view. Philip Lindsay (*Kings of Merry England*, p. 591) makes Elizabeth Woodville the originator of the proposed marriage between her daughter and Richard III, thereby attempting to prove that Richard was innocent of the murder of the Princes in the Tower.

14. Hall, *Chronicle*, p. 409.

15. Cf. J. Gairdner's opinion in his *Richard III*, p. 204, n. 1, in which he refers to 'the weakness of which Elizabeth Woodville was actually guilty in yielding to Richard III'. See also Sir Clements Markham (*Richard III*, p. 238), who takes the queen's letter to Dorset as a proof that the two little princes were alive at this time. Nevertheless when, about ten years later, the Impostor, Perkin Warbeck, appeared, he claimed to be not Edward V, but his younger brother, Richard, Duke of York. This would seem to imply that by 1495 there was no longer any doubt regarding the fate of Edward V. Furthermore, one must not overlook the fact that Perkin Warbeck did not sail for England till July 1495, three years after the death of Elizabeth,

his pretended mother. Had Elizabeth been still living, she, above all others, would have been able to prove to Henry VII the utter futility of Warbeck's claims. It may not have been mere coincidence that Warbeck's expedition sailed after her death. For the best account of Perkin Warbeck see J. Gairdner, 'The Story of Perkin Warbeck' in his *Richard III*, pp. 263–335.

16. According to some accounts (Great Chronicle, fol. 209 *verso*; Polydore Vergil, p. 707; Rous, p. 215) her end was hastened by foul play. It would appear, however, more probable that she died a natural death, as she had been ailing for some considerable time. Once again Shakespeare (*Richard III*, Act IV, scenes II and III) must be held responsible for the general belief that Richard caused his queen to be poisoned, so that he would be free to marry his niece Elizabeth.

17. Great Chronicle, fol. 210; *Cont. Croyland*, p. 572; *Harl. MS.*, 541, fol. 217 b. Cf. Sir R. Baker, *Chronicle of the Kings of England*, p. 231. There does not seem to be an atom of truth in the letter printed by Buck in Kennett's *History of England* (I, 568), in which he quotes a so-called 'authentic' letter written by the princess Elizabeth to Richard III stating that she was willing to become his wife. It seems rather peculiar that Buck is the only erspon to mention this letter, and that its contents were invaluable to him in his attempt at defending Richard III's character. Cf. Gairdner, *Richard III*, pp. 203–4. This is, perhaps, the 'definite proof' offered us by Philip Lindsay (*Kings of Merry England*, p. 591) that Elizabeth Woodville 'had every intention of pushing through the marriage if she could'.

18. Cf. chapter 14 note 16.

19. *Cont. Croyland*, p. 572.

20. Edward Plantagenet, Earl of Warwick, son of George, Duke of Clarence.

21. See Ramsay, II, 532, n. 2.

22. G. E. C., *Complete Peerage* (New Series), IX, 718.

23. Hall, p. 410.

24. See P. Pelicier, *Essai sur le Gouvernement de la Dame de Beaujeu*, p. 103 and n. 1; G. Temperley, *Henry VII*, p. 15; Gairdner, *Richard III*, 213; *idem.*, *Henry VII*, p. 24; J. S. C. Bridge, *History of France from the Death of Louis XI*, I, 132. Cf. Alfred Spont, 'La marine francaise sous le regne de Charles VIII, 1483–93', *Revue des questions historiques*, LV. These troops were commanded by Philibert de Shaunde, who was created Earl of Bath on 6 January 1486. See W. Campbell, *Materials for a History of Henry VII*, II, 152; Gairdner, *Richard III*, pp. 246, 363; G. E. C., *Complete Peerage*, II, 15. Cf. Hall, p. 424; Temperley, *Henry VII*, P. 42.

25. Great Chronicle, fol. 219. See also Gairdner, *Richard III*, p. 213, n. 2.

26. Before Novemebr 1482. See G. E. C., *Complete Peerage*, II, 207.

27. For a description of this battle see J. Gairdner, 'The Battle of Bosworth', *Archaeologia*, LV, 159–79.

28. Hall in *Historical Magazine*, III, 71.

29. Great Chronicle, fol. 219.

## *15 The Accession of Henry VII & the Restitution & Death of Elizabeth*

1. Gairdner, *Henry VII*, p. 31.

2. See previous chapter.

3. Bacon's *History of the Reign of Henry VII*, p. 4.

4. Philip Lindsay (*King's of Merry England*, p. 585), however, states that Elizabeth 'was to prove by her schemes that she respected Richard and perhaps loved him'. In view of the many insults heaped on Elizabeth this would appear to be somewhat unlikely. Cf. chapter 14, n. 11.

5. *Harl. MS*, 541, fol. 217b.

6. Bacon, *l.c.*, p. 4.

7. Great Chronicle, fol. 221.

8. *Rot. Parl.*, VI, p. 228.

9. *Ibid*, p. 289.

10. Cf. S. B. Chrimes, *English Constitutional Ideas in the Fifteenth Century*, p. 266, n. 4.

11. *Rot. Parl.*, p. 289. Cf. Sir Nicholas Harris Nicolas, *Privy Purse Expenses of Elizabeth of York*, p. lxviii, n. 2.

12. *Rot. Parl.*, VI, 270.

13. *Ibid*.

14. Dorset did not take part in Henry's expedition to England, as the latter, who still mistrusted him, left him behind at Paris with Sir John Bourchier in the hands of Charles VIII as surety for

a loan of money. It was not till four months after his victory at Bosworth that Henry finally recalled Dorset to England. Hall, p. 402; cf. Gairdner, *Richard III*, p. 212, and *Henry VII*, p. 41.

15. Like William III after him, Henry did not wish it to appear that he owed his title of king to his wife's claims, and he therefore did all he could in order to keep her name out of the Act of Settlement. His long delay in marrying Elizabeth of York was due more to this fact than to the reason given by Sir Clements Markham (*Richard III*, p. 254) that Edward IV's two sons were still alive, and that by marrying their sister Elizabeth and declaring her illegitimate, he would have made his future wife's brother Edward, King of England. For a full account of Henry VII's claim to the crown, see S. B. Chrimes, *English Constitutional Ideas in the Fifteenth Century* p. 33, n. 1. Cf. also K. Pickthorn, *Early Tudor Government*, I, 1–10; A. D. Innes, *England under the Tudors*, App. B., pp. 437–40; Stubbs, *Seventeen Lectures on the Study of Medieval and Modern History*, pp. 395–6; Charles Williams, *Henry VII*, pp. 40–4.

16. Cf. Bacon, *Henry VII*, p. 9. 'And it is true that all his lifetime, while the Lady Elizabeth lived with him, he shewed himself no very indulgent husband towards her, though she was beautiful, gentle, and fruitful. But his aversion towards the House of York was so predominant in him, as it found place not only in his wars and counsels but in his chamber and bed.'

17. *Portraits of Illustrious Personages of Great Britain*, II, 3.

18. *Cal. Pat. Rolls, Henry VII*, I, 75. Cf. W. Campbell, *Materials for a History of Henry VII*, I, 338.

19. Patent Roll, 5 March, I Henry VII, p. 3, m. 3; *Cal. Pat. Rolls*, I, 75. See also W. Campbell, *Materials*, I, 347–50; Gairdner, *Letters and Papers*, II, 368.

20. J. Armitage Robinson, *The Abbot's House at Westminster*, pp. 13 and 22–3. The lease can still be seen at the Muniment Room and Library, Westminster (Register I. f.3). The house is described as the 'mansion of Cheynegates'.

21. *Lelandi Collectanea*, IV, 204–7.

22. Bacon, *Henry VII*, p. 11.

23. Great Chronicle, fol. 222 *verso*.

24. Hall, *Chronicle*, p. 431.

25. See p. 152–4.

26. **p. 154.**

27. Cf. Polydore Vergil, p. 571; Bacon, *Henry VII*, p. 16.

28. *Rot. Parl.*, VI, 289.

29. Cf. Gairdner, *Henry VII* p. 50, who refers to a 'very mysterious decision about the queen dowager', but further adds that there is no reason to think there is any truth in the statement that Elizabeth encouraged Lambert Simnel's rebellion. Cf. also Sir R. Baker, *Chronicle of the Kings of England*, p. 238; William B. Hannon, *The Lady Margaret*, p. 70.

30. Jon de la Pole, Earl of Lincoln, eldest son of John de la Pole, 2nd Duke of Suffolk and Elizabeth, sister of Edward IV. G. E. C., (New Series), VII, 688–9.

31. Rous, p. 218; Lingard, IV, 251; Ramsay, II, 522; Gairdner, *Richard III*, PP. 183 and 208; Oman, *Political History*, IV, 487.

32. For the best account of Lambert Simnel's rebellion see W. Busch, *England under the Tudors*, I, 34–7, 326. Cf. Gairdner, *Henry VII*, pp. 48–6.

33. *Rot. Scot.*, II (ed. D. Macpherson), 480–2; A. E. Conway, *Henry VII's Relations with Scotland and Ireland*, p. 11.

34. There does nto appear to be any truth in the statement made by Commynes (ed. Mandrot, II, 65) that Richard III had previous planned to marry Elizabeth to Bishop Stillington's son. It seems almost certain that Commynes referred to Elizabeth's eldest daughter. Cf. B. de Mandrot's edition of Commynes, II, 65, n. 1.

35. Rymer, *Foedera*, XII, 329; Lingard, IV, 287. Cf. *Dict. Nat. Biog.*, X, 580; Conway, *Henry VII's Relations with Scotland and Ireland*, p. 11. This three-fold marriage had already been agreed to by a clause in the Three Years' Truce signed on 3 July 1486. *Rot. Scot.*, II, 475–7; Conway, *Henry VII's Relations with Scotland and Ireland*, 10.

36. Sir Clements Markham (*Richard III*, p. 257) and Philip Lindsay (*Richard III*, p. 319, and *Kings of Merry England*, p. 584) are the principal advocates of this opinion. Lingard (IV, 287–7) and Sir Nicholas Harris Nicolas (*Privy Purse Expenses of Elizabeth of York*, pp. 77–81) are, however, of the opinion that Elizabeth Woodville was always well treated by Henry VII. An impartial hsitorian, R. Pauli (*Geschichte von England*, V, 536), agrees with Lingard and Sir Harris Nicolas.

37. William Drummond of Hawthornden, *History of Scotland, 1423–1542*, p. 175.

38. Hall, *Chronicle*, pp. 439–41; Morice, *Histoire de Bretagne*, III, 594; Alain Bouchard, *Les Grandes Cronicques de Bretaigne*, Bk IV, 243; D'Argentre, *Histoire de Bretaigne*, 972; St Gilles, *Les Grandes Cronicques et Annales de France*, p. 422; Polydore Vergil, pp. 577–9; Dupuy, *Reunion de la Bretagne a la France*, pp. 124–7; Fisher, *Political History*, V, 29; W. Busch, *England under the Tudors*, p. 44, n. 1; G. Temperley, *Henry VII*, p. 77, n. 3; Gairdner, *Henry VII*, p. 64; P. Pelicier, *Essai, etc.*, p. 144; J. S. C. Bridge, *History in France*, I, 164–7. R. B. Merriman in his 'Edward Woodville: Knight-Errant', *Proceedings of the American Antiquarian Society*, XVI, 127–44, mentions that Sir Edward Woodville's career was to a graet extent responsible for the ultimate completion of the marriage between Henry VIII and Cahterine of Aragon, 'which was destined to have incalculable importance for Europe and for Christendom'. Cf. Marquis de Beauchesne, 'L'Expedition d'Edouard Wydeville en Bretagne', *Revue de Bretagne*, XLVI, 185–214; B. A. Pocquet du Haut-Jusse, 'Francois II, duc de Bretagne, et l'Angleterre', *Memoires de la Societe d'Histoire et d'Archeologie de Bretagne*, IX, 458–63.

39. Esc. 7 Henry VII, n. 39; Doyle, *Baronage*, III, 145; G. E. C., V, 362, n.c. Cf. Baker, *Northamptonshire*, II, 166.

40. In Sir Richard Woodville's Will, dated 20 February 1490/1, and proved at Lambeth on 23 March, Catherine alone is mentioned. The other heirs are named as being Henry, son and heir of her sister Anne and the Earl of Essex; William, son and heir of Margaret Lady Maltravers; Elizabeth, daughter of her sister Mary and Lord Herbert; Joan, daughter of her sister Jacquetta Lady Strange of Knockyn. Thus it would appear that all her other sisters were already dead. Esc. 7 Henry VII, n. 39; G. E. C. (New Series), V, 362, n.c.; cf. G. E. C. (New Series), VII, 166, n.f; Baker, II, 166.

41. *Lelandi Collectanea*, IV, 249. This François de Bourbon, Comte de Vendome, had, in 1487, married Marie, daughter of Pierre II of Luxembourg, second son of Louis, Comte de St Pol, connetable de France, Elizabeth Woodville's uncle. See Anselme, *Histoire genealogique et chronologique de la Maison Royale de France*, I, 325–6; A. Stokvis, *Manuel d'Histoire, de Genealogie, etc.*, II, 45, 70.

42. Pat. 5 Henry VII, m. 20; *Cal. Pat. Rolls*, I, 302; N. Harris Nicolas, *Privy Purse Expenses*, p. lxxix.

43. Public Record Office, Museum, Pedestal 20, Ancient Deeds, A. 15109.

44. 'The XXI day of May the vjth yere King Henry VIIth'. Cf. *Archaeologia Cantiana*, I, 147–9; W. J. Harvey, *Handwriting of the Kings and Queens of England*, p. 38.

45. Signed Bills. See W. Campbell, *Materials for a History of Henry VII*, II, 555.

46. Bacon, *Henry VII*, p. 14. Cf. also R. Wilkinson, *Londina Illustrata*, II, 8; Charles Knight, *London*, III, 8; Clements Markham, *Richard III*, p. 257 and n. 3; Philip Lindsay, *Richard III*, p. 319.

47. British Museum, *Harl. MS.* 231, fol. 37B; see also *Annales Monasterii de Bermundessia* (ed. H. R. Luard), III, 460.

48. See J. H. Round's article in the *Dict. Nat. Biog.*, X, 375–6. Cf. G. E. C., *Complete Peerage*, III, 246; *Archaeological Journal*, LVI, 221–31.

49. G. W. Phllips, *History and Antiquities of the Parish of Bermondsey*, 41–2; Edward T. Clarke, *Bermondsey*, p. 123. Cf. Strickland, *Queens of England*, II, 368–9, and Janetta C. Sorley, *Kings' Daughters*, p. 166.

50. At the time of Elizabeth's entry to Bermondsey the abbot's name was John de Marlow, who, in 1483, officiated as deacon at the obsequies of Edward IV.

51. See Knight's *London*, III, 7.

52. See N. Harris Nicolas, *l.c.*, p. lxxxi. There seems no proof of the assertions made by Hall (p. 431) and Gairdner (*Henry VII*, p. 51) that she lived 'a wretched and miserable life'. Cf. Gladys Temperley, who in her *Henry VII* (p. 386) says, 'The theory to which Bacon has lent the support of his great name, that Henry treated his wife badly and her mother worse, long held the field, but it now so discredited that it is hardly worth dwelling on.'

53. These worsd have frequently been quoted as a proof that Elizabeth was reduced to destitution by Henry VII; since, however, she had only a life interest in property, she consequently had little to leave.

54. J. Nichols, *Wills of the Kings and Queens of England*, pp. 350–1. See also Sir H. Nicolas, *Memoirs of Lady Jane Grey*, pp. vii–ix; R. Wilkinson, *Londina Illustrata*, II, 8; G. W. Philips, *Bermondsey*, pp. 42–4; Knight's *London*, III, 11; T. Clarke, *Bermondsey*, pp. 123–4; G. Baker, *Northamptonshire*, II, 181; *Court Magazine* for 1841, XVIII, 201.

55. 'Vij Junii Obiit domina Elizabetha Regina Anglie uxor Edwardi quarti Regis Anglie.' Obituary of Christ Church, Canterbury – compiled about 1 504. Lambeth MS. no. 20. Cf. G. E. C., *Complete Peerage*, V, 362, n.a. 8 June is the day usually given. Cf. *Dict. Nat. Biog.*, VI, 617.

56. *Arundel MS.* 26, fol. 29b.

57. *Ibid.*: 'And the said queen desired in her dethe bedde that assoone as she shud be decessed she shuld in all goodly hast without any worldly pompe be conveied to Wyndesore and ther be beried in the same vaut that her husband the kyng was beryed in.' Cf. R. Tighe and J. E. Davis, *Annals of Windsor*, I, 415–6.

58. *Arundel MS.* 26, fols 29b–30. Cf. R. R. Tighe and J. E. Davis, *Annals of Windsor*, I, 415–6; G. E. C., *Complete Peerage*, V, 362.

59. The child, Princess Elizabeth, was born on 2 July 1492. See Sandford, *Genealogical History*, p. 477. Cf. N. Harris Nicolas, *Privy Purse Expenses of Elizabeth of York*, p. lxxxv; Lane, *Royal Daughters of England*, I, 325.

60. Edward IV's tomb is in the north aisle at the east end of St George's Chapel, Windsor.

61. *European Magazine* (5 March, 1789), vol. 15, p. 344. See also *Vetusta Monumenta*, vol. III, pp. 1–4 and pl. VII–IX.

62. Robert Southley, *Complete Works*, p. 765.

## Conclusion

1. A. F. Prevost d'Exiles, *Histoire de Marguerite d'Anjou*, I, 2nd part, 40–7. Cf. *Dict. Nat. Biog.*, VI, 617.

## Miscellanea

1. *Royal MS.* 14 E. III, fol. 162.

2. Public Record Office, S.C.I./XLVI, 151. This Sir William Stonor later held the office of Constable of Wallingford Castle. *Pat. Rolls*, 4 Henry VII, memb. 28 (4); *Cal. Pat. Rolls*, I, 273.

3. Two letters now in the Public Record Office (S.C.I/XLVI, 218, 219) show that Sir William Stonor was out of favour with the queen in this year.

4. Printed in the *Royal History Society*, Camden Series III, vol. XXX, p. 150. See also Miss Strickland, *Lives of the Queens of England*, vol. II, p. 337; M. A. E. Wood (later Green), *Letters fo Illustrious Ladies*, vol. I, p. 110.

5. Public Record. Museum. Pedestal 20. (Ancient Deeds A. 15109). Cf. *Archaeologia Cantiana*, I, 147; W. H. Harvey, *Handwriting of the Kings and Queens of England*, 38.

6. S.C.I./XLIV, 64. Printed in *Royal Historical Society*, Camden Series III, XXX, 127–8.

7. See Caxton's Memoir of Rivers in the *Cordyalae* printed in W. Blades's *William Caxton*, I, 149; *Excerpta Historica*, p. 245. Cf. Ramsay, II, 493.

8. See. W. Blades, *William Caxton*, I, 163.

9. See the Account Book of her Receiver-General, Miscellaneous Books, Exchequer T. of R., no. 207.

10. British Museum, *Royal MS.* 14 E. III.

11. Ames, *Typographical Antiquities*, I, 27. Cf. Scofield, II, 452 and n. 1.

12. *Hist. MSS. Comm. Report 6*, App. 353, 357–8; Scofield, II, 452, n. 1.

13. W. Blades, *William Caxton*, II, 34. Cf. Scofield, II, 457.

14. Caxton's Prologue to his *History of Jason* (ed. J. Munro), p. 2. Cf. W. Blades, *William Caxton*, I, 139–40.

15. C. H. Cooper, *Memorials of Cambridge*, I, 289–90; W. J. Searle, *History of Queens College*, pp. 69–72; J. B. Mullinger, *The University of Cambridge*, I, 315–6; J. H. Grey, *Queen's College*, 12–13, 27–32; R. Willis, *The Architectural History of Cambridge University* I, lxiv.

16. Vol. II, 315.

## Appendix 1

1. Patent Rolls. For an account of John Stratford see Dr W. A. Shaw's most interesting article 'An Early English Pre-Holbein School of Portraiture', *Connoisseur*, XXXI, 76–7.

2. The Ashmolean Portrait has been reproduced in the *Illustrated Catalogue of the Oxford Portrait Exhibition*, no. 8, p. 20, 1904.

3. See William A. Shaw, 'The Early English School of Portraiture', *Burlington Magazine*, LXV, no. ccclxxix; p. 184.

4. Reproduced by J. Nichols in *The History andAntiquities of the County of Leicester*, III, pt. 2, pl. LXXXVIII, p. 662.

5. See Bernard Rackham in *The Sixth Annual Report of the Friends of Canterbury*, p. 33, 1933.

6. See *Tenth Annual Report of the Friends of Canterbury*, p. 20, 1937. Cf. *Sixth Annual Report*, p. 35.

7. This portrait has been engraved in J. Fenn's edition of the *Paston Letters*, V, lxxv, 1823.

8. This portrait has been reproduced in colour by John Jas. Lambert in *Recorsd of the Skinners of London, Edward I to James I*, p. 82. It has also been reproduced in Herbert Norris's *Costume and Fashion*, p. 415, fig. 570; *Tenth Annual Report of the Friends of Canterbury*, p. 56, 1937.

9. Cf. *Tenth Annual Report of the Friends of Canterbury*, p. 56.

10. No. 265, fol. I.b. This miniature has been reproduced in Horace Walpole's *Royal and Noble Authors* as a frontispiece to vol. II; in colour in Joseph Strutt's *Regal and Ecclesiastical Antiquities*, pl. 47. An engraving of this portrait has been reproduced in Miss Strickland's *Queens of England*, II, 315.

11. R. Willis, *Architectural History of Cambridge*, II, 47. An engraving of this portrait has been reproduced in Miss Strickland's *Queens of England*, II, 315.

12. J. H. Grey, *Queens' College*, App. 301–2; T. D. Atkinson, *Cambridge Described and Illustrated*, pp. 384–5.

13. The Department of Prints and Drawings, British Museum, has several engravings, including one by Facius (*c.* 1780). Further reproductions are to be found in Massue de Ruvigny, *Blood Royal of Britain*, p. 176; C. R. L. Fletcher, *Historical Portraits*, p. 174; Emily Riching, *White Roseleaves*; E. Thornton Cook, *Her Majesty*, p. 123. This portait has also been engraved in E. Samuel Johnson's and G. Stevens's *Shakespeare*, X, 305. Many other mediocre engravings have been made. Cf. Knight's *London*, III, 8.

14. The Department of Prints and Drawings has three copies of this engraving, which is unlike any other portrait of Elizabeth.

*Appendix 2*

1. *Add. MS.* 4614, fols 222–3. Printed by Sir Henry Ellis in *Original Letters*, 2nd series, vol. I, pp. 140–2; *Genealogist*, IV, 126–7.

*Appendix 3*

1. Sandford, *Genealogical History*, p. 418; G. E. C., *Complete Peerage* (Old Series), VIII, 79; Doyle, *Official Baronage*, III, 611; N. H. Nicolas, *Privy Purse Expenses*, xix; Green, *Princesses of England*, III, 422; Clements Markham, p. 86; Stratford, *Edward IV*, p. 319.

2. *Rot. Parl.*, VI, 544; Sandford, p. 418; Green, *ut. sup.*, III, 433; Ramsay, II, 469; H. M. lane, *Royal Daughters of England*, I, 312.

3. G. E. C. (Old series), VIII, 79; Lane, *ibid.*, I, 312 and 313, n. 4.

4. G. E. C., VIII, 79, Ramsay, II, 469; Green, III, 436; Lane, *ibid.*, I, 312.

5. G. E. C. (New Series), IX, Doyle, II, 594; T. Madox, *Formulare Anglicanum*, pp. 109–10; Sandford, p. 418; Nicolas, p. xxiii; Green, IV, 7; Ramsay, II, 469; Clements Markham, p. 86; Stratford, p. 319; Lane, *ibid*, I, 315.

6. G. E. C. (New Series), IX, 619; Ramsay, II, 469; Lane, I, 315.

7. G. E. C. (New Series), IV, 330; *Rot. Parl.*, VI, 481; Nicolas, xxv; Green, IV, 18; Markham, p. 87; Stratford, p. 319; Lane, I, 316.

8. G. E. C. (New Series), IV, 330; Doyle, I, 581; Sandford, p. 418; Green, IV, 39; Ramsay, II, 469; Lane, I, 316.

9. Sandford, p. 418; Nicolas, p. xviii; Green, III, 401; Ramsay, II, 469; Tighe and Davis, *Annals of Windsor*, I, 385; Lane, I, 311.

10. Sandford, p. 419; Nicolas, p. xxii; Green, III, 437; Ramsay, II, 469; Lane, I, 314.

11. Sandford, p. 418; Nicolas, p. xxx; Green, IV, 447; Ramsay, II, 470; Lane, I, 308.

12. G. E. C. (New Series), I, 250; Doyle, I, 79; Baker, *Northamptonshire*, II, 161; Ramsay, II, 321; Oman, *Political History*, IV, 424; Stratford, p. 97; Scofield, I, 397; George Smith, *Coronation*, pp. 51–2.

13. G. E. C. (New Series), V, 138; *Cal. Pat. Rolls*, II, 25; Doyle, II 282. Cf. Ramsay, II, 321, n. 4; Oman, IV, 424; Stratford, p. 97; Scofield, I, 397.

14. G. E. C., V, 138; VII, 167; Doyle, II, 282; Lane, I, 245.

15. G. E. C. (Old Series), VII, 274; cf. G. E. C. (New Series), VII, 166, n.f. Baker, II, 161; Oman, IV, 424; Stratford, p. 97; Smith, 51–2; Lane, I, 245.

16. G. E. C. (New Series), VI, 160; VII, 166; Ramsay, II, 321; Oman, IV, 424; Stratford, p. 97; Smith, p. 51.

17. G. E. C. (New Series), II, 390; Doyle, I, 255; Baker, II, 161; Ramsay, II, 321; Oman, IV, 424; Stratford, p. 97; Scofield, I, 397; Smith, 51.

18. G. E. C. (New Series), II, 73; Doyle, I, 153. *Dict. Nat. Biog.*, XIX, 1217.

19. Sandford, p. 293; Lodge, *Peerage of Ireland* V, 266; *Dict. Nat. Biog.*, XXI, 660, 887.

20. *Dict. Nat. Biog.*, XXI, 661.

21. G. E. C. (Old Series), VI, 214; Doyle, III, 17; Baker, II, 161; Ramsay, II, 321; Oman, IV, 424; Stratford, p. 97; Scofield, I, 397; Smith, pp. 51–2.

22. *Harleian Society: Visitation of Shropshire in 1623*, p. 75. Cf. Dugdale, II, 231; *Dict. Nat. Biog.*, XXI, 887; Smith, *Coronation*, p. 52.

23. G. E. C. (Old Series), VII, 73; VI, 371. Anthony Woodville married, in 1461 or 1462, Elizabeth, Baroness Scales, in her own right, and from 22 December 1462, was, in her right, summoned to Parliament as Baron Scales. Cf. *Genealogist* (New Series), V, 103. He married secondly Mary, daughter and co-heir of Sir Henry Fitz Lewis of Horndon (Essex) and Elizabeth, fifth daughter of Edmund (Beaufort), 2nd Duke of Somerset. G. E. C. (Old Series), VI, 372; Doyle, III, 144; *Dict. Nat. Biog.*, XXI, 884.

24. G. E. C. (New Series), IX, 606.

25. See Baker, *Northamptonshire*, II, 166; cf. Bridges, I, 300.

26. F. Sandford, *Genealogical History of the Kings and Queens of England*, p. 407. Reproduced in Sandford's *Genealogical History, etc.*, p. 374; also in W. St John Hope's *Heraldry for Craftsmen and Designers*, pl. XXV. See also T. Willement, *Royal Heraldry*, pp. 47–8, and plate XI. The Arms of Elizabeth Woodville are also to be seen in the North Transept of Canterbury Cathedral. Cf. also *Genealogist*, IX, 240. The Seal is in possession of the Society of Antiquaries. For full details of the history and genealogy of the Hosue of Luxembourg see Nicolas Vignier, *Histoire de la maison de Luxembourg*; Andre du Chesne, *Histoire de la Maison de Luxembourg*; P. Anselme, *Histoire genealogique et chronologique de la maison royale de France*, III; James Anderson, *Royal Genealogies*; S. P. Ernst, 'Dissertation historique et critique sur la maison royale des comtes d'Ardennes', *Bulletin de la Commission Royale d'Histoire*, 2nd Series, X; G. Pertz, *Monumenta Germaniae Historica*, II and IX; Johann Schotter, *Einige Kirtische Erorterungen uber die Fruhere Geschichte der Graffschaft Luxemburg; Geschichte des Luxemburger Landes*; A. M. H. J. Stokvis, *Manuel d'Histoire, de Genealogie etc.*, vols II, III; Robert Parisot, *Le Royaume de Lorraine sous les Carolingiens*; Alfred Lefort, *La Maison Souveraine de Luxembourg*; Leon Vanderkindere, *La Formation Territoriale des Principautes Belges au Moyen Age*, 2 vols; Robert Parisot, *Les Origines de la Haute-Lorraine*. See also Louis Chantereau-Le Fevre, *Considerations historiques sur la genealogie de la maison de Lorraine*; S. P. Ernst, *Histoire du duche de Limbourg*; E. Dummler, *Geschichte des Ostfrankischen Reiches*; Emil Kruger, 'Uber die Abstammung Henrichs I von den Karolingern' in Ludwig Quidde's *Deutsche Zeitschrift fur Geschichtswissenschaft*, IX; ed. Favre, 'La Famile d'Evrard, Marquis de Frioul' in *Etudes d'histoire du Moyen Age dediees a G. Monod* (ed. Lavisse). For Elizabeth's pedigree see also *The Genealogist*, IX, 239–40 (New Series), in which is reproduced a pedigree drawn up in 1601 and signed by William Dethick, Garter King of Arms. The original is quoted as being 'at Rome in the possession of Prince Orsini'. Cf. also Baker, *Northamptonshire*, II, 1 66; J. Bridges, *Northamptonshire*, I, 300.

# BIBLIOGRAPHY

*Manuscripts*
*British Museum*
Add. MSS. 4614, fols 222–3.
Add. MSS. 4791, fol. 139.
Add. MSS. 6113, fols 48b *et seq.*
Add. MSS. 19,398, fol. 33.
Add. MSS. 23,938 (Computus J. Breknoke).
Add. MSS. 37,447, fol. XLIX Hardwyck Annals.
Arundel MSS. 26, fols 29b–30.
Arundel MSS 28, fol. 25 *verso.*
Cott. MS. Faustina B. VIII, fol. 4 *verso.*
Cott. MS. Nero C. IX.
Cott. MS. Vespasian C. XIV, fols 122–3.
Cott. MS. Vitellius A. XVI, fols 129 *verso et seq.*
Harleian MSS. 48, fols 78–91. Re-interment of the Duke of York.
Harleian MSS. 231, fol. 37b.
Harleian MSS. 433, fols 6 *et seq.*
Harleian MSS. 541, fol. 217b.
Harleian MSS. 543, fols 130, 172.
Harleian MSS. 545, fol. 132 *verso* (Chron. Tewkesbury).
Harleian MSS. 1431, fol. 4.
Harleian MSS. 4780, fol. 2 *et seq.* (Wardrobe Accounts of Edward IV)
Landsowne MS. 285, fol. 2 *et seq.*
Royal MS. 14 E. III, fol. 162.
Royal MS. 17 B XLVII, fols 165–166.
Sloane MS. 3479.

*Guildhall*
Great Chronicle (MS. 3313 in course of publication) fols 158 *verso*–222 *verso.*
London Journal 7, fols 198b and 223–224.
London Journal 8, fols 4 *et seq.*
London Journal 9, fol. 23 *verso.*
London Bridge Masters' Accounts, 1460–84, fols 94–95, Letter-Book L.

*Public Record Office*
Chancery Records: Early Chancery Proceedings.

Charter Rolls.
French Rolls.
Fine Rolls.
Patent Rolls.
Pardon Rolls.
*Inquisitiones post mortem.*
Warrants for the Great Seal, Series I.
Writs of Privy Seal.
Bills of Privy Seal.
Warrants under the Signet.
Signed Bills.
Treasurer of Wars' Accounts

Exchequer Records: Exchequer K.R.
Customs Accounts.
Household Accounts.
Miscellanea.
Exchequer L.T.R.
Enrolments of Wardrobe Accounts.
Exchequer T.R.
Miscellaneous Books.
Council and Privy Seal.
Warrants for Issues.
Issue Rolls.
Tellers' Rolls.

Duchy of Lancaster: 28 5/8. Household Accounts of Queen Margaret.

Ancient Correspondence: S.C.I./XLIV, No. 64.
S.C.I./XLV, No. 236.
S.C.I./XLVI, Nos 151, 206, 207, 218, 219.

Museum: Pedestal 20. Ancient Deeds. A. 15109.

*Lambeth Palace*
Lambeth MS. No. 20, *Obituary of Christ Church, Canterbury.*
No. 265, *Dictes and Sayings of the Philosophers.*

*National Library, Paris*
MS. Fonds fr. 4054, fol. 229.
MS. Fonds fr. 6759, fol. 144 *verso.*
MS. Fonds fr. 10,187²,* fols 123–4.
MS. F. ital. 1649, fol. 168.

*Printed Books*
*Acts of the Parliaments of Scotland,* 1424–1567, vol. II (London, 1814).
*American Antiquarian Society, Proceedings of the,* vol. XVI (Worcester, Mass., 1905).
Ames, J., *Typographical Antiquities* (London, 1749).
*Ancestor, The,* vol. III (London, 1902).
Anderson, James, *Royal Genealogies* (London, 1736).
*Annales Monasterii de Bermundessia* in *Annales Monastici* (ed. H. R. Luard), vol. III (London, 1866).
*Annals of the Kingdom of Ireland by the Four Masters* (ed. J. O' Donovon), vol. IV (Dublin, 1851).
Anon., *Crown Jewels* (London, 1897).
Anselme, P., *Histoire genealogique et chronologique de la maison royale de France* (3rd ed., 9 vols: Paris, 1726–33).
Arber, E., An English Garner, vol. II (London, 1879).

*Archaeologia*, vols I, XIII, XXI, XXVI, XXIX, XXXI, XLVII, LV, LXII (2), LXXXIV (London, 1790–1935).

*Archaeologia Cantiana*, vols I, XXXVII (London, 1858–1925).

*Archaeological Journal*, vol. LVI (London, 1899).

Armstrong, C. A. K., *The Usurpation of Richard III*, being the first edition of Dominic Mancini's *De Occupatione Regni Anglie* (Oxford, 1936).

Ashmole, E., *The Order of the Garter*, 2 vols (London, 1672).

*Athenaeum, The*, 16 November 1844.

Atkinson, T. D., *Cambridge Described and Illustrated* (London, 1897).

Auden, T., *Shrewsbury* (London, 1923).

Bacon, Francis, 'The History of the Reign of King Henry the Seventh' in *Works* (ed. Spedding, Ellis and Heath), vol. VI (London, 1858).

Baker, Goerge, *History of Northamptonshire*, 2 vols (London, 1822–41).

Baker, Sir R., *Chronicle of the Kings of England* (London, 1830).

Barante, Brugière de, *Histoire des Ducs de Bourgogne* (ed. Gachard), 2 vols (Brussels, 1838–40).

Basin, Thomas, *Histoire des regnes de Charles VII et de Louis XI* (Societe de l'Histoire de France) (ed. J. Quicherat) (Paris, 1855–9).

Baudot, Jules, *Les Princesses Yolande et les Ducs de Bar: Melusine* (Paris, 1900).

Bayley, A. R., 'Edward IV and Lady Elizabeth Butler' in *Notes and Queries*, vol. 151 (London, 1926).

Bazeley, Canon William, in *Transactions of the Bristol and Gloucestershire Archaeological Society*, vol. XXVI (Bristol, 1903).

Beachesne, Marquis de, 'L'expedition d'Edouard Wydeville en Bretagne', in *Revue de Bretagne*, vol. XLVI (Vannes, 1911).

Beaucourt, G. Du Fresne de., *Histoire de Charles VII*, 10 vols (Paris, 1881–91).

Behault de Dornon, Armand de., *Bruges: Sejour d'exil des rois d'Angleterre Edouard IV et Charles II* (Bruges 1931).

Bensemann, Walter, *Richard Neville, der Konigmacher* (Strasbourg, 1898).

Berry, H. F., *Statute Rolls of the Parliament of Ireland, 1–12 Edward IV* (Dublin, 1914).

*Biographia Britannica*, vol. 12 (London, 1789).

Bistici, Vespasiano da, *Lives of Illustrious Men of the Fifteenth Century* (ed. W. G. and E. Waters) (London, 1926).

Black, W. H., *Historical Illustrations of the Reign of Edward IV* (London, 1830).

Black, W. H., *Illustrations of Ancient State and Chivalry* (Roxburghe Club, 50) (London, 1840).

Blades, W., *The Life and Typography of William Caxton*, 2 vols (London, 1861–63).

Blakeway, J. A., *see* Owen, H.

Bliss, T. and G. Francis, *Some Account of Sir HughJ Johnys* (Swansea, 1845).

Blomefield, Francis, *Norfolk*, 11 vols (London, 1805–10).

Bloxham, A., *Broadgate Park* (Leicester, 1820).

Botfield, B., *Manners and Household Expenses of England in the Thirteenth and Fifteenth Centuries* (London, 1841).

Bouchard, Alain, *Les grandes Croniques de Bretagne* (Rennes, 1886).

Brayley, E. W., *History and Antiquities of Westminster*, 2 vols (London, 1818–23).

Bridge, J. S. C., *History of France from the Death of Louis XI*, 2 vols (Oxford, 1921).

*Bristol and Gloucestershire Archaeological Society*, vol. XXVI (Bristol, 1903).

Brooke, Richard, *Visits to Fields of Battle in England* (London, 1857).

Bullet, J. P., *Dissertation sur la Mysthologie francaise* (Paris, 1771).

*Burlington Magazine*, vol. LXV (London, 1934).

Burton, William, *Leicestershire* (Lynn, 1777).

Busch, W., *England under the Tudors* (London, 1895).

But, Chronique d'Adrien de (ed. Baron Kervyn de Lettenhove), *Chroniques relatives a l'histoire de Belgique sous la domination des ducs de Bourgogne*, vol. I (Brussels, 1870).

*Calendar of Patent Rolls preserved in the Public Record Office*:

*Edward II*, 1361–74 (Rolls Series 163) vols XII, XIII, XV (London, 1912–14).

*Richard II*, 1385–9 (Rolls Series 164) vol. III (London, 1900).

*Henry VI*, 1422–61 (Rolls Series 167) vols I, II, III, V, VI (London, 1901–10).

*Edward IV*, 1461–7 (Rolls Series 168) (London, 1897).

*Edward IV*, Henry VI, 1467–77 (Rolls Series 168) (London, 1900).

*Edward IV*, Edward V, Richard III, 1476–85 (Rolls Series 168) (London, 1901).

*Henry VII*, 1485–94 (Rolls Series 169) vol. I (London, 1914).

*Calendar of State Papers and MSS. Existing in the Archives and Collections of Milan* (ed. A. B. Hinds) (Rolls Series 158) vol. I (London, 1912).

*Calendar of State Papers and MSS. Relating to English Affairs existing in the Archives and Collections of Venice*, 1202–1509 (ed. Rawdon Brown) vol. I (Rolls Series 181) (London, 1864).

Calmette, J. and Georges Perinelle, *Louis XI et l'angleterre: Societe de l'Ecole des Chartes: Memoires at Documents*, vol. XI (Paris, 1930).

Campbell, John Lord, *Lives of the Lord Chancellors of England*, vol. I (London, 1845).

Campbell, W., *Materials for a History of Henry VIII*, 2 vols (Rolls Series 60) (London, 1873–7).

'Carew Manuscripts, 1575–88' in *Calendar of State Papers* (ed. J. Brewer and W. Bullen) (Rolls Series 192) (London, 1868).

Cartellieri, Otto, *The Court of Burgundy* (London, 1929).

Caxton, William, 'Prologue' in *History of Jason* (ed. J. Munro) (London, 1913).

*Cely Papers* (ed. H. E. Malden) (Camden Society, 3rd Series, I) (London, 1913).

Chantereau-Le Febvre, Louis, *Considerations historiques sur la Genealogie de la Maison de Lorraine* (Paris, 1642).

Chastellain, Georges, 'Chronique' (ed. Kervyn de Lettenhove), *Academie imperiale et royale*, 8 vols (Brussels, 1863–5).

Chrimes, S. B., *English Constitutional Ideas in the Fifteenth Century* (Cambridge, 1936).

Christie, Mabel E., *Henry VI* (London, 1922).

*Chronicle of the Rebellion in Lincolnshire* (ed. J. G. Nichols) (Camden Miscellany, Vol. I) (London, 1847).

*Chronicles of the White Rose* (ed. J. A. Giles) (London, 1845).

Churchill, George B., 'Richard the Third up to Shakespeare'in *Palaestra*, X (Berlin, 1900).

Clarke, Edward T., *Bermondsey* (London, 1901).

Cobbett, W., *State Trials*, vol. I (London, 1809).

C[okayne], G. E., *Complete Peerage*, new edition, ed. Vicary Gibbs, A–G, 5 vols (1910–13), G–Nuneham, 4 vols (1926–36), ed. H. A. Doubleday and Lord Howard de Walden, old edition, N–Z, vols VII–IX (London, 1895–8).

*Collection de Documents inedits sur l'Histoire de France*, Series 1, Histoire Politique: Journal des Etats Generaux tenus a Tours en 1484 redige en Latin par Jehan Masselin (ed. A. Bernier) (Paris, 1835).

*Collection of Ordinances and Regulations for the Government of the Royal Household* (ed. Society of Antiquaries) (London, 1790).

*Commission royale d'Histoire* (Belgium), *Bulletins*:

Series I, vol. V (1842).

Series II, vol. X (1858).

Commynes, Philippe de, *Memoires* (ed. B. de Mandrot), 2 vols (Paros, 1901–3).

Commynes, Philippe de, *Memoires* (ed. Lenglet), 3 vols (Paris: Societe de l'Histoire de France, 1840–7).

Commynes, Philippe de, *Memoires* (ed. J. Calmette), 3 vols (Paris, 1924–5).

*Connoisseur, The*, vol. XXXI (October 1911).

Conway, Agnes E., 'The Maidstone Sector of Buckingham's Rebellion', *Archaeologia Cantiana*, XXXVII (London, 1925).

Conway, Agnes E., *Henry VII's Relations with Scotland and Ireland* (Cambridge, 1932).

Cook, E. Thornton, *Her Majesty* (London, 1926).

Cooper, C. H., *Annals of Cambridge*, 5 vols (Cambridge, 1842–1908).

Coore, H., *Elizabeth Woodville* (Halifax, 1845).

*Court Magazine, The*, vol. XVIII (London, 1841).

*Coventry Leet Book or Mayor's Register*, ed. M. D. Harris, 2 parts (Early English Texts Society, Nos CXXXIV, CXXXV) (London, 1907–8).

Craik, G. L., *Pictorial History of England*, 9 vols (London, 1849–50).

*Croyland Abbey Chronicle of, Continuations*, (ed. T. Gale) in *Rerum Anglicarum Scriptorum Veterum*, I (Oxford, 1684).

Cunningham, George G., *Lives of Eminent and Illustrious Englishmen*, vol. I (Glasgow, 1837).

Cusack, M. F., *History of the Irish Nation* (London, 1876).

Cust, Henry, *Gentlemen Errant* (London, 1909).

D'Argentre, Bernard, *Histoier de Bretaigne* (Paris, 1618).

Davies, J. S., *An English Chronicle* (London: Camden Society, LXIV, 1856).

Davies, R., *Extracts from the Municipal Records of the City of York during the reigns of Edward IV, Edward V, and Richard III* (London, 1843).

Davis, James E., *see* Tighe, Robert R.

Devon, F., *Issues of the Exchequer* (London, 1837).

*Dictionaries of National Biography* (Reissue), vols VI, VII, VIII, IX, X, XIII, XIV, XV, XVI, XVIII, XIX, XX, XXI (London, 1908, etc.).

Doyle, J. E., Official Baronage of England, 3 vols (London, 1886).

Drake, Francis, *Eboracum* (London, 1736).

Drummond, William, of Hawthornden, *History of the Five James's* (London, 1681).

Du Chesne, Andre, *Histoire de la maison de Luxembourg* (Paris, 1631).

Du Clercq, Jacques, *Memoires, 1448–67* (ed. J. A. Buchon) vols XXXVII–XL of the *Collection des Chroniques Nationales Francaises* (Paris, 1826–7).

Dugdale, Sir William, *Baronage of England*, 2 vols (London, 1675–6).

Dummler, E., *Geschiste des ostfrankischen Reiches* (Leipzig, 1887–8).

Dupuy, A., *Histoire de la Reunion de la Bretagne a la France*, 2 vols (Paris, 1880).

Ellis, Sir Henry, *Original Letters*, 3 series (London, 1825–46).

*English Historical Magazine*, vols III, VI (London, 1791, 1891).

*English Historical Review*, vols IV, XXI, XXIV, XXX, XXXVII, XXXIX, XLI (London, 1889–1926).

*Epistolae Academicae Oxon*, vol. II (ed. H. Anstey) [*Oxford Historical Society*, XXXVI, 1898].

Erlanger, Philippe, *Marguerite d'Anjou* (Paris, 1931).

Ernst, S. P., *Histoire du duche de Limbourg*, 3 vols (Liege, 1837–9).

Ernst, S. P., 'Dissertation historique et critique sur la maison royale des comtes d'Ardennes' in *Bulletin de la Commission royale d'Histoire*, 2nd series, X (Brussels, 1858).

*Etudes d'histoire du Moyen Age dediees a G. Monod* (ed. Lavisse) (Paris, 1896).

*European Magazine*, XV (London, 1789).

*Excerpta Historica* (ed. S. Bentley) (London, 1831).

Fabyan, R., *Chronicle* (ed. Ellis) (London, 1811).

Favre, Ed., 'La Famille d'Everard, Marquis de Frioul' in *Etudes d'Histoire du Moyen Age dediees a G. Monod* (ed. Lavisse) (Paris, 1896).

Fisher, H. A. L., Political History, 1485–1547, vol. V (London, 1906).

Flenley, Ralph, *Six Town Chronicles of England* (Oxford, 1911).

Fletcher, C. R. L. and E. Walker, *Historical Portraits* (Oxford, 1909).

Fortescue, Sir John, *The Governance of England* (ed. Charles Plummer) (Oxford, 1885).

Foss, E., *The Judges of England*, vol. IV (London, 1851).

Francis, J. Grant, *see* Bliss, T.

Francis, René, *Warwick the Kingmaker* (London, 1916).

Friends of Canterbury Cathedral, The, *Sixth Annual Report, Tenth Annual Report* (Canterbury, 1933, 1937).

Fuller, T., *The Worthies of England*, 2 vols (London, 1811).

Gachard, L. P., *Itinéraire de Philippe de Bon, Collection de Chroniques Belges Inedites: Voyages des Souverains des Pays-Bas*, vol. I (Brussels, 1874).

Gairdner, James, *Letters and Papers Illustrative of the Reigns of Richard III and Henry VII*, 2 vols (Rolls Series 24) (London, 1861–3).

Gairdner, James, *Three Fifteenth-Century Chronicles* (London: Camden Society, 119, 1876).

Gairdner, James, 'The Battle of Bosworth', *Archaeologia*, LV (London, 1897).

Gairdner, James, *Richard III* (Cambridge, 1898).

Gairdner, James, *Henry VII* (London, 1902).

*Genealogist, The*, New Series, vols I, III, IV, V, IX (London, 1884, etc.).

*Gentleman's Magazine*, January 1831, September 1832, December 1839, September, October, December 1844.

*Gesta Henrici V* (ed. Benjamin Williams), *English Historical Society* (London, 1850).

Gilbert, J. T., *History of the Viceroys of Ireland* (Dublin, 1865).

Gilliodts-van-Severen, L., *Inventaire des Archives de Bruges: Recueil de Chroniques Publie ... par la Societe d'Emulation de Bruges*, series 3 (Bruges, 1899).

Gould, S. Baring, *Curious Myths of the Middle Ages* (1872).

Grafton, R., *Chronicle* (ed. Ellis) (London, 1809).

Grainge, William, *The Battles and Battlefields of Yorkshire* (Ripon, 1896).

Graves, J., *see* Hayman, S.

Green, Mary A. E., *Letters of Royal and Illustrious Ladies of Great Britain* (London, 1846).

Green, Mary A. E., *Lives of the Princesses of England*, 6 vols (London, 1849–55).

Gregory, *Chronicle*, see J. Gairdner, *Historical Collections of a London Citizen* (London: Camden Society, 119, 1876).

Grey, J. H., *Queens' College* (London, 1899).

Habington, William, 'Life and Reign of King Edward IV' in *Complete History of England*, vol. I (London, 1706).

Hall, E., *Chronicle* (ed. Ellis) (London, 1809).

Halliwell, J. D., *see* Warkworth.

Hannon, William B., *The Lady Margaret* (London, 1816).

Harben, H. A., *Dictionary of London* (London, 1918).

Harcourt, L. W. Vernon, *His Grace the Steward and Trial of Peers* (London, 1907).

Hardyng, John, *Chronicle ... Together with the Continuation by R. Grafton* (ed. Ellis) (London, 1812).

Hardwycke-Jones, J. W., *Hardwycke of Hardwycke and Burcott* (1911)

Harleian Society, *Visitation of Shopshire in 1623* (London, 1889).

Harrod, Henry in *Norfolk Archaeology*, vol. V (Norwich, 1859).

Harvey, W. G., *Handwriting of the Kings and Queens of England* (London, 1893).

Hasted, E., *History of Kent*, 4 vols (Canterbury, 1778–99).

Hatcher, Henry, *Old and New Sarum* (R. C. Hoare, *History of Modern Wiltshire*) (London, 1843).

Hayward, Winifred I., 'Economic Aspects of the Wars of the Roses in East Anglia', *English Historical Review*, XLI (London, 1926).

Hayman, S. and J. Graves, *Unpublished Geraldine Documents*, 4 parts (Dublin, 1870).

Haynin, Jean de, *Memoires* (ed. D. D. Brouwers, *Societe des Bibliophiles Liegois*), 2 vols (Liege, 1905–6).

Hearne, T., 'Fragment' in his edition of Sprott's *Chronica* (Oxford, 1719).

Hearne, T., *Liber Niger Scaccarii* (London, 1771).

Hickmore, Mary A. S., 'A Royal Pageant' in *Tenth Annual Report of the Friends of Canterbury Cathedral* (Canterbury, 1937).

Hirsch, Theodor, *see* Weinrech, Caspar.

*Historical Manuscripts Commission*:

*Appendix to 4th Report* (London, 1874).

*6th Report, Appendix IV* (London, 1878).

*9th Report* (London, 1884).

*12th Report, Appendix IV* (London, 1888).

*Historie of the Arrivall of Edward IV* (ed. J. Bruce, Camden Society, 1) (London, 1838).

Hoare, R. C., *Itinerary of Giraldus Cambrensis* (London, 1806).

Holinshed, Raphael, *Chronicles* (ed. Ellis) (London, 1807).

Holinshed, Raphael, *Chronicles* (ed. Hooker), 3 vols (London, 1587).

Hook, W. F., *Lives of the Archbishops of Canterbury*, vol. V (London, 1867).

Hope, W. H. St John, *Stall Plates of the Knights of the Garter* (London, 1901).

Hope, W. H. St John, *Heraldry for Craftsmen and Beginners* (London, 1913).

*Household Books of John, Duke of Norfolk, and Thomas, Earl of Surrey, 1481–90* (ed. Payne Collier, Roxburghe Club, 55) (London, 1844).

*Howth, Book of*, in *Calendar of the Carew MSS.* (ed. J. Brewer and W. Bullen, Rolls Series 192) (London, 1871).

Hudson, W. and J. C. Tingey, *The Records of the City of Norwich*, 2 vols (Norwich, 1906–10).

Hull, Eleanor, *History of Ireland* (London, 1926).

Innes, Arthur D., *England under the Tudors* (London, 1932).

*Inquisitiones post mortem, Henry VII*, 2 vols (Rolls Series 154) (London, 1898–1915).

K[empe], A. J., in *Gentleman's Magazine*, September 1844.

Kennet, White, *Complete History of England*, 3 vols (London, 1706).

Kingsford, C. L., *Chronicles of London* (MS. Cott. Vitell. A. XVI) (London, 1905).

Kingsford, C. L., *English History in Contemporary Poetry: Lancaster and York* (London, 1913).

Kingsford, C. L., *English Historical Literature in the Fifteenth Century: The Record of Bluemantle Pursuivant* (Oxford, 1913).

Kingsford, C. L., *English Historical Review*, vol. XXXIX (London, 1924)

Kirk, James F., *Charles the Bold*, 3 vols (London, 1863–8).

Knight, Charles, *London*, vol. III (London, 1876).

Kruger, Emil, 'Uber die Abstammung Heinrichs I von den Karolingern' in Quidde, L., *Deutsche Zeitschrift fur Geshichstswissenschaft*, vol. IX (Leipzig, 1893).

La Marche, Olivier de, *Memoires* (ed. H Beaune and J. d'Arbaumont, Societe de l'Histoire de France), 4 vols (Paris, 1883–8).

Lambert, John James, *Records of the Skinners of London, Edward I to James I* (London, 1933).

Lane, H. Murray, *Royal Daughters of England*, 2 vols (London, 1910–11).

Lappenberg, J., *Urkundliche Geschichte des Hansischen Stahlhofes zu London* (Hamburg, 1851).

Lefort, Alfred, *La Maison souveraien de Luxembourg* (Luxembourg, 1902).

Leland, J., *De Rebus Britannicis Collectanea* (ed. Hearne), 6 vols (London, 1770).

Lindsay, Philip, *Richard III* (London, 1933).

Lindsay, Philip, *On Some Bones in Westminster Abbey* (London, 1934).

Lindsay, Philip, *Kings of Merry England* (London, 1933).

Lingard, John, *History of England*, 11 vols (London, 1849).

Lodge, E., *The Peerage of Ireland* (7 vols) (London, 1789).

Lodge, E., *Portraits of Illustrious Personages of Great Britain*, 8 vols (London, 1821).

Lodge, E. C. and G. A. Thornton, *English Constitutional Documents, 1307–1485* (Cambridge, 1935).

Longnon, A., *Paris Pendant la Domination Anglaise* (Paris, 1878).

Lyte, Maxwell, *History of the University of Oxford* (London, 1886).

Lytton, Lord E. Bulwer, *The Last of the Barons* (ed. F. C. Romilly) (Oxford, 1913).

Madden, Sir Frederick, *see Gentleman's Magazine*, January 1831.

Madox, Thomas, *Formulare Anglicanum* (London, 1702).

Mancini, Dominic, *see* Armstrong, C. A. J.

Mandrot, Bernard de, *Depeches des Ambassadeurs Milanais en France sous Louis XI et Francois Sforza*, vols I–II (Paris, 1916–9).

Mandrot, Bernard de, *see also* Commynes, Philippe de.

Markham, Sir Clements, *Richard III* (London, 1906).

Mason, R. H., *History of Norfolk* (London, 1884).

Massue de Ruvigny, Marquis M. A., *The Blood Royal of Britain* (London, 1903).

Merriman, R. B., 'Edward Woodville – Knight-Errant', *Proceedings of the American Antiquarian Society*, vol. VXI (Worcester, Mass., 1905).

Michelet, Jules, *Histoire de France*, 19 vols [IX] (Paris, 1879).

Mitchell, R. J., *John Tiptoft (1427–1470)* (London, 1938).

Molinet, Jean, *Chroniques* (ed. J. Buchon), 5 vols (vols XLIII–XLVII of the *Colelction de Chroniques Nationales Francaises*) (Paris, 1827–8).

Monstrelet, Enguerrand de, *Chronique* (ed. Douet d'Arcq), 6 vols (Societe de l'Histoire de France) (Paris, 1857–62).

More, Sir Thomas, *Life of Richard III* (ED. J. R. Lumby) (London, 1883).

Morice, Pierre H., *Memoires pour servir a l'histoire ecclesiastique et civile de Bretagne* (Paris, 1742–6).

Morice, Pierre H., *Histoire de la Bretagne*, 2 vols (Paris, 1750–6).

Mowat, R. B., *The Wars of the Roses* (London, 1914).

Muller, J. A., *Stephen Gardiner and the Tudor Reaction* (London, 1926).

Mullinger, J. B., *The University of Cambridge to 1669*, 3 vols (Cambridge, 1873–1911).

Munch, E., *Die Furstinnen des Hauses Burgund-Osterreich*, 2 vols (Leipzig, 1832).

Nichols, J., *Royal Wills* (London, 1780).

Nichols, J., *History and Antiquities of the County of Leicester*, 4 vols (London, 1795–1815).

Nichols, J. G, *Grants of King Edward V* (London: Camden Society, 58, 1854).

Nicolas, Sir N. Harris, *Privy Purse Expenses of Elizabeth of York* (London, 1830).

Nicolas, Sir N. Harris, *A Chronicle of London* (London, 1827).
Nicolas, Sir N. Harris, *Memoirs of Lady Jane Grey* (London, 1832).
*Norfolk Archaeology*, V (Norwich, 1859).
Norris, Herbert, *Costume and Fashion* (London, 1924).
Notar Giacomo, *Cronica di Napoli* (ed. P. Garzilli) (Naples, 1845).
*Notes and Queries*, 2nd series, vol. VIII, 5th series, vols VII, VIII, IX, 8th series, vols II, X, 11th series, vol. II, vols 151, 153, 166 (London, 1859–1934).
Oman, Sir Charles W., *Warwick the Kingmaker* (London, 1891).
Oman, Sir Charles W., *Political History*, vol. IV, 1377–1485 (London, 1906).
Oman, Sir Charles W., *A History of the Art of War in the Middle Ages*, 2 vols (London, 1924).
Orpen, G. H. in *English Historical Review*, XXX (London, 1915).
Orridge, B. B., *The Citizens of London* (London, 1867).
Orridge, B. B., *Illustrations of Jack Cades's Rebellion* (London, 1869).
Owen, H. and J. B. Blakeway, *History of Shrewsbury*, 2 vols (London, 1825).
Paget, Guy, *The Rose of London* (London, 1934).
Parisot, Robert, *Le Royaume de Lorraine sous le Carolingiens* (Paris, 1899).
Parisot, Robert, *Les Origines de la Haute-Lorraine* (Paris, 1909).
*Paston Letters* (ed. James Gairdner), 4 vols (London, 1900–1); 6 vols (London, 1904).
Pauli, Reinhold, *Geschischte von England*, vol. V (Gotha, 1858).
Pelicier, P., *Essai sur le Gouvernement de la Dame de Beaujeu* (Chartres, 1882).
Perinelle, Georges, *see* Calmette, J.
Pertz, G., *Monumenta Germanica Historica*, vols II and IX (Hannover, 1828).
Philipott, T., *Villare Cantianum* (Lynn, 1776).
Phillips, G. W., *History and Antiquities of the Parish of Bermondsey* (London, 1841).
Pickthron, Kenneth, *Early Tudor Government*, 2 vols (Cambridge, 1934).
Picot, Georges, *Histoire des Etats Generaux*, 4 vols (Paris, 1872).
Plancher, U., *Histoire de Bourgogne*, 4 vols (Dijon, 1739–81).
Pocquet du Haut-Jusse, B.A., 'Francois II, duc de Bretagne, et l'Angleterre', *Memoires de la Societe d'Histoire et d'Archeologie de Bretagne*, IX (Paris, 1928).
*Political Poems and Songs relating to English History* (ed. T. Wright) (Rolls Series 14), 2 vols (London, 1859–61).
Pollard, A. F., *The Reign of Henry VII from Contemporary Sources*, 3 vols (London, 1913).
Pollard, A. F., 'The Making of Sir Thomas More's *Richard III*' in *Historical Essays in Honour of James Tait* (Manchester, 1933).
Potter, T. R., *The History and Anitquities of Charnwood Forest* (London, 1842).
Praet, J. B. van, *Recherches sur Louis de Bruges* (Paris, 1831).
Prevost, A. F. d'Exiles, *Histoire de Marguerite d'Anjou*, 4 parts (Amsterdam, 1740).
*Proceedings and Ordinances of the Privy Council of England* (ed. Sir H. Nicolas), 6 vols (London, 1834–7).
Prynne, William, *Aurum Reginae* (London, 1668).
Putnam, R., *Charles the Bold* (London, 1908).
Quidde, Ludwig, *Deutsche Zeitschrift fur Geschichtswissenschaft*, IX (Leipzig, 1893).
Rackham, Bernard, in *Sixth Annual Report of the Friends of Canterbury* (Canterbury, 1933).
Ramsay, Sir James, *Lancaster and York*, 2 vols (Oxford, 1892).
*Reports of the Deputy Keeper of the Public Records: Third, Seventh and Ninth Reports* (1824–8).
Robinson, J. Armitage, *The Abbot's House at Westminster* (London, 1811).
Roquefort, J. B. B., *Glossaire de la Langue Romane*, 3 vols (Paris, 1808–20).
Ross, John, *Historia regum Anglie* (ed. T. Hearne) (2nd ed.: Oxford, 1745).
Ross, John, *Rows Roll* (ed. W. Courthope) (London, 1859).
*Rotuli Parliamentorum* (Rolls of Parliament), vols IV, V, VI (ed. J. Strachey) (London, 1777). Quoted as *Rot. Parl.*
*Rotuli Scotiae, 1291–1516*, vol. II (ed. D. Macpherson) (London: Record Commission, 1819).
Routh, E. M. G., *Lady Margaret* (Oxford, 1924).
Roy, C., *Melusine* (Liguge, 1898).
*Royal Historical Society* (Camden Series III), XXX (London, 1919).
Rozmital, Leo von, *Ritter- Hof- und Pilger-Reise, 1465–7* (Stuttgart, 1843).
Russell, W., *Extraordinary Women* (London, 1857).

Rymer, T., *Foedera, 1420–1502*, vols X, XI, XII (London, 1710–11).

St Gilles, Nicole, *Les Grandes Cronicques et Annalse de France* (ed. F. de Bellforest) (Paris, 1573).

Sandford, F., *Genealogical History of the Kings and Queens of England* (London, 1707).

Schotter, Johann, *Einige Kritische Erorterungen uber die Fruhere Geschichte der Graffschaft Luxembourg* (Luxembourg, 1859).

Schotter, Johann, *Geschichte des Luxemburger Landes*(Luxembourg, 1882).

Scofield, C. L., 'Elizabeth Wydeville in the Sanctuary at Westminster, 1470', *English Historical Review*, XXIV (London, 1909).

Scofield, C. L., 'The Capture of Lord Rivers and Sir Anthony Woodville in 1460', *English Historical Review*, XXXVII (London, 1922).

Scofield, C. L., *Edward IV*, 2 vols (London, 1923).

Scott, Benjamin J., *The Norman Balliols in England* (London, 1914).

Scott, J. R., *Memorials of Scott of Scotts Hall* (London, 1876).

Searle, W. G., *Queens' College* (Cambridge, 1867).

Sergeant, Philip W., *Anne Boleyn* (London, 1935).

Shakespeare, *Henry VI*, parts I and II.

Shakespeare, *Richard III*.

Sharpe, R. R., *London and the Kingdom*, 3 vols (London, 1894–5).

Shaw, Dr William A., 'An Early English Pre-Holbein School of Portraiture', *Connoisseur*, XXXI (London, 1911).

Shaw, Dr William A., 'The Early English School of Portraiture', *Burlington Magazine*, LXV (London, 1934).

*Shropshire Archaeological Society Transactions*, 1st series, vol. III (Shrewsbury, 1880).

Smith, George, *The Coronation of Elizabeth Woodville* (London, 1935).

*Somerset Record Society, Feet of Fines* (ed. E. Green), 4 vols (London, 1982–1906).

Southey, Robert, *Complete Works* (London, 1850).

Sorley, Janetta C., *Kings' Daughters* (Cambridge, 1937).

Spont, Alfred, 'La marine francaise sous le regne de Charles VIII, 1483–93', *Revue des Questions Historiques*, LV (Paris, 1894).

Stevenson, J., *Letters and Papers Illsutrative of the Wars of the English in France* (Rolls Series 22), 2 vols (London, 1861–4).

Stovkis, A. M. H. J., *Manuel d'Histoire, de Genealogie, etc.*, vols II, III (Leide, 1889–93).

*Stone, Chronicle of John* (ed. W. G. Searle) (Cambridge Antiquarian Society, 1902).

*Stonor Letters and Papers 1290–1483* (ed. C. L. Kingsford), 2 vols (Camden Society, 3rd Series, vols XXIX and XXX) (London, 1919).

Stow, John, *Annals of England* (London, 1615).

Stow, John, *Survey of London* (ed. J. Strype), 2 vols (London, 1720).

Stow, John, *Ibid.* (ed. C. L. Kingsford), 2 vols (London, 1908).

Stratford, Laurence, *Edward IV* (London, 1910).

Strickland, Agnes, *Lives of the Queens of England*, vol. II (London, 1851).

Strutt, Joseph, *Regal and Ecclesiastical Antiquities* (London, 1842).

Stubbs, W., *Constitutional History of England*, 3 vols (Oxford, 1895–7).

Stubbs, W., *Seventeen Lectures on the Study of Medieval and Modern History* (Oxford, 1900).

Swallow, H. K., *De Nova Villa, or the House of Nevill* (London, 1885).

Tanner, Lawrence E. and Professor William Wright, 'Recent Investigations Regarding the Fate of the Princes in the Tower', *Archaeologia*, LXXXIV (London, 1935).

Temperley, Gladys, *Henry VII* (London, 1917).

Thompson, C. J. S., *The Witchery of Jane Shore* (London, 1933).

Thornton, G. A., *see* Lodge, E. C.

Tighe, Robert R. and James E. Davis, *Annals of Windsor*, 2 vols (London, 1858).

*Times, The*, 1 and 12 December 1933; 26 May 1934.

Tingey, J. C., *see* Hudson, W.

*Topographer, The and Genealogist* (ed. J. G. Nichols), vol. I (London, 1846).

Turner, A. T., *Hardwycke Annals* (1905).

Turner, Sharon, *History of England during the Middle Ages* (London, 1825).

Vanderkindere, Leon, *La Formation Territoriale des Principautes Belges au Moyen Age*, 2 vols (Brussels, 1902).

Vergil, Polydore, *History* (ed. Sir H. Ellis) (London: Camden Society, XXIX, 1844).
*Vetusta Monumenta*, vol. III (London, 1796).
Vickers, K. H., *England in the Later Middle Ages* (London, 1930).
Vignier, Nicolas, *Histoire de la Maison de Luxembourg* (Paris, 1619),
Walker, E., *see* Fletcher, C. R. L.
Wallis, W., *English Regnal Years and Titles* (London, 1921).
Walpole, Horace, *A Catalogue of the Royal and Noble Authors*, 4 vols (London, 1806).
Warkworth, John, *Chronicle* (ed. J. O. Halliwell) (London: Camden Society, X, 1839).
Watts, Alaric A., *Literary Souvenir* (London, 1827).
Waurin, Jean de, *Chronique* (ed. Dupont), 3 vols (Paris: Societe de l'Histoire de France, 1858–63).
Waurin, Jean de, *Ibid.* (ed. W. and E. L. Hardy), vols IV and V (Rolls Series 39) (London, 1884–91).
Weever, John, *Ancient Funerall Monuments* (London, 1767).
Weinreich, Caspar, 'Danziger Chronik' in Hirsch, Theodor, *Scriptores Rerum Prussicarum*, vol. IV (Leipzig, 1870).
West, Gilbert, 'The Children of Edward IV', *Notes and Queries*, 153, 166 (London, 1927–34).
Whellan, F., *History of Northamptonshire* (London, 1874).
Whethamstede, *Registrum* (ed. H. T. Riley) (Rolls Series 28 (vi)) (London, 1873).
Widmore, R., *History of Westminster Abbey* (London, 1751).
Wilkinson, R., *Londina Illustrata* (London, 1819).
Willement, T., *Royal Heraldry* (London, 1821).
Williams, C. H., 'The Yorkist Kings', *Cambridge Medieval History*, VIII ch. XII (Cambridge, 1936).
Williams, Charles, *Henry VIII* (London, 1837).
Willis, Browne, *History of the Mitred Parliamentary Abbies*, 2 vols (London, 1718–9).
Willis, R., *The Architectural History of the University of Cambridge*, 4 vols (Cambridge, 1886).
Wood, Antony à, *History of the Colleges and Halls of Oxford* (ed. J. Gutch), 2 vols (Oxford, 1786–90).
Wood, Anthony à, *History of the University of Oxford* (ed. J. Gutch), 2 vols (Oxford, 1792–6).
Woodhouse, R. J., *The Life of John Morton* (London, 1895).
Worcester, William of, 'Annales Rerum Anglicarum' (ed. T. Hearne) in *Liber Niger Scaccarii* (2nd ed.), vol. II (London, 1771).
Wright, Professor William, *see* Tanner, Lawrence E.

# Also available from Amberley Publishing

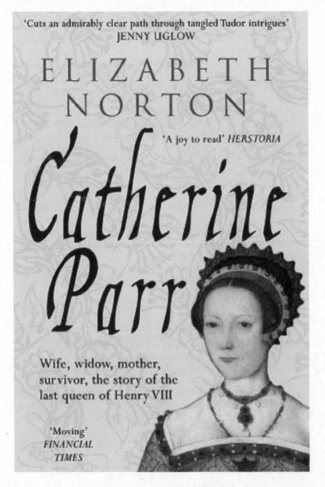

*Wife, widow, mother, survivor, the story of the last queen of Henry VIII*

'Scintillating' THE FINANCIAL TIMES
'Norton cuts an admirably clear path through the tangled Tudor intrigues' JENNY UGLOW
'Wonderful, an excellent book, a joy to read' HERSTORIA

The sixth wife of Henry VIII was also the most married queen of England, outliving three husbands
before finally marrying for love. Catherine Parr was enjoying her freedom after her first two arranged
marriages when she caught the attention of the elderly Henry VIII. She was the most reluctant of all
Henry's wives, offering to become his mistress rather than submit herself to the dangers of becoming
Henry's queen. This only served to increase Henry's enthusiasm for the young widow and Catherine
was forced to abandon her lover for the decrepit king.

£9.99 Paperback
49 illustrations (39 colour)
304 pages
978-1-4456-0383-4

## Also available as an ebook
Available from all good bookshops or to order direct
Please call **01453-847-800**
**www.amberleybooks.com**

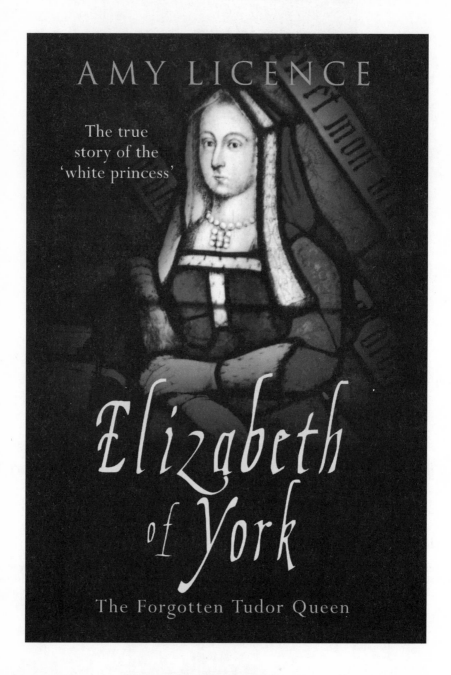

# Also available from Amberley Publishing

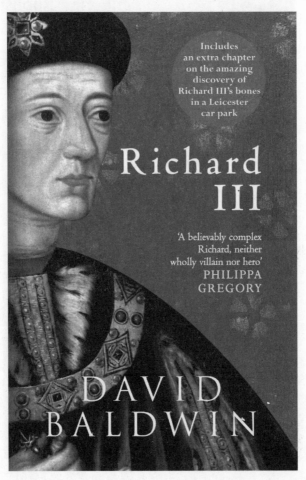

Includes an extra chapter on the amazing discovery of Richard III's bones in a Leicester car park

*Includes an extra chapter on the amazing discovery of Richard III's bones in a Leicester car park*

'A believably complex Richard, neither wholly villain nor hero' PHILIPPA GREGORY

'David Baldwin correctly theorised the final resting place of Richard... 27 years ago' *LEICESTER MERCURY*

Some would argue that a true biography is impossible because the letters and other personal documents required for this purpose are simply not available; but David Baldwin has overcome this by an in-depth study of his dealings with his contemporaries. The fundamental question he has answered is 'what was Richard III *really* like'.

£9.99 Paperback
80 illustrations (60 colour)
296 pages
978-1-4456-1591-2

## Also available as an ebook
Available from all good bookshops or to order direct
Please call **01453-847-800**
**www.amberleybooks.com**

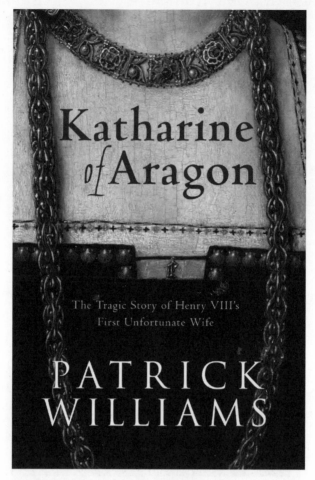

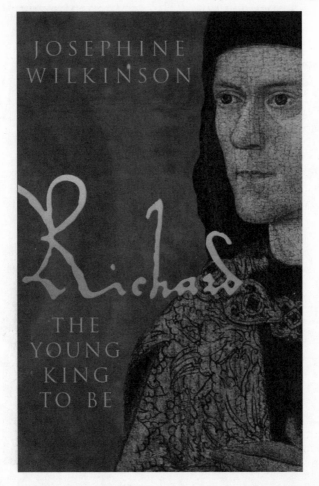

Forthcoming May 2013 from Amberley Publishing

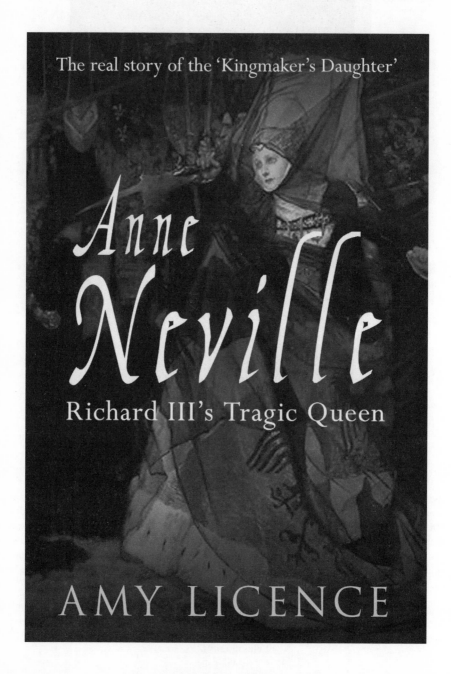

The real story of the 'Kingmaker's Daughter'

# Anne Neville

## Richard III's Tragic Queen

### AMY LICENCE

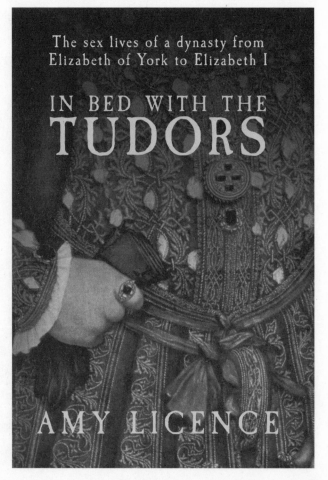

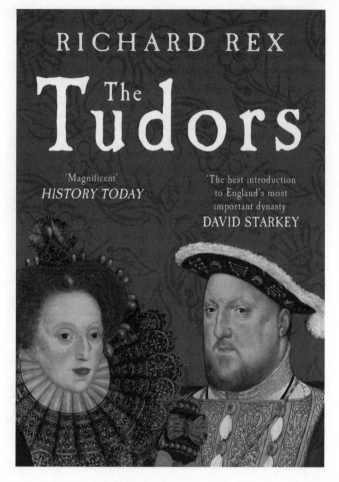

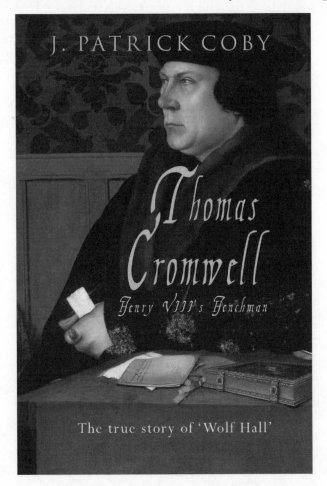

The Tudor femmes fatales
who changed English history

The Boleyn Women

ELIZABETH NORTON

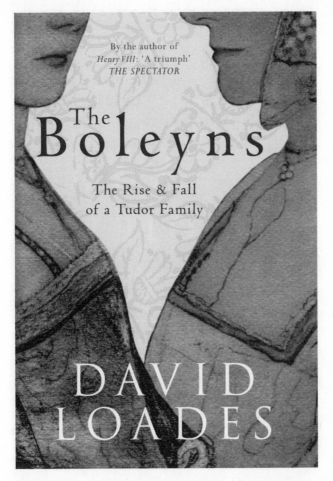

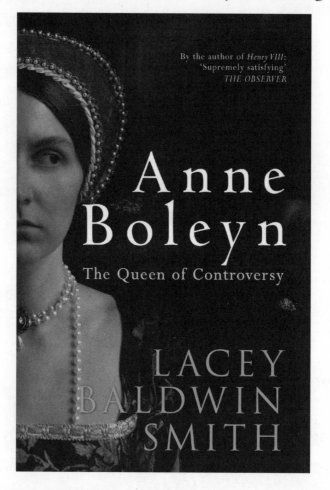

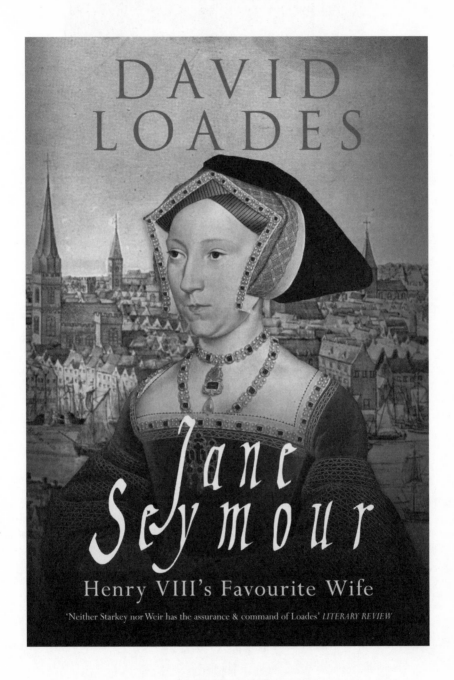

# Also available from Amberley Publishing

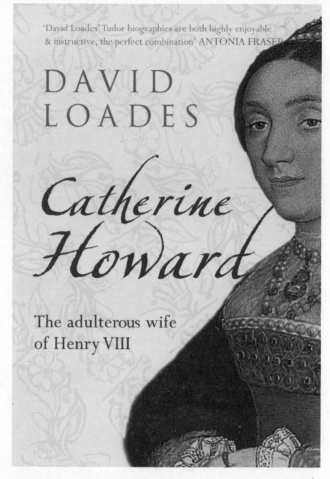

'David Loades' Tudor biographies are both highly enjoyable & instructive, the perfect combination' ANTONIA FRASER

## DAVID LOADES

# Catherine Howard

The adulterous wife of Henry VIII

## *The sorry tale of the fifth wife of Henry VIII*

Henry's fifth Queen is best known to history as the stupid adolescent who got herself fatally entangled with lovers, and ended up on the block. However there was more to her than that. She was a symptom of the power struggle which was going on in the court in 1539-40 between Thomas Cromwell and his conservative rivals, among whom the Howard family figured prominently.

Politics and sexuality were inextricably mixed, especially when the King's potency was called in question. It is time to have another look at her brief but important reign.

£20 Hardback
27 illustrations (19 colour)
240 pages
978-1-4456-0768-9

## Also available as an ebook
Available from all good bookshops or to order direct
Please call **01453-847-800**
**www.amberleybooks.com**